Asset Pricing Models and Market Efficiency

James W. Kolari · Wei Liu · Jianhua Z. Huang · Huiling Liao

Asset Pricing Models and Market Efficiency

Using Machine Learning to Explain Stock Market Anomalies

palgrave
macmillan

James W. Kolari
Mays Business School
Texas A&M University
College Station, TX, USA

Wei Liu
Mays Business School
Texas A&M University
College Station, TX, USA

Jianhua Z. Huang
School of Artificial Intelligence
and School of Data Science
The Chinese University of Hong
Kong, Shenzhen
Shenzhen, Guangdong, China

Huiling Liao
Applied Mathematics
Illinois Institute of Technology
Chicago, IL, USA

ISBN 978-3-031-92900-7 ISBN 978-3-031-92901-4 (eBook)
https://doi.org/10.1007/978-3-031-92901-4

This Palgrave Macmillan imprint is published by the registered company Springer Nature Switzerland AG
The registered company address is: Gewerbestrasse 11, 6330 Cham, Switzerland

KOLARI—To my wife Karie and son Wes and his wife
LIU—To my wife Na and daughters Ashley and Chelsea
HUANG—To my wife Lan and sons Tian-shu and Tian-da
LIAO—To my parents Zhi-qiang and Kam-yee

Preface

Anomalies are relatively high stock market portfolio returns that cannot be explained by asset pricing models. They are most commonly portfolios with long positions in stocks with specific firm or market characteristics and short positions in other stocks with different characteristics. The most puzzling of all anomalies is the momentum anomaly. A momentum portfolio is long stocks that earned the highest returns over the past year and short stocks that earned the lowest returns last year. Winners in the recent past tend to continue winning and losers continue losing. Surprisingly, this simple investment strategy (known for centuries) generates abnormally high stock returns. As another example, a size anomaly exists wherein small stocks earn higher average returns than large stocks. The size anomaly can be measured by holding long stocks with small market capitalization and selling short stocks with large market capitalization.

A major controversy has emerged in the finance literature about what explains anomalies. Efficient market proponents argue that anomalies can be explained by risk factors in asset pricing models. Rational investors assess the risks of assets in the financial market and then price assets per unit risk. To assess risks, the asset pricing approach seeks to supplement the now famous Capital Asset Pricing Model (CAPM) of Sharpe (1964) with multifactors, including (for example) the size and value factors of Fama and French (1992, 1993). Like the anomalies, these factors are long/short portfolios based on firm and market characteristics. While augmenting the CAPM with multifactors was initially successful at accounting for their risks and thereby explaining anomalies, a major problem arose over time—namely, researchers started to find hundreds of anomalies in the stock market. Given the large number of anomalies, asset pricing models have fallen behind in terms of keeping up with their diverse returns and risks.

Due to the breakdown of asset pricing models' ability to explain anomalies, behavioral finance theories have sought to fill the void. Behavioralists argue that psychological human biases explain the anomalies. Irrational human behavior can arise due to cognitive biases, over- and under-confidence, hindsight bias, emotional bias, under-diversification, etc. If investor irrationality is prevalent in the market, then the efficient market hypothesis cannot hold. Is the stock market inefficient such that anomalies can only be explained by behavioral theories? Or, is the market efficient but bad asset pricing models are to blame for their inability of explain anomalies?

In forthcoming chapters, we explore these questions by investigating almost 300 anomalies identified by researchers over the past 30 years or more. Chapter 1 overviews the efficient markets and behavioral finance debate. Chapter 2 reviews research studies on the identification and measurement of anomalies over time. Interestingly, some researchers believe the anomalies gradually disappear after their publication in academic journals. However, others find that they are not diminishing and are replicable over time. Chapter 3 surveys the most prominent multifactor asset pricing models that seek to explain anomalies' abnormal return performance.

Chapter 4 introduces our asset pricing model explanation for anomalies. We employ the *ZCAPM* of Kolari, Liu, and Huang (2021), a lesser known asset pricing model containing only two factors. The ZCAPM has a market factor similar to multifactor models plus a market return dispersion factor. The former market factor is the average or mean return of stocks in the market on any day. The latter return dispersion factor is measured as the cross-sectional standard deviation of returns for all stocks in the market on any given day. Unlike other multifactor models estimated using ordinary least squares (OLS) regression methods, the ZCAPM is estimated via regression analyses using an expectation-maximization (EM) algorithm.

While the EM algorithm is little known in economics and finance, it is widely applied in the hard sciences, including biology, chemistry, meteorology, physics, etc. The key advantage of EM is the estimation of hidden or latent parameters for independent variables with missing data. In the case of the ZCAPM, a latent parameter associated with the probability of positive versus negative sensitivity of stocks' returns to market return dispersion is estimated by the EM algorithm. This directional sensitivity is hidden and therefore not observable from stock return data. The EM algorithm utilizes machine learning (ML) based on observable variable data in the market to estimate this latent probability and associated risk factor. As we document in this book, ML is crucial to the ZCAPM's success in explaining stock market anomalies.

It is important to recognize that the science of artificial intelligence (AI) is predictive by nature. That is, out-of-sample tests are consistent with AI, as opposed to in-sample tests. In this book, we focus on predictive, out-of-sample tests of different asset pricing models. By contrast, most researchers rely much more on nonpredictive, in-sample tests of models (e.g., the Gibbons, Ross, and Shanken (GRS) (1989) test of the equality of joint alphas of stock portfolios). Here we seek to deepen our understanding of the predictive AI abilities of asset pricing models.

Chapters 5 and 6 report empirical evidence on the ability of different asset pricing models to explain hundreds of anomalies. All empirical tests are predictive in the sense of using out-of-sample analyses—that is, risk parameters in models are measured in a 1-year estimation period and then tests are performed of their association with stock returns in the next month. No manipulation or cheating is possible in these out-of-sample tests, which are tantamount to investable stock strategies of investors in the real world.

Chapter 5 provides empirical tests of large online databases of stock anomalies provided by researchers in recent years. We implement often-used cross-sectional regression tests of the risk estimates of leading multifactor asset pricing models. If the risk loadings (or beta risks) of factors in these models are predictive, they will exhibit significance and good explanatory power in accounting for anomalies in the out-of-sample next month. Not surprisingly, often-used multifactor models generally fail in explaining anomalies on an out-of-sample basis. In stark contrast, the ZCAPM well explains all of the anomalies in out-of-sample tests. This evidence strongly favors the efficient market hypothesis; consequently, behavioral theories are not needed. In effect, the anomalies are anomalous to many leading asset pricing models but not to the ZCAPM. Anomalies have high stock returns due to inherent systematic risks measured by the

ZCAPM. The anomalies are no longer unexplained—as such, the long-standing anomalies debate for long/short stock portfolios is settled by and large in our opinion.

Chapter 6 extends the empirical tests of anomaly portfolios to further analyses. We test constituent portfolios in anomalies, i.e., the long portfolios and short portfolios themselves are studied. Also, we test industry portfolios that are difficult for asset pricing models to explain. Finally, anomaly portfolios in the Japanese stock market are tested. In all these tests, the ZCAPM well outperforms OLS multifactor models popular in the finance literature. These tests confirm that anomalies can be explained by the ZCAPM but not other asset pricing models. By implication, the stock market is efficiently priced by rational investors.

Chapter 7 performs empirical tests on the validity of different asset pricing models. A recently published cross-sectional regression test for the validity of a model is implemented. Tests using different anomaly portfolios are reported. We find that the ZCAPM is the only valid model. Leading multifactor models are rejected due to evidence of missing factors. In general, the ZCAPM did not exhibit a missing factor (or factors). These results help to reconcile our anomaly portfolio tests. Other asset pricing models do a poor job of explaining anomalies due to missing factor problems. Contrarily, the ZCAPM succeeds in explaining anomalies due to being complete for the most part with no missing factors.

Lastly, Chapter 8 summarizes the material in the book. Additionally, we discuss the implications of our findings to asset pricing and market efficiency. A major unanswered question is the repeated rejection of the ZCAPM in top tier finance journals over the past decade. The authors have published three books (including this book) on the ZCAPM plus two academic journal publications and made numerous finance conference presentations (earning some Best Paper in Investments awards) but have not gained acceptance at the major finance journals. Given its ability to resolve the growing problem of anomalies in the finance literature as well as mounting evidence of its success in previous books and works, the continued rejection of the ZCAPM by the academic community is disconcerting. Are referees at top finance journals biased by models published in their journals? Are editors influenced by Nobel winners and other highly recognized professors with competing models? From a scientific point of view, the ZCAPM clearly dominates the predictive ability of all of the models in the top tier finance journals. The authors hope that the ZCAPM will someday be widely recognized within the academic and professional finance community as a quantum leap in field of asset pricing.

College Station, USA — James W. Kolari
College Station, USA — Wei Liu
Shenzhen, China — Jianhua Z. Huang
Chicago, USA — Huiling Liao

Acknowledgements The authors gratefully acknowledge financial support from the following academic institutions: Mays Business School, Texas A&M University, College Station, Texas; School of Data Science, The Chinese University of Hong Kong, Shenzhen, China; and Applied Mathematics, Illinois Institute of Technology, Chicago, Illinois.

We have benefited from helpful comments about the ZCAPM at a number of regional and local conferences. We thank participants at the Financial Management Association 2012 conference in Atlanta, GA, Midwest Finance Association 2012 conference in New Orleans, LA, Multinational Finance Society 2012 conference in Krakow, Poland, Southern Finance Association 2020 virtual conference, Southwestern Finance Association 2021 virtual conference, Academy of Finance 2021 virtual conference, invited presentation at the University of Ortego, Dunedin, New Zealand, Academy of Finance 2022 conference in Chicago, IL, Southwestern Finance Association 2023 conference in Las Vegas, NV, Western Economic Association International 2023 conference in San Diego, CA, Southern Finance Association 2024 conference in Palm Beach Gardens, FL, and Southwestern Finance Association 2025 conference in San Antonio, Texas. We are grateful for being awarded the Best Paper in Investments at the Financial Management Association 2012 conference as well as the Southwestern Finance Association 2025 conference.

Also, we are thankful for financial support and real world experience in collaboration with the Teachers Retirement System of Texas and Texas A&M University. Through our joint work in 2013 and 2014 on applying the ZCAPM to investment in a diversified stock portfolio, we gained important knowledge that contributed to our understanding of the ZCAPM.

We have been conducting research on the ZCAPM since 2010. Over the years, we have been fortunate to have useful conversations with many researchers at academic institutions and professional managers at investment firms, including Ali Anari, Will Armstrong, Ihsan Badshah, Geert Bekaert, Grant Birdwell, Saurabh Biswas, Jaap Bos, Andrew Chen, Yong Chen, Gjergji Cici, Brett Cornwell, Lammertjan Dam, Huaizhang Deng, Bilal Ertuk, Wayne Ferson, Paige Fields, Tristan Fitzgerald, Markus Franke, Wesley Gray, Klaus Grobys, Yao Han, Britt Harris, Tim Jones, Hagen Kim, Johan Knif, Sudhir Krishnamurthi, Anestis Ladas, Scott

Lee, Qi Li, Yutong Li, Kelly Newhall, Chris Pann, Francisco Penaranda, Fabricio Perez, Ralitsa Petkova, Mike Pia, Seppo Pynnönen, Liqian Ren, Kyle Rusconi, Katharina Schüller, Clemens Sialm, William Smith, Mikhail Sokolov, Ty Sorrel, Tahir Suleman, Jene Tebeaux, Ahmet Tuncez, David Veal, Jack Vogel, Ivo Welch, Mark Westerfield, Toni Whitehead, Jian Yang, Nan Yang, Christopher Yost-Bremm, Jun Zhang, Zhao Xin, Tony van Zijl, Yangru Wu, Zhaodong Zhong, and Yuzhao Zhang.

We are thankful for the assistance of Ph.D. students while at Texas A&M University. Yao Han (Assistant Professor of Finance, Jiangxi University of Finance and Economics, Jiangxi, China) provided assistance with early cross-sectional statistical tests of the ZCAPM. Also, Huiling Liao (Assistant Professor of Applied Mathematics, Illinois Institute of Technology, Chicago, Ilinois) composed the R package for free online ZCAPM software on the GitHub website, and assisted with additional tests.

Finally, we would like to express our sincere gratitude to Executive Editor Tula Weis at Palgrave Macmillan for her continued support without which this book would not have been possible. Also, expert assistance from Production Editor/Senior Executive Supraja Yegnaraman enabled the manuscript preparation and production. An anonymous referee provided helpful comments.

Competing Interests The authors have no competing interests to declare that are relevant to the content of this manuscript.

Contents

About the Authors

James W. Kolari is the JP Morgan Chase Professor of Finance in the Department of Finance at Texas A&M University, College Station, Texas, USA. He has taught money and capital markets as well as banking classes there since earning his PhD in finance from Arizona State University in 1980. With more than 100 articles published in refereed journals, numerous other papers and monographs, 25 co-authored books, and many competitive papers presented at academic conferences, he ranks in the top 1–2% of finance scholars in the United States. He is a co-author of leading college textbooks in introductory business, commercial bank management, and asset pricing. Numerous scholarly/professional books have been published in banking, financial markets, investments, and asset pricing.

Wei Liu received his first PhD in Physics in 2004 from Texas A&M University. His research focused on particle physics theory. After working as a postdoc, he changed his career path and earned a second PhD in Finance in 2013 from Texas A&M University with an emphasis on asset pricing. From 2013 to 2016, he served as the manager and part owner of a small investment company. He created U.S. equity investment strategies to manage 100 million for the Teachers Retirement System of Texas. Subsequently, he has worked at IberiaBank Corporation in Birmingham, Alabama, USAA Bank in San Antonio, Texas, and Texas A&M University.

He has published research in academic journals as well as asset pricing and investments books.

Jianhua Z. Huang is Presidential Chair Professor and Director of Technology and Innovation Center for Digital Economy at School of Data Science, The Chinese University of Hong Kong, Shenzhen. He received his BS (1989) and MS (1992) in Probability and Statistics from Beijing University, and Ph.D. in Statistics (1997) from University of California at Berkeley. He worked in the Wharton School, University of Pennsylvania and in Texas A&M University before his current position. His main research interest is statistics and interdisciplinary research. He is a Fellow of American Statistical Association, a Fellow of Institute of Mathematical Statistics, and an Elected Member of International Statistical Institute. Recently, he was awarded the 2022 INFORMS Impact Prize. He has published over 100 refereed papers.

Huiling Liao received a Bachelors Economics degree in Statistics from Renmin University of China (2015) and completed her PhD in Statistics (2022) from Texas A&M University. She began working as a Postdoctoral Associate with the Division of Biostatistics and Health Data Science at the University of Minnesota in 2022. In summer 2024, she moved to the Illinois Institute of Technology. Her research interests include machine learning, causal inference, and statistical applications in various areas such as genetics and finance.

List of Figures

List of Tables

PART I

Introduction

CHAPTER 1

The Rise of Anomalies: Challenging Theory and Practice in Finance

Abstract This chapter introduces the basic issues and problems of anomalies, asset pricing, and behavioral finance. Long/short portfolios of stocks not explained by an asset pricing model are considered to be anomalies. However, other important characteristics of anomalies are abnormally high return performance as well as return predictability. Anomalies with high returns that are persistent over time are particularly attractive to investors. According to the efficient market hypothesis (EMH), anomalies with high returns should be arbitraged away by investors and therefore are only transitory in nature. Unfortunately, despite some controversy, empirical evidence has been accumulating over the past 40 years or more that long/short portfolio anomalies are real and not going away. If anomaly portfolios are not efficiently priced, we need to consider the possibility that inefficiencies exist in the market. Behavioralists argue that human psychology allows for irrational investor behavior, which accounts for inefficiencies in the pricing of anomaly portfolios. Other potential sources of anomalies are information asymmetries and market structure. These sources of abnormal returns should be arbitraged away by profit-seeking investors. However, the effects of irrational investor behavior driven by human behavior are likely more difficult to eliminate via arbitrage. The main purpose of this book is to present new stock market evidence on the ability of asset pricing models to explain large datasets of long/short anomaly portfolios. Also, we review published studies on stock market anomalies and asset pricing models. In this chapter, we provide background discussion on the EMH-behavioralist debate. Later chapters review previous empirical tests and report new evidence us-

J. W. Kolari et al., *Asset Pricing Models and Market Efficiency*,
https://doi.org/10.1007/978-3-031-92901-3_1

ing open source (online) datasets of long/short anomaly portfolios. Which school of thought does the market evidence support? Efficient markets? Behavioral finance? Or are both schools useful to our understanding of stock prices? As we will see, based on a new asset pricing model dubbed the ZCAPM by Kolari et al. (2021), our empirical evidence in forthcoming chapters strongly favors the EMH.

1.1 The Anomalies Debate

Professor Fama (1965, 1970) earned the Nobel Prize in Economics in 2013 in large part due to the efficient markets hypothesis (EMH). This hypothesis says that security prices in financial markets fully reflect all available information, including price trends over time as well as accounting, financial, economic, and other market information. Market participants are assumed to be rational in making investment decisions about securities and have homogeneous expectations about the price implications of information that they receive. The financial market is characterized by freely available information to all market investors, no transactions costs, and price taking investors. While these assumptions might seem restrictive or unrealistic, they are reasonable nowadays due to the internet, computers, telecommunications, online databases, and other technologies.[1]

Building on the EMH, the renowned *Capital Asset Pricing Model* (CAPM) was developed by Treynor (1961, 1962), Sharpe (1964), Lintner (1965), Mossin (1966), and Black (1972). The CAPM posits that security prices are explained by the market portfolio, a portfolio on the efficient frontier of the mean-variance investment parabola proposed by Markowitz (1959). Covariances between security returns and market portfolio returns enable the estimation of beta risk, a measure of systematic market risk. Professor William Sharpe earned the Nobel Prize in Economics in 1990 for this elegantly simple model of equilibrium asset prices in an efficient capital market. However, due to weak empirical evidence by Black et al. (1972) and others in early tests of the CAPM using U.S. stock market data, many researchers sought to develop variants of the CAPM in an effort to better

[1] See Lo (2008) for an excellent discussion of the EMH, including its origins in the random walk hypothesis (RWH) and the martingale model that made statistical propositions about the inability to forecast asset price changes. Also, an interesting discussion of anomalies and the EMH versus behavioral debate is provided.

explain stock returns.[2] Unfortunately, these alternative forms of the CAPM did not improve matters for the most part.

Even worse for the CAPM, Fama and French (1992, 1993, 1995) published a series of papers in the 1990s that documented extensive evidence that beta risk was not related to the cross-section of average stock returns. They found that size and value portfolios were anomalous to the CAPM. That is, beta risk could not explain why small stocks persistently had higher average returns over time than large stocks, and why high book-to-market-equity ratio (value) firms had higher returns than low book-to-market-equity ratio (growth) firms. When these differences in returns were regressed on the market factor in the CAPM, they found significant alpha intercepts and little or no explanatory power. In this regard, Jensen (1968) proposed that the significance of alpha in a CAPM regression model (or so-called *market model*) could be used to test the CAPM. If alpha was positive and significant, mispricing error exists that implies other factors are needed to more completely explain security returns.

Given significant CAPM alphas, Fama and French proposed innovative size and value factors to augment the market factor in the CAPM to explain these anomalies. The size factor is a zero-investment portfolio that is long small stocks' returns and short big stocks' returns, where size is measured by market capitalization. The value factor is long value firms' stock returns and short growth firms' stock returns, where the book-to-market equity ratio is high (low) for value (growth) firms. When they added these new *multifactors* to the CAPM, the alpha estimates decreased to approximately zero for test assets portfolios sorted on size and book-to-market ratio firm characteristics. They inferred that this *three-factor model* better explained stock returns than the CAPM.

What happened next was surprising. Researchers began to increasingly identify long/short portfolios that were not explained by Fama and French's three-factor model. Rather than going down the traditional path of efficient markets, many researchers looked to behavioral finance for explanations of these anomalies. Behavioralists broke away from the traditional assumptions of rational investors and Fama's EMH. Instead, they argued that human psychology plays an important role in explain-

[2] See the consumption CAPM (CCAPM) of Lucas (1978) and Breeden (1979), intertemporal CAPM (ICAPM) of Merton (1973), conditional CAPM of Ferson and Harvery (1991), production-based asset pricing model (PAPM) of Cochrane (1991), and international CAPM of Stulz (1981, 1995).

ing anomalies—for example, see Kahneman and Tversky (1979), Shiller (1981), Debindt and Thaler (1985), Debindt and Thaler (1995), Daniel et al. (1997), Barberis et al. (1998), and many others. Human behavior can be irrational due to cognitive biases, over- and under-confidence, hindsight bias, emotional bias, under-diversification, etc.

Countering the behavioralist school, researchers proposed new multifactors to explain anomaly portfolio returns. Fama and French (2015, 2018, 2020) constructed five- and six-factor models to explain profitability and capital investment anomalies. To account for the puzzle of persistently high returns for momentum portfolios, Carhart (1997) proposed a four-factor model that included a momentum factor (i.e., long stocks with high past returns and short stocks with low past returns). Other multifactor models were developed by researchers. Even so, the list of anomaly portfolios kept growing into the hundreds that Cochrane (2011) described as a *factor zoo*.

At the time of this writing, the debate between efficient markets and behavioral schools has become increasingly intense. "We're right and you're wrong" seems to be an attitude that has taken hold in the field of asset pricing. Rational investors and the EMH argue that asset pricing models using multifactors can explain the anomaly portfolio returns. Behavioralists counterargue that asset pricing models fail to explain most anomalies and, therefore, human psychology is responsible for these anomalies. Who's right? Efficient markets advocates, behavioralists, or both?[3]

In this book, we will show that a new asset pricing model dubbed the ZCAPM by Kolari et al. (2021) can explain hundreds of anomaly portfolio returns on an out-sample basis. The ZCAPM takes advantage of machine learning to estimate a hidden or latent variable that is crucial to its empirical success. Our tests reveal that systematic risks measured by the ZCAPM are related to future one-month-ahead returns of anomaly portfolios. These out-of-sample tests are not exposed to any kind of tampering, data snooping, or other nefarious manipulation of the data to favor the ZCAPM. Interestingly, prominent multifactor models, such as the three-, five-, and six-factor models of Fama and French as well as other widely accepted models, do not well explain anomaly portfolio returns in our out-of-sample tests. Thus, many anomaly portfolios are indeed anomalous to commonly used multifactor models but not to the ZCAPM.

[3] For those interested in a comprehensive review of stock market anomalies, Schwert (2003) surveyed the literature and related efficient markets and behavioral views. See also Osterrieder and Seigne (2023).

Contrary to behavioral theories, we infer that efficient markets can explain large numbers of anomaly portfolios. At least in the context of long/short anomaly portfolio returns, the EMH appears to hold such that behavioralist explanations are superfluous. Also, the ZCAPM proves to be a superior, parsimonious asset pricing model relative to other multifactor models that are so popular nowadays. There is no need for a factor zoo to build robust asset pricing models as the ZCAPM only has two market factors. Of course, from a scientific perspective, additional research is warranted to replicate our anomaly findings, extend our analyses to other countries, and conduct further tests of asset pricing models including the ZCAPM. That being said, our results bode well for the efficient market hypothesis.

1.2 The CAPM and Anomalies

The Capital Asset Pricing Model (CAPM) of Sharpe (1964) and others posits the following relationship between the expected returns of the ith asset and market risk:

$$E(R_i) = R_f + \beta_i[E(R_M) - R_f], \tag{1.1}$$

where R_f is the riskless rate of interest, $E(R_M)$ is the expected return on the market portfolio, and β_i (known as *beta*) is a measure of *systematic market risk* related to the market portfolio M. Portfolio M contains all assets in the market and, therefore, is a general market index.[4] Notice that, if we set asset i to be the market portfolio M, its beta would be $\beta_M = 1$. If beta $<$ 1 or beta $>$ 1 for the i asset, it has lower or higher risk, respectively, than the market portfolio.

A key takeaway from the CAPM is that the risk of any asset can be measured solely by beta. More formally, Sharpe defined beta as:

$$\beta_i = \frac{Cov(R_i, R_M)}{\sigma^2(R_M)}. \tag{1.2}$$

where $Cov(R_i, R_M)$ is the covariance of asset i returns with market portfolio returns, and $\sigma^2(R_M)$ is the variance of market portfolio returns associated

[4] In a two-dimensional graph of expected returns (Y) and beta (X), Sharpe identifies M as the tangent portfolio of the ray extending from the riskless rate of interest to the efficient frontier of Markowitz (1959) mean-variance investment parabola

with the total risk of the market. Given the total risk of the market as measured by $\sigma^2(R_M)$, the covariance term in the numerator determines whether an asset has a low or high beta systematic risk.

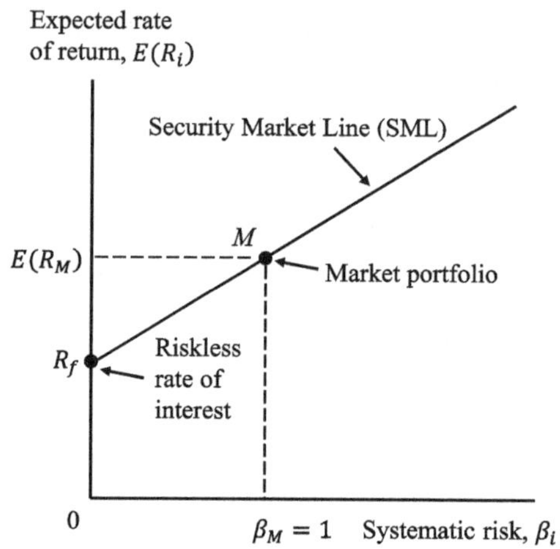

Fig. 1.1 The Capital Asset Pricing Model (CAPM) with market portfolio M, the riskless rate of interest R_f, and market beta risk β

Figure 1.1 provides an illustration of the CAPM. The Security Market Line (SML) connects the points at R_f and M to show the linear relationship between the expected rate of return $E(R_i)$ and beta risk β_i for individual assets. The difference $E(R_M) - R_f$ captures the *market risk premium* or market return in excess of the riskless rate. According to Eq. (1.1), the risk premium for the i asset, or $E(R_i) - R_f$, equals beta times the market risk premium, or $\beta_i[E(R_M) - R_f]$. A tour de force in equilibrium pricing theory, the CAPM is the most well-known asset pricing model in the world that is widely taught in university finance classes, applied by finance practitioners, and frequently used in academic studies.

Because the CAPM is a purely theoretical model, for the purpose of testing it in the real world, Markowitz (1959), Sharpe (1963), and Fama (1968) proposed its empirical counterpart dubbed the *market model*:

$$R_{it} - R_{ft} = \alpha_i + \beta_i(R_{mt} - R_{ft}) + e_{it}, \tag{1.3}$$

where $R_{it} - R_{ft}$ is the excess realized rate of return on asset i in time period t (e.g., daily or monthly), and $R_{mt} - R_{ft}$ is the realized excess average rate of return on the stock market as a whole. Economically speaking, intercept

α_i measures the excess realized rate of return in the case that there is no beta risk (i.e., $\beta = 0$). According to CAPM theory, $\alpha = 0$. Notice that we have changed the lower case notation. Now we use m to denote the market portfolio, which is typically proxied using a general market index such as the S&P 500 index, CRSP index (available from the Center for Research in Security Prices at the University of Chicago), etc. Unfortunately, the true theoretical market portfolio M is not readily observable in the real world.

A major advantage of the market model is that it can be estimated using well-known linear ordinary least squares (OLS) regression. OLS seeks to estimate the parameters α_i and β_i such that residual error terms e_{it} have the property $E(e_{it}) = 0$ (viz., the average of the sum of residuals error terms around the regression line is zero). Also, the intercept parameter α_i is set to increase the goodness-of-fit (i.e., R-squared) of the OLS regression.

Conveniently, Jensen (1968) observed that the market model affords an empirical test of the CAPM. He hypothesized that *alpha* embodies a joint test of both the efficiency of the market portfolio proxy and possible mispricing error due to missing factors. If the market portfolio proxy m is a poor representative of the theoretical market portfolio M, then α would be nonzero. Emphasizing this point, Roll (1977) argued that, without a good proxy for market portfolio M, the CAPM could not be tested—AKA the *Roll critique*. Additionally, while a single factor offers simplicity in the market model, it is reasonable to believe that investors use additional information in the financial market to price assets. As such, other systematic risk factors in the market may well exist.

Anomaly portfolios fit into the framework of the market model. If a portfolio of stocks' returns is regressed on excess market returns, and $\alpha > 0$, we can infer that these returns cannot be fully explained and, therefore, are anomalous to the CAPM. The risk-adjusted return α can be interpreted as an abnormally high anomalous return. In forthcoming Chapter 2, we discuss a recent study by Jensen et al. (2023), who used α to measure risk-adjusted returns for 153 anomalies in the U.S. plus over 90 other countries.

Fama and French (1992, 1993, 1995) showed that the cross-section of average returns in the U.S. stock market are not explained by beta risk over a long period of time. Figure 1.2 illustrates the theoretical CAPM in comparison to a hypothetical depiction of Fama and French's evidence on the relationship between beta risk (β) and excess stock returns. Since beta is unrelated to the cross-section of stock returns, Fig. 1.2 implies that most stock portfolios are anomalous to the CAPM. However, as mentioned earlier, additional qualities are needed to define an anomaly portfolio. It must have abnormally high predictably returns that are persistent over time.

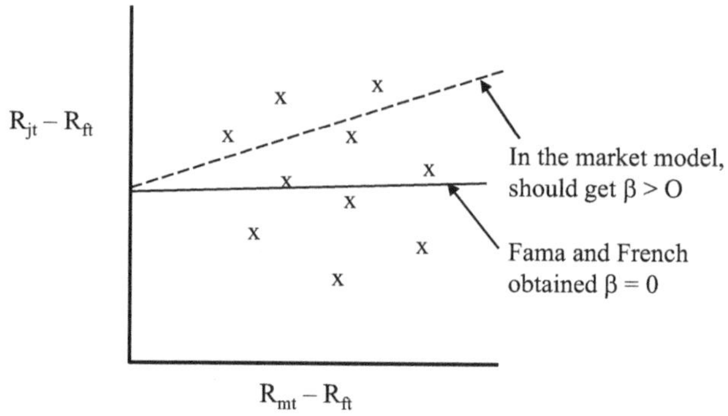

Fig. 1.2 Beta risk (β) in the market model according to CAPM theory and Fama and French (1992, 1993, 1995) evidence

For example, Fama and French found that small stocks (value stocks) had average returns over time that tended to exceed those of big stocks (growth stocks). Continued patterns of outperformance or underperformance by portfolios of stocks are exemplary of an anomaly.

To explain the size and value portfolio anomalies, Fama and French innovated factors constructed as long/short portfolios based on size and value firm characteristics. These so-called *multifactors* were added to the market model to create a three-factor model. In this expanded model, three different beta risks related to market, size, and value factors exist. Consistent with the EMH, Fama and French found that the size and value anomalies could be explained by the size and value multifactors and their associated beta risks.

As new anomalies were discovered by researchers, asset pricing models were augmented to include additional multifactors. However, as discussed in forthcoming Chapter 2, there has been a growing proliferation of long/short portfolio anomalies. The explosion of anomaly portfolios has outpaced the ability of asset pricing models to explain them via new multifactors. To fill the gap, behavioralists have offered other non-EMH explanations for the persistent stock return patterns of anomaly portfolios.

1.3 Two Pillars of Asset Pricing

As highlighted earlier, Professor Eugene Fama at the University of Chicago was awarded the Nobel Prize in Economics in 2013 for empirical work on asset pricing. His Nobel lecture was entitled, "Two Pillars of Asset Pricing." Efficient capital markets and asset pricing models comprise these two pillars. Market efficiency says that prices reflect all available information available to investors. As defined by Fama (1970), there are three forms of market efficiency: weak, semi-strong, and strong. Weak form efficiency means that past prices cannot be used to predict future prices. Semi-strong efficiency says that investors utilize all publicly available information (e.g., accounting statements, business and economic information, etc.) to set prices of assets in the market. Lastly, strong form efficiency implies that even private information affects asset prices.

This efficient market hypothesis (EMH) can be restated in terms of the expected returns of assets given some information set employed by market participants. Fama was careful in his Nobel lecture to make clear that the efficiency of prices and expected returns with respect to market information is not directly observable and therefore not testable. What is needed is an equilibrium asset pricing model that relates rational expected returns to risk characteristics. Even so, as discussed above per Jensen, a joint hypothesis problem exists. If the model fails, we do not know if the market is inefficient or the model is bad (i.e., large mispricing errors). Conversely, if an asset pricing model is valid, then alpha mispricing error is trivial or zero, and we can infer that the market is efficient.

Because they offer insights into market efficiency, event studies are interesting. One of the earliest event studies by Fama et al. (1969) investigated price changes of stocks around the announcement of stock splits by companies. To do this, they employed the market model in Eq. (1.3). Their focus was on the residual term e_{it} defined as:

$$e_{it} = R_{it} - R_{ft} - [\alpha_i + \beta_i(R_{mt} - R_{ft}], \tag{1.4}$$

where $R_{it} - R_{ft}$ is the realized excess return for the ith event stock, and $\alpha_i + \beta_i(R_{mt} - R_{ft})$ is the predicted (fitted) return based on the market model. The residual error represents the ***abnormal return*** (AR) of the stock that is not explained by the model.[5] They found that cumulative abnor-

[5] Consistent with Jensen, note that the alpha term in the market model is another measure of abnormal returns not explained by beta risk.

mal returns (CARs) exhibited a definite pattern over time. CARs gradually increased in the months prior to the split announcement and then became approximately zero thereafter. They interpreted this abnormal return pattern to mean that companies split their stock after good times. Thus, investors in the stock market efficiently process information about the firm during good times and anticipate the split. After the split, there is no additional new information to move the stock price. In this sense the split is a market signal by the firm to investors that confirms their recent success.

Short-run event studies that focus on the days surrounding an event became very popular in finance due to their ability to explore the economic implications of corporate decisions, including dividends, mergers and acquisitions, stock issuance and repurchase, etc.[6] A vast literature exists today with detailed analyses of many different news events. Applying different asset pricing models to adjust returns for risk, these studies generally support market efficiency. Interestingly, the ARs computed from the market model and various multifactor models are very similar to one another (e.g., see Kolari and Pynnonen 2010). The reason is that the alpha parameter adjusts ARs for missing factors in addition to other sources of mispricing error.

Over time, traditional short-run event studies were extended to long-run studies. The latter studies explored abnormal returns spanning one-to-five years (for example) after corporate events. Surprisingly, long-run CARs appeared to persist for years after many corporate events. These findings raised questions about market efficiency. Not only should prices adjust to information, but they should adjust somewhat rapidly. Long-run, slow-moving CARs are contrary to efficient markets. Consequently, behavioralists argued that long-run CARs are attributable to irrational human behavior in financial markets. In his Nobel lecture, Fama was careful to point out that the market model parameters α_i and β_i are not constant over such long periods and must be continuously adjusted to accurately measure these parameters, compute predicted returns, and then calculate abnormal returns (e.g., see also Fama 1998).

In an effort to more accurately estimate risk of event stocks, a recent paper by Han et al. (2023) implemented a market model that dynamically adjusts the market model parameters on a daily basis (by rolling the esti-

[6] Typically, event studies compute abnormal returns (ARs) somewhat differently than in Eq. (1.4). For example, the market model is computed in an estimation window ending prior to the event (e.g., 11 days prior). Then ARs are computed by subtracting the actual returns of a stock from the predicted return on each of the event days (e.g., days −10 to +10).

mation period for the model forward one day at a time in the days after a corporate event). Upon doing so, long-run CARs in post-event years for a variety of corporate events were revealed to decline to approximately zero. Thus, while bad model problems plague long-run event studies as Fama has contended, such problems can be largely mitigated by dynamically adjusting model parameters over time.

We should caution that event studies are not without potential pitfalls. A major problem in the asset pricing models is the alpha parameter α_i. If nonzero, then the model risk parameters do not fully explain returns. That is, something is missing. If α_i were dropped in the computation of predicted returns in Eq. (1.4), abnormal returns would become quite large with magnitudes that would be difficult to explain. Hence, we propose that the bad model problem is deeper than Fama appears to concede. The existence of economically large and statistically significant alphas in the CAPM suggests that it is a bad model, which should not be used in event studies and other applications even if the alpha parameter captures mispricing errors and thereby adjusts ARs for them.

Of course, as discussed earlier, Fama and French and other researchers have sought to improve asset pricing models by reducing alphas to near zero. But this common approach to improving asset pricing models does not totally resolve the alpha problem in event studies. The alpha for a firm experiencing a significant corporate event is likely affected and itself may well contain abnormal returns (ARs) (e.g., returns associated with behavioral influences rather than systematic risk factors). When this alpha is included in the computation of predicted (fitted) returns, it could introduce bias in the estimation of ARs. For example, predicted returns are overestimated due to the inclusion of alpha, such that ARs computed as actual returns minus predicted returns are underestimated. Of course, one way to avoid such bias is to use a valid asset pricing model, for which the alpha should be zero as Jensen has asserted. In other words, to more accurately estimate ARs in event studies, we should apply a valid asset pricing model that contains little or no alpha mispricing error. To the authors' knowledge, no previous event studies acknowledge this pre-condition to computing ARs. Without a valid asset pricing model, ARs in event studies can be biased by bad model problems related to nonzero alpha intercepts.[7]

[7] In forthcoming Chapter 4 we review a recent asset pricing model by Kolari et al. (2021) dubbed the ZCAPM that, unlike other models, contains no intercept parameter. In Chapters

In search of a valid asset pricing model, researchers typically test for alpha near zero on an in-sample basis using some estimation period to compute and compare models. For example, they will estimate a multifactor model in a five-year estimation period, and then estimate α_is for stocks within this sample period. Another way to test asset asset pricing models is to use an out-of-sample setup that is potentially less prone to data mining. Fama and MacBeth (1973) invented a cross-sectional regression approach for testing different asset pricing models. The test can be conducted on an in-sample or out-of-sample basis. As Fama recognized, this cross-sectional regression approach solves problems in the cross-correlation of residuals in asset pricing regression models as well as multicollinearity between multifactors in models.

In forthcoming empirical analyses of long/short anomaly portfolios, we will rely on out-of-sample, cross-sectional regressions rather than in-sample, time-series regressions. Anomaly portfolios are economically interesting and represent a particularly high bar for testing asset pricing models. After all, researchers have exhaustively sifted through large stock return databases to identify anomalies. In our cross-sectional regression tests, we use out-of-sample rather than in-sample analyses to not only reduce potential data mining but be more consistent with real world investor behavior in the market. That is, investors initially measure the risk parameters of a stock using an asset pricing model; subsequently, they use this risk information to invest in stocks. To be an investable strategy, returns in the next month (for example) should be related to previously estimated risk parameters. If not, the model is not valid from the perspective of investors.

The primary question that we address in this book is: Can asset pricing models explain the out-of-sample returns of the cross-section of average anomaly portfolio returns? If one or more models can do this, market efficiency is supported. As Fama emphasized, the two pillars of efficient markets and asset pricing models are inextricably linked to one another.

5 to 7 we show that this model appears to be a valid model with exceptional ability to explain the cross-section of average stock returns when compared to prominent multifactor models.

However, if asset pricing models cannot explain anomaly portfolios on an out-of-sample basis, the door is open to behavioralists to better explain asset prices. We next provide a brief discussion of behavioral finance.

1.4 Behavioral Finance

In the 1980s and 1990s, numerous studies reported evidence that stock returns overreact to market information, including Debindt and Thaler (1985), (1987), Howe (1986), Brown and Harlow (1988), Ball and Kothari (1989), Zarowin (1990), Chopra et al. (1992), Jegadeesh and Titman (1993), and others. These studies generally found that extreme stock price movements were followed by reversals in direction over time. As elucidated by DeBondt and Thaler, a commonly accepted explanation of this anomaly is that, in investment decisions, individuals "...overweight recent information and underweight base rate data ... " (1987, p. 557). They credited previous authors, including Keynes (1936), Shiller (1984) and others, for similar ideas concerning this short-run behavioral bias in investor behavior that tended to be irrational in nature. Known as *prospect theory*, another behavioral phenomenon posited by Kahneman and Tversky (1979) is that investors are more sensitive to losses than gains (i.e., loss aversion). Later work by Barbaries et al. (2021) used prospect theory to develop a new asset pricing model that proved able to explain a majority of 23 well-known stock market anomalies.[8]

In 2013 Professor Robert Shiller was awarded the Nobel Prize in Economics at the same time as Professor Fama. However, Shiller (1981) argued that, contrary to the EMH, stock prices fluctuated over time much more than corporate dividends. Working with Thalor as directors of the National Bureau of Economic Research program in behavioral economics, they read hundreds of studies that tended to contradict rational markets and instead favor behavioral finance. Shiller observed that speculative bubbles in stock markets are indicative of psychological contagion among market participants that fuels excessive price increases. Emotions, epidemiology, sociology, social psychology, news media and journalism, etc. play important roles in bubbles. He discerned that bubbles are not about the craziness of

[8] In the Barberis et al. model, asset prices are determined by the asset's volatility, its return skewness, and capital market overhang related to the investor's average prior gain or loss from holding the asset. Investors have not only CAPM mean-variance preferences but prospect theory preferences (in addition to narrow framing of new risks separate of other risks).

investors but epidemic-like swings in investor behavior due to "irrational exuberance" and other psychological factors. Shiller concluded his Nobel lecture by proposing that, by their intelligent design, financial innovations and financial institutions could help to mitigate market excesses, bubbles, and crashes caused by psychological forces in markets.

Two often-cited and well-known studies of behavioral theory that incorporate investor psychology in analytical models were published by Daniel, Hirshleifer, Subrahmanyam (1997) and Barberis et al. (1998). These studies are exemplary of behavioral finance and therefore worth discussion. A key proposition in the DHS paper is that investors overreact to private information and underreact to public information. Alternatively, BSV posited that investors overweight the strength of information (i.e., the tendency to view events as typical of some class) and underweight statistical probabilities of events. In both DHS and BSV, similar to arguments by DeBondt and Thaler and others, the overreaction phase is marked by momentum in stock prices that is eventually reversed in a correction phase wherein public information gradually pulls prices back toward fundamentals.

The stock price implication of the DHS and BSV propositions is that a hump-shaped impulse response function would be produced. In tandem with changing investor confidence or sentiment over time, stock prices initially rise and later fall to some long-run, full-information equilibrium price level. The authors indicated that their propositions might help to explain an extensive list of firm-specific stock price anomalies. For example, they cited a litany of associated published research studies, including underreaction to public news events, short-term momentum, long-term reversal, unconditional excess volatility, and abnormal stock price movements. These theories allow for the possibility that price overreaction reflects (to some extent) human behavior in response to information flows in the financial market. In this sense, stock price overreaction does not imply mispricing due to poor information or lack of attention to market information so much as human patterns of behavior in response to information. We summarize these propositions below.

DHS Propositions

The DHS model assumes that there are informed and uniformed investors. Informed investors are exposed to judgment biases but not uniformed investors. As contended by DHS, an initial overreaction phase occurs due to overconfidence on the part of informed investors using private information. Overreaction here means that the magnitude of stock price responses to unexpected movements in fundamental variables (i.e., determinants of future firm cash flows) is substantially larger than justified by the full (or true) information signals. If subsequent public information signals confirm the private signal, overconfidence increases and leads to greater overreaction. This continued overreaction is a source of short-run momentum in the overreaction phase. Of course, if investors receive public signals that disagree with their private signals, prices will adjust by reversing direction, but this reversal is understated due to cognitive dissonance that causes investors to suppress negative events. This tendency for people to overweight events that confirm their actions and underweight contradictory events is known as *self-attribution bias* in the psychology literature. The underreaction to negative public signals causes the correction phase to be extended over more periods than the overreaction phase. We might add that, to the extent that public signals are slow or inconclusive, the overreaction and correction phases will be exaggerated. Nonetheless, given private information discovery by investors with self-attribution bias, a hump-shaped impulse response function is generated by positive and negative private news.

Figure 1.3 graphically illustrates the hump-shaped curves of stock price dynamics over time corresponding to overreaction and underreaction by investors, respectively. Assuming investors are rational, the expected value of the asset is shown well below and above these curves, respectively. Notice that, after this over- and underreaction phase, there is a correction phase that reverses the price to the rational price over time. These price patterns are symptomatic of overconfident investors in their responses to public and private information.

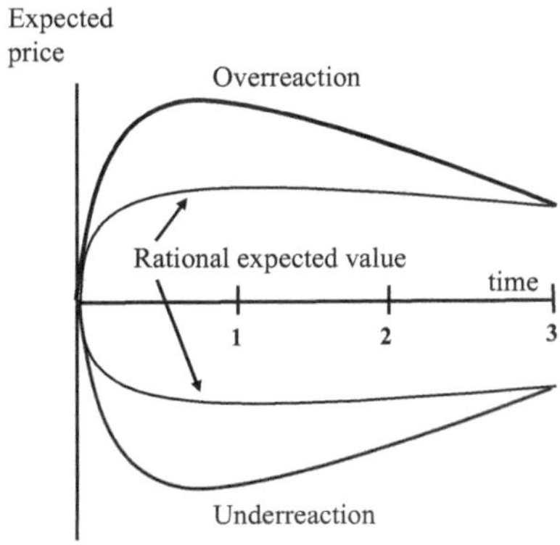

Fig. 1.3 Stock price dynamics over time to investors' cverreaction and underreaction in the behavioral theory of Daniel, Hirshleifer, Subrahmanyam (1997)

BSV Propositions

The BSV behavioral model is similar but yet distinct from DHS in some important ways. BSV posited that under- and overreaction are possible due to overweighting recent patterns in data and underweighting other data that is relevant to investor decisions. They consider two possible earnings regime patterns: (1) mean reversion (associated with underreaction) and (2) trending (associated with overreaction). Focusing on the trending regime, BSV noted that, "In the stock market, for example, investors might classify some stocks as growth stocks based on a history of consistent earnings growth, ignoring the likelihood that there are few companies that just keep growing." Barberis et al. (1998, pp. 308–309) Apparently, investors pay closer attention to the strength of information (due to a so-called representativeness heuristic) and forecast future values based on extrapolating trends in data. They give less attention to the entire set of information or statistical weight of the data which may simply follow a random walk. An important implication of BSV's investor sentiment theory is that, when information flows with high strength and low weight trend in favorable or unfavorable directions, an overreaction response is possible. Of course, long-term reversal occurs as this bias in forecasting judgment is eventually identified and corrected by investors.[9]

Trading Strategies

Over time the behavioral finance literature has become a major branch of financial economics with many subfields of study. To appreciate the depth and breadth of this literature, it is useful to consider the following different areas of study: cognitive and emotional biases, confirmation bias, hindsight bias, illusion of knowledge, illusion of control, overoptimism, overconfidence, status quo bias, the endowment effect, affect heuristics, availability heuristics, anchoring, familiarity, representativeness, debiasing, choices under uncertainty, and framing effects such as loss aversion, aversion to sure loss, mental accounting, hedonic editing, and cognitive and emotional aspects. Fairly comprehensive reviews of this behavioral literature

[9] We should mention that Fama (1998, p. 285) has criticized the DHS and BHS propositions on grounds that post-event continuation of returns occurs about as frequently as post-event reversal. However, these theories are consistent with many anomalies characterized by reversals. Other behavioral theories may well explain post-event continuation.

can be found in Schoenhart (2008), Cervellati et al. (2024), and citations therein. It is beyond the scope of the present book to review this large body of work.

Relevant to our interest in anomalies, a natural evolution of behavioral research has been the development of trading strategies to exploit market anomalies. As noted by Schoenhart, many strategies are being applied by practitioners, including momentum trading, contrarian (reversal) strategies, daylight saving anomaly trading, seasonal affective disorder (SAD) trading, and integrated strategies based on multiple approaches.[10] Among these trading strategies, many researchers have proposed long/short portfolios that persistently earn abnormal returns. Some examples are: long winner stocks/short loser stocks (viz., momentum portfolios), long small size stocks/short big size stocks (viz., size factor), long value stocks/short growth stocks (viz., value factor), etc.

Bali et al. (2012) investigated different decision rules to assess the investment practice of five popular anomaly strategies. They found that some anomaly investment strategies, such as short-term reversal, long-term reversal, and momentum, produced efficient investment returns. Edelen et al. (2016)) studied institutional investor demand for stock return anomalies. Unexpectedly, institutions tended to buy (not sell) stocks in the short position of a long/short stock portfolio anomaly. Hence, these informed, sophisticated investors traded contrary to anomaly strategies. On the other hand, Calluzo et al. (2019) showed that institutional investors increased their trading of 14 prominent anomalies due to academic publications and availability of related accounting data. Particularly institutions with high turnover, such as hedge funds, tended to increase their anomaly trading. Other research by Birru et al. (202) reported evidence that quantitative equity research analysts (known as *Quants*) identify stock market anomalies that benefit analysts and mutual fund clients. Additionally, a recent working paper by Lazo-Paz et al. (2024) found that anomaly risk-adjusted returns only occur among the most crowded stocks, which are held by many investors. A trading strategy that is long most crowded stocks and short least crowded stocks earned significant abnormal returns.

In forthcoming Chapter 2, we review studies that investigate the growing number of anomaly portfolios. As we will see, there is no concensus among researchers on the existence of anomalies. Some authors contend

[10] See Zacks (2011) for an in-depth review of behavioral trading strategies.

that they either vanish over time or were not there in the first place (i.e., false discoveries). Other authors argue that anomalies are replicable and persist over time (i.e, real phenomena). Anomalies not characterized by tradable long/short portfolios are not addressed in this book.

1.5 Summary

The debate between efficient markets and behavioralist schools in finance has increasingly intensified over the past half century. Led by Professor Eugene Fama, the efficient markets hypothesis (EMH) posits that rational investors price assets in the market based on available information. Of course, advances in technology, such as computers, the internet, communications, etc., should improve efficiency over time. However, many stock price patterns do not appear to be consistent with rational investor behavior. In response to this gap in the literature, behavioralists have argued that human psychology plays an important role in asset pricing.

Related to the EMH, the Capital Asset Pricing Model (CAPM) of Sharpe (1964) and others relies upon rational investor behavior to price assets in the market. Elegant in design, the CAPM says that the expected return of an asset is a function of market portfolio expected returns and its associated beta risk. To empirically test the CAPM in the real world, the market model was developed. Jensen (1968) observed that the intercept term (alpha or α) in the market model affords a test for mispricing error, which should should be zero under the theoretical CAPM. A nonzero alpha for an asset implies that the CAPM cannot explain it—that is, something is missing. As such, researchers used alpha as a way to identify anomalies in the stock market (e.g., see Jensen et al. (2023)). An anomaly has a nonzero alpha and tends to have persistently high returns over time.

In an effort to explain anomalies, asset pricing researcher augmented the single market factor CAPM with other factors. Seminal work by Fama and French (1992, 1993, 1995) introduced long/short factors to explain size and value anomalies. After adding these multifactors to the market model, the alpha was reduced to near zero for portfolios sorted on size and value firm characteristics. In his 2013 Nobel lecture, Fama advocated for two pillars in asset pricing—namely, market efficiency and asset pricing models. A valid asset pricing model with zero alpha mispricing error implies market efficiency. Unfortunately, researchers began to identify in increasing number of anomalies in the stock market that were unexplained by the three-factor model. Asset pricing modelers responded by adding more multifactors in attempt to explain new discoveries of anomalies. However, due to the rapid proliferation of anomalies over time, the ability of asset pricing models to keep up has became realistically untenable. Behavioralists appear to be winning the battle. Many anomalies must be attributable to irrational human behavior that does not fit into the traditional EMH framework.

In forthcoming chapters, we survey existing literature on asset pricing models and their ability to explain stock market anomalies. Also, we conduct asset pricing tests of large datasets of anomaly portfolio returns. We show that prominent asset pricing models fail to explain most of these anomaly returns. However, a lesser known model dubbed the ZCAPM by Kolari et al. (2021) that takes advantage of machine learning well explains large numbers of anomaly portfolio returns. Exceptionally, in out-of-sample tests of their returns, almost 300 anomalies are explained by systematic risks estimated by the ZCAPM. This explanatory power is outstanding in the sense that even random chance would predict some anomalies do not fit the model. Hence, our empirical evidence strongly supports the EMH of Fama. At least for long/short anomaly portfolios, the behavioralists will need to find anomalies not explained by the ZCAPM to stand their ground against the EMH. We hope that this book stimulates new research to replicate our findings, expand our tests to other anomaly portfolios, and further study the ZCAPM.

References

Bali, Tar., Bro., and Dem. 2012. Investing in stock market anomalies, Working paper at Baruch College, SUNY and New York University (available on SSRN with abstract ID 1996681).

Ball, R., and Kot. 1989. Nonstationary expected returns: Implications for tests of market efficiency and serial correlation in returns. *Journal of Financial Economics* 25: 51–74.

Barberis, N., L. J. Jin, and B. Wan. 2021. Prospect theory and stock market anomalies. *Journal of Finance* 56: 2639–2687.

Barberis, N., A. Shleifer, and R. Vishny. 1998. A model of investor sentiment. *Journal of Financial Economics* 49: 307–343.

Birru, J., S. Gokkaya, X. Liu, and S. Markov. 2024. Quants and market anomalies. *Journal of Accounting and Economics* 78 (101688): 1–27.

Black, F. 1972. Capital market equilibrium with restricted borrowing. *Journal of Business* 45: 444–454.

Black, F., M. C. Jensen, and M. Scholes. 1972. The capital asset pricing model: Some empirical tests, in Jen., M. C., ed., *Studies in the Theory of Capital Markets* (Praeger, New York, NY).

Breeden, N. D. 1979. An intertemporal asset pricing model with stochastic consumption and investment opportunities. *Journal of Financial Economics* 7: 265–296.

Brown, K. C., and W. V. Harlow. 1988. Market overreaction: Magnitude and intensity. *Journal of Portfolio Management* 14: 6–13.

Calluzo, P., F. Moneta, and S. Topaloglu. 2019. When anomalies are publicized broadly, do institutions trade accordingly? *Management Science* 65: 4555–4574.

Carhart, M. M. 1997. On persistence in mutual fund performance. *Journal of Finance* 52: 57–82.

Cervellati, E. M., N. Angelini, and G. P. Stella. *Behavioral Finance and Wealth Management: Market Anomalies, Investors' Behavior and the Role of Financial Advisors* (Virtus Interpress, Sumy, Ukraine). https://doi.org/10.22495/bfwm

Chopra, N., J. Lokonishok, and J. R. Ritter. 1992. *Journal of Financial Economics* 31: 235–268.

Cochrane, J. H. 1991. Production-based asset pricing and the link between stock returns and economic fluctuations. *Journal of Finance* 46: 209–237.

Cochrane, J. H. 2011. Presidential address: Discount rates. *Journal of Finance* 56: 1047–1108.

Daniel, K., D. Hirshleifer, and A. Subrahmanya. 1997. A theory of overconfidence, self-attribution, and security market under- and over-reactions. Unpublished working paper. University of Michigan.

DeBondt, W., and Thaler. 1985. Does the stock market overreact? *Journal of Finance* 40: 793–805.

DeBondt, W., and Thaler. 1995. Financial decision-making in markets and firms: A behavioral perspective. In *Handbooks in OR and MS*, vol. 9, ed. R. Jarrow, et al., 385–410. Amsterdam: Elsevier.

Edelen, R. M., O. S. Ince, and G. B. Kadlec. 2016. Institutional investors and stock return anomalies. *Journal of Financial Economics* 119: 472–488.

Fama, E. F. 1965. The behavior of stock-market prices. *The Journal of Business* 38: 34–105.

Fama, E. F., 1968. Risk, return, and equilibrium: Some clarifying comments. *Journal of Finance* 23: 29–40.

Fama, E. F. 1970. Efficient capital markets: A review of theory and evidence. *Journal of Finance* 35: 383–417.

Fama, E. F. 1998. Market efficiency, long-term returns, and behavioral finance. *Journal of Financial Economics* 49: 283–306.

Fama, E. F., L. Fisher, M. C. Jensen, and R. Roll. 1969. The adjustment of stock prices to new information. *International Economic Journal* 10: 1–21.

Fama, E. F., and K. R. French. 1992. The cross-section of expected stock returns. *Journal of Finance* 47: 427–465.

Fama, E. F., and K. R. French. 1993. The cross-section of expected returns. *Journal of Financial Economics* 33: 3–56.

Fama, E. F., and K. R. French. 1995. Size and book-to-market factors in earnings and returns. *Journal of Finance* 50: 131–156.

Fama, E. F., and K. R. French. 2015. A five-factor asset pricing model. *Journal of Financial Economics* 116: 1–22.

Fama, E. F., and K. R. French. 2018. Choosing factors. *Journal of Financial Economics* 128: 234–252.

Fama, E. F., and K. R. French. 2020. Comparing cross-section and time-series factor models. *Review of Financial Studies* 33: 1892–1926.

Fama, E. F., and J. D. MacBeth. 1973. Risk, return, and equilibrium: Empirical tests. *Journal of Political Economy* 81: 607–636.

Ferson, W. E., and C. R. Harvey. 1996. Conditioning variables and the cross-section of stock returns, Working paper, Duke University, 1996.

Han, Y., J. W. Kolari, and S. Pynnonen. 2023. Dynamic risk adjustment in long-run event study tests. *Applied Economics* 56: 744–764. Available online at: https://doi.org/10.1080/00036846.2023.2287554.

Howe, J. S. 1986. Evidence on stock market overreaction. *Financial Analysts Journal* 42: 74–77.

Jensen, M. C. 1968. The performance of mutual funds in the period 1945–1964. *Journal of Finance* 23: 389–416.

Jensen, T. I., B. Kelly, and L. H. Pedersen. 2023. Is there a replication crisis in finance? *Journal of Finance* 78: 2465–2518.

Jegadeesh, M., and S. Titman. 1993. Returns to buying winners and selling losers: Implications for stock market efficiency. *Journal of Finance* 48: 65–91.

Kahneman, D., and A. Tversky. 1979. Prospect theory: An analysis of decision under risk. *Econometrica* 47: 263–291.

Kolari, J. W., W. Liu, and J. Z. Huang. 2021. *A New Model of Capital Asset Prices: Theory and Evidence.* Cham, Switzerland: Palgrave Macmillan.

Kolari, J., and S. Pynnonen. 2010. Event study testing with cross-sectional correlation of abnormal returns. *Review of Financial Studies* 23: 3996–4025.

Lazo-Paz, R., F. Moneta, and L. B. Chincarin. 2024. Crowded spaces and anomalies, Working paper at the University of Ottawa and University of San Francisco.

Lintner, J. 1965. The valuation of risk assets and the selection of risky investments in stock portfolios and capital budgets. *Review of Economics and Statistics* 47: 13–37.

Lo, A. W. 2008. Efficient market hypothesis. In *The New Palgrave Dictionary of Economics*, 2nd ed., ed. S. N. Durlauf and L. E. Blume. New York, NY: Palgrave Macmillan.

Lucas, R. E. 1978. Asset prices in an exchange economy. *Econometrica* 46: 1429–1445.

Markowitz, H. M. 1959. *Portfolio Selection: Efficient Diversification of Investments.* New York, NY: Wiley.

Merton, R. C. 1973. An intertemporal capital asset pricing model. *Econometrica* 41: 867–887.

Mossin, J. 1966. Equilibrium in a capital asset market. *Econometrica* 34: 768–783.

Osterrieder, J., and M. Seigne. 2023. Unraveling market mysteries: A comprehensive review of financial anomalies and puzzles, Working paper, Bern Business School and Candor Partners Limited.

Roll, R. 1977. A critique of the asset pricing theory's tests, part I: On past and potential future testability of the theory. *Journal of Financial Economics* 4: 129–176.

Schoenhart. 2008. *Behavioral Finance and Market Anomalies: An Academic Review*. Saarbuecken, Germany: VDM.

Schwert, G. W. 2003. Anomalies and market efficiency. In Constantinides, *Handbook of the Economics and Finance*, vol. 1, ed. M. Harris, and R. M. Stulz, 939–974.

Sharpe, W. F. 1963. A simplified model for portfolio analysis. *Management Science* 9: 277–293.

Sharpe, W. F. 1964. Capital asset prices: A theory of market equilibrium under conditions of risk. *Journal of Finance* 19: 425–442.

Shiller, R. J. 1981. Do stock prices move too much to be justified by subsequent changes in dividends. *American Economic Review* 71: 421–436.

Shiller, R. J., 1984. Stock prices and social dynamics. *Brookings Papers on Economic Activity* 2: 457–510.

Stulz, R. M. 1981. A model of international asset pricing. *Journal of Financial Economics* 9: 383–406.

Treynor, J. L. 1961. Market value, time, and risk, Unpublished manuscript.

Treynor, J. L. 1962. Toward a theory of market value of risky assets, Unpublished manuscript.

Zacks, L. 2011. *The Handbook of Equity Market Anomalies: Translating Market Inefficiencies into Effective Investment Strategies*, 1st ed. Hoboken, NJ: Wiley.

Zarowin, P. 1990. Size, seasonality, and stock market overreaction. *Journal of Financial and Quantitative Analysis* 25: 113–125.

CHAPTER 2

Anomaly Stock Portfolios

Abstract This chapter surveys the finance literature on anomalous stock portfolios. These portfolios have long positions in selected stocks and short positions in other stocks. Early examples are the size and value anomaly stock portfolios. To explain these anomalies, Fama and French (1992), Fama and French (1993) famously created a three-factor model comprised of a market factor, a size factor that is long small capitalization stocks and short big capitalization stocks, and a value factor that is long high book-to-market equity ratio stocks and short low book-to-market equity ratio stocks. Many subsequent research papers have been published on a wide variety of other long/short anomaly portfolios over the past three decades. In the last few years, work on anomaly stock portfolios has accelerated with some excellent comprehensive studies of hundreds of such anomalies in top finance journals. To encourage research on anomalies, authors of some of recent studies are making available their stock return data series on the internet for hundreds of anomaly portfolios—for example, Chen and Zimmermann (2022) and Jensen et al. (2023). We have downloaded data from these studies via their online websites. This open source data are publicly available to researchers. In forthcoming chapters of this book, we employ this data to conduct empirical tests on the ability of alternative asset pricing models to explain almost 300 anomaly stock portfolios.

J. W. Kolari et al., *Asset Pricing Models and Market Efficiency*,
https://doi.org/10.1007/978-3-031-92901-4_2

2.1 Disappearing Anomalies

An often-cited paper on anomalies was published by McLean and Pontiff (2016). Interestingly, the authors found that many anomalies based on long/short portfolios have disappeared over time. One reason is statistical bias. Persistent anomalies over time can be detected using in-sample stock return data; however, the anomalies noticeably diminished when measured on an out-of-sample basis. This decline in return predictability means that investors would earn less than in-sample tests would suggest.

Another potential source of declining anomaly returns over time is mispricing. Upon publication of an anomaly in academic journals, market investors revise their pricing to eliminate the anomalous return. However, if risk rather than mispricing explains the anomaly, as observed by Cochrane (1999), returns to investors will be the same pre- and post-publication. In this case, rational expectations account for anomaly returns, which are not anomalous after risk adjustment.

McLean and Pontiff studied 97 long/short anomaly portfolios contained in 79 academic studies. They found that out-of-sample returns were on average 26 percent lower than in-sample returns in line with statistical bias. On a post-publication basis, the average anomaly returns declined by 58 percent. Subtracting the statistical bias effect, they inferred that the publication effect had a lower bound of 32 percent. Thus, while return predictability of anomaly portfolios did not disappear entirely in their tests, it was greatly diminished by statistical bias and publication effects.

Concerning diminishing anomaly returns, anomalies with the highest in-sample returns and construction based on price data (e.g., momentum portfolios) had the largest declines in returns over time.[1] Consistent with these findings, they documented increased trading activity among stocks in anomaly portfolios as well as increased differences in short interest among stocks in the long and short sides of anomaly portfolios. These and other findings led them to infer that academic publication of anomalies draws

[1] High in-sample returns are likely in high risk small stocks. Earlier research by Cederburg and O'Dougherty (2015) showed that anomalies associated with small stocks tended to diminish over time to a much greater extent that those for large stocks. They inferred that transaction costs and liquidity problems prevent investors from exploiting anomalies among small stocks.

the attention of sophisticated investors. These investors arbitrage away a substantial portion of anomaly returns.[2]

A closely related study by Jacobs and Müller (2020) examined 241 anomalies in 39 stock markets around the world. Confirming McLean and Pontiff, anomaly returns decreased after publication in the U.S. stock market. Using equal-weighted (value-weighted) anomaly returns, post-publication percentage decline in returns was a fairly large at 62 percent (66 percent). However, very different results were observed in other stock markets. Post-publication returns did not significantly or economically decrease after anomaly publications in 39 international markets. For large stocks there was a decline in anomaly returns in some countries after publication; nonetheless, U.S. stock returns declined noticeably more than other markets.

They interpreted the disparity between U.S. and international markets to be due to cross-country investment barriers that tend to segment markets. Additional analyses revealed that out-of-sample anomaly returns in global stock markets are approximately two-thirds of the magnitude of original U.S. in-sample anomalies. Thus, anomalies are not simply due to chance.

The authors compared the anomaly returns of anomalies with high versus low arbitrage costs. Predictably, the high arbitrage cost anomalies had higher returns that the low cost anomalies. Both in-sample and post-publication tests confirmed these results. They noted that behavioral finance theories propose that anomalies can arise due to both behavioral biases and impediments to arbitrage (Barbaris and Thaler 2003). In general, they inferred from their findings that anomalies are real and not the product of data mining.

2.2 Publication Bias-Adjusted Returns

Chen and Zimmermann (2020) developed a method for adjusting anomaly returns for publication bias. Their in-sample adjustment applied Bayes rule. More specifically, the distribution of anomaly returns are compared to the distribution based on pure chance. In this way, they assessed the extent to which the cross-sectional dispersion anomaly returns were due to chance.

[2] See also Cotter and McGeever (2018), who investigated five well-known anomalies, including accruals, asset growth, book-to-market ratio, new equity issuances, firm profitability, return reversal, momentum, firm size, and stock turnover. They found that the significance of these anomalies declined from 1990 to 2013. With the exception of firm profitability and stock turnover, anomalies became insignificant over time in different empirical tests.

For 156 published long/short anomaly portfolios, they found that publication bias-adjusted returns were only 12.3 percent smaller that otherwise. Whereas the average predictor anomaly earned about 8 percent per year, the bias-adjusted return was not much reduced at about 7 percent. Thus, according to their findings, publication did not materially reduce anomaly returns. Some out-of-sample tests were conducted that increased the upper bound on the publication bias to 23 percent (from about 12 percent using in-sample tests). However, only 3 percent of this decrease in returns was due to publication bias as other effects accounted for most of the declines.

It is worth mentioning that Chen and Zimmerman contended that out-of-sample tests of anomalies are contaminated by changing economic conditions across large samples of anomalies. These changes account for widely varying estimates of deteriorating out-of-sample anomaly portfolio performance in previous studies. As such, they believed that their in-sample tests provided a more accurate estimate of publication bias in anomaly returns.

We interpret their analyses to have similar implications to those of a more recent study discussed below by Bowles, Reed, Ringgenberg, and Thornock (2024) on anomaly time. That is, anomalies are real, not the result of data mining, and persist over time despite academic publication.

2.3 Failure to Replicate Anomalies in Previous Studies

Hou et al. (2020) sought to replicate a large database of 452 anomalies. Their paper provided a detailed appendix with details of how these anomalies were constructed. Taking into account very small microcap stocks, 65 percent of the anomalies were not statistically significant with an absolute t-statistic of 1.96. At the 5 percent significance level (i.e., t-statistic of 2.78), 82 percent of the anomalies failed replication. Among those that passed these statistical tests, average returns were much smaller than originally published. In replication experiments, they computed anomaly returns for the same population, used both different and the same samples, and implemented similar but not identical methods.

Some anomalies were replicable, including well-known value, profitability, capital investment, and momentum anomalies. However, anomalies based on trading frictions (e.g., liquidity, market microstructure, etc.) tended to fail replication as well as many anomaly portfolios containing microcaps.

This study seriously challenged the anomalies literature. Apparently, most anomalies published in academic studies are false discoveries.[3] They conjectured that researchers have difficulty publishing insignificant findings in journals. Hence, those findings are not published but a smaller set of significant findings is published. Also, they criticized the finance journals for not publishing replication studies, which is so common in the hard sciences. Without replication, findings cannot be verified and potentially taint inferences drawn from data in studies. They cited Harvey (2017), who argued that editors seek to boost citation-based impact factors of their journals by selecting papers with highly significant findings. Faced with this situation, researchers may well engage in *p*-hacking, wherein they run different samples with different test methods until a significant results is found. Hou, Xue, and Zhang conjectured that these editorial behaviors and researcher data mining efforts help to explain the poor replicability of anomaly portfolio returns. Another relevant issue is the economic importance of anomalies. Cederburg and O'Doherty (2015) argued that many anomalies occur in small, illiquid stocks that are not economically important. Hence, the existence of large numbers of anomalies is "overblown."

2.4 Reproducing Anomalies in Previous Studies

Chen and Zimmermann (2022) replicated 319 firm-level characteristics used to obtain long/short portfolio returns in original published papers using the same sample periods. Only three anomalies were not accurately reproduced. Unlike Hou, Xue, and Zhang, they "reproduced" the anomalies using the same sample and same computer code. As Welch (2019) has observed, there are important differences between reproducing and replicating empirical findings. Replication seeks to mimic sample and test procedures; by contrast, reproduction exactly duplicates the findings. Replication allows for much wider scope of analyses than reproduction in terms of samples, methods, etc. Admittedly, replication would seem to be useful in determining the degree of *p*-hacking in the literature. However, reproduction seeks to verify the accuracy of published results. It is common for researchers to reproduce major scientific discoveries to ensure the validity of the findings. Whether the tests can be extended to other samples and methods is subject to further study but does not disprove the original findings.

[3] More generally, the authors cited an earlier study by Harvey et al. (2016) that claimed most findings in financial economics studies are false.

With close to 100 percent accuracy in terms of reproducing anomaly portfolio results, in addition to other out-of-sample tests and different methodological choices as robustness checks, the authors concluded that their study restores trust in the empirical asset pricing literature. To emphasize this point, the authors made available their anomaly returns as an open source dataset on the internet for researchers around the world. The main takeaway of their findings is that long/short portfolio return anomalies are not false discoveries due to the publication process, data mining, or other potential sources of bias; on the contrary, anomaly portfolio returns demonstrate cross sectional predictability and therefore are real.

2.5 Trading Costs

Chen and Velikov (2023) examined the expected returns of long/short anomaly portfolios after taking into account bid-ask spreads, post-publication effects, and trading costs. The average anomaly return of 8 percent per year should be attractive to investors. Of course, these returns are only generated in academic studies and not the real world. Disappointingly, they found that expected returns are near zero.

The authors studied 204 return predictors (anomalies) in Chen and Zimmermann (2022). Summarizing their findings:

- the average return is 68 basis point (bps) in their sample of 204 anomalies;
- the average return falls to 44 bps per month after trading costs;
- taking into account post-publication effects, the average return falls dramatically to 9 bps per month; and
- restricting the analyses to post-2005 when trading technology had substantially advanced, they estimated an average return of only 4 bps per month.

Like McLean and Pontiff, they found that anomaly returns decayed post-publication by about 50 percent in general and 72 percent in the post-2005 period. Even the strongest anomalies experienced low expected returns after these adjustments. Altogether, at least from a real world perspective, these results paint a dim picture of anomalies. Academic anomalies do not translate into tradable investment strategies due to publication of anomalies in addition to investors arbitraging away mispricing using modern trading technology.

The authors cited a number of other studies that reported profitable anomalies after taking into account trading costs, including Frazzini et al. (2015), Novy-Marx and Velikov (2016), Briere et al. (2019), and DeMiguel et al. (2020). However, they observed that these studies relied upon pre-2006 data that has stronger return predictability than in their post-2005 analyses. The implication is that anomalies are shrinking over time to the point that, net of trading cost, publication, and other effects, there are no tradable profits to be realized. They added a caveat that profitable long/short portfolio strategies may well exist in an world with some degree of imperfectly efficient pricing. However, they are not as ubiquitous as the literature would portray.

2.6 Anomaly Time

Bowles et al. (2024) examined 28 anomalies in the McLean and Pontiff study that are based on earnings announcements and 10-K accounting statements. These anomalies are related to information that arrives at infrequent but discrete periods of time. They collected real-time data available from the Compustat Snapshot database to construct panel data series around anomaly event dates from 1990 to 2019. Using these events, the authors found that anomaly returns did not decline over time as much as previously believed. Anomaly portfolio returns were economically and statistically significant after news announcements but decayed rapidly thereafter. The latter decay can be attributed to arbitrage by investors.

How can we reconcile these findings with those in McLean and Pontiff? Bowles et al. found that the informativeness of anomaly returns degraded over time due to stale information in their computation. Previous studies that rebalance anomaly portfolios on a weekly, monthly, or even annual basis incorporate stale information. By focusing on the return predictability of anomaly portfolios immediately after the release of relevant information, they were able to show that stale information can explain the diminution of anomaly returns over time in McLean and Pontiff. They argued that, due to stale information, prior studies substantially underestimated anomaly returns.

Bowles et al. concluded that, unlike researchers that argue anomalies tend to vanish over time or simply do not exist due to failure to replicate, anomalies are real and do predict returns if portfolios are constructed immediately after information is released. They are not simply the results of data mining efforts of researchers, who are dredging for patterns in stock returns. In their words, "Our event-based approach finds evidence that the anomaly zoo is alive and well in the information age ... " (Bowles et al. 2024, p. 3578)

2.7 Anomalies and Alphas

In an effort to address the growing skepticism about the persistence of anomalies in financial economics, Jensen et al. (2023) developed an innovative Bayesian model to show that anomalies are more replicable than previously believed (i.e., pass standard statistical t-tests for significant differences from zero returns). They compared their replicability to the 35 percent rate obtained by Hou et al. (2020). They found:

- 55.6 percent baseline replication based on 153 long/short anomaly portfolios referred to as *factors* in their study; and
- after dropping anomalies that were insignificant in original studies, the replication rate rises to 61.3 percent.

Most importantly, Jensen et al. departed from earlier anomaly studies by computing the alphas using the CAPM (see Eq. (1.3) in Chapter 1) instead of raw returns. Based on these risk-adjusted returns, the replication rate was even higher at 82.4 percent. Other tests using a fairly sophisticated Bayesian model that includes a multiple testing (MT) correction again generated a 82.4 percent replication rate. We summarize their findings in Fig. 2.1.

The authors expanded their analyses to 93 countries. For this large global sample, the replication rate was again 82.4 percent. In terms of post-publication performance, anomalies with higher pre-publication alphas had higher post-publication alphas too. And, higher in-sample alphas was associated with higher out-of-sample alphas. Post-publication alphas decreased but due to expected Bayesian outcomes rather than diminishing due to arbitrage. When collectively evaluating anomalies, they proposed that they tend to cluster into 13 or so *themes*. The factor zoo is not as big as it might seem with hundreds of anomalies. Anomalies within each theme are correlated with one another.

Summarizing in their words:

> The majority of factors do replicate, do survive joint modeling of all factors, do hold up out-of-sample, are strengthened (not weakened) by the large number of observed factors, are further strengthened by global evidence, and the number of factors can be understood as multiple versions of a smaller number of themes. (Jensen et al. 2023, p. 2466)

In other results, they showed that investors could have profited from anomalies (factors) that were significant based on their Bayesian method but not other Bayesian methods used by previous authors. Also, further tests indicated that the Sharpe ratios of these anomaly portfolios increased over time. This trend means that the risk-return profile of anomalies has increased as more discoveries have been made. In view of these substantive findings, they concluded that their empirical results markedly contrast with those of previous studies. The use of risk-adjusted returns via CAPM alphas yielded very different results than obtained by previous returns using raw returns.

A related study by Favero et al. (2023) computed risk-adjusted anomaly returns also. Somewhat differently from Jensen et al., they estimated the CAPM market model and then computed risk-adjusted returns as residuals in forthcoming days, i.e., actual returns minus predicted returns using the estimated alpha and beta parameters of the market model. Subsequently, they summed up the residuals over time to get cumulative risk-adjusted returns. Their test assets consisted of 90 portfolios comprised of the top and bottom deciles of 45 characteristics sorted portfolios. Assuming a no arbitrage condition, risk-adjusted anomaly returns should be unpredictable. However, based on long-run returns and a mean-variance framework, they found that future risk-adjusted portfolio returns were predictable in terms of a negative relation to current price deviations. As such, the latter current price deviations were attributable to under- or over-pricing of stocks relative to mean-variance portfolio prices. They then exploited this finding by implementing a zero-investment portfolio that buys (sells) under-priced (over-priced) portfolios. Significant gains were achieved with this simple investment strategy. In short, the anomaly portfolio findings in this study agree with those in Jensen et al., who found that risk-adjusted anomaly returns exist.

Earlier work by Lu et al. (2017) measured the alphas for nine often-cited anomalies in five countries: Canada, France, Germany, Japan, and the U.K. Risk-adjusted alphas were computed using the Fama and French (1993) three-factor model. Because the anomalies' alphas were significant in all five non-U.S. countries in the 1980 to 2015 sampler period, the authors inferred that they are not spurious or due to data mining. Also, evidence of mispricing among anomalies was documented due to the significance of idiosyncratic volatility in explaining anomalies.

Finally, a recent paper by Anginer et al. (2024) showed that anomaly returns tend to be higher for stocks with a growth orientation (cheap) rather than a value (expensive) orientation. Also, those anomalies with both value and momentum orientations had higher returns than other anomalies. We interpret their findings to suggest that risk-adjusted alphas continue to persist over time for anomaly stock portfolios.

2.8 Online Anomaly Portfolios

For purposes of our empirical tests in forthcoming chapters, daily returns for large datasets of long-short portfolio anomalies are generously made available by Chen and Zimmermann (2022) and Jensen et al. (2023)). Out of a total of 172 portfolios in the Chen and Zimmerman dataset, we retain 133 anomaly portfolios with complete daily return data in the full sample period July 3, 1972 to December 31, 2021 (see Appendix A).[4] As a robustness check, we replicate our empirical tests using 153 anomaly portfolios in the Jensen et al. dataset (see Appendix B).

In total we investigate 286 anomalies. This large dataset of anomaly portfolio returns allows fairly comprehensive analyses of the explanatory power of asset pricing models. Can these anomalies be explained by asset pricing models? Alternatively, are they indeed anomalies based on real mispricing not taken into account in the models and better explained by behavioral theories? In forthcoming Chapters 5–7, we report empirical evidence in an effort to answer these questions.

2.9 Surveys of Anomalies Research

Due to large body of studies on anomalies in finance, some authors have provided surveys of the literature. Latif et al. (2011) discussed research in different countries on calendar anomalies,[5] technical anomalies,[6] and fundamental anomalies.[7] The market efficiency hypothesis (EMH) and behavioral theories are reviewed in the context of these anomalies. Another survey study by Woo, Mai, McAleer, and Wong (2020) similarly sought to provide a comprehensive discussion of the EMH, behavioral theories,

[4] As mentioned by Chen and Velikov (2023), this database contains most if not all anomalies studied by Harvey et al. (2016), McLean and Pontiff (2016), Green, Hand, and Zhang (2013), and Hou et al. (2020).

[5] Some examples of calendar anomalies are weekend, turn-of-the-month, turn-of-the-year, and January effects.

[6] For, example, moving averages and trading range breaks in technical analysis techniques.

[7] Long-short portfolios based on accounting and financial information, such as the size, value, profit, capital investment, dividend, and many other anomalies. These anomalies are the focus of the present book.

and the growing number of stock market anomalies. A long list of anomaly studies are cited in their paper, which is a useful resource for academics and professionals interested in learning more about anomalies.

2.10 Summary

Over the last 30 years, the number of anomalies in finance has risen into the hundreds. There are so many anomalies that asset pricing models have fallen behind in their ability to explain them. While this problem appeared to insurmountable for asset pricing modelers, McLean and Pontiff (2016) found that the anomalies vanished for the most part over time after their academic publication. Post-publication returns declined by about 58 percent. Also, out-of-sample anomaly returns were 26 percent lower than in-sample returns. Combining these publication and statistical effects, anomalies would appear to be overblown. However, a related study by Jacobs and Müller (2020) found that post-publication returns declined in the U.S. but not 38 other countries. Hence, anomalies are still an issue in international stock markets. Moreover, empirical tests by Chen and Zimmermann (2020) adjusted anomaly returns for publication bias via Bayesian methods and found that returns did not materially decline over time.

The controversy surrounding the existence of anomalies deepened with evidence reported by Hou et al. (2020). When they attempted to replicate a large dataset of 452 anomalies, 82 percent of these anomalies could not be replicated. They inferred that most anomalies published in academic studies were false discoveries. Editorial behaviors at academic journals and data mining by researchers were contributing issues that explained the factor zoo comprised of hundreds of anomalies. Another study by Chen and Velikov (2023) found that, after taking into trading costs to implement anomaly portfolios in practice as well as post-2005 stock return data series, anomaly returns vanished for the most part.

Other studies documented evidence in favor of the existence of anomalies. Chen and Zimmermann (2022) found that almost all of 319 anomalies could be reproduced using the identical samples and methods of original researchers. Bowles et al. (2024) added further evidence to support anomalies by showing that stale information used in their computation tended to underestimate anomaly returns. When accurate information was used surrounding major corporate events of firms, anomaly returns did not diminish over time. Looking more broadly at anomalies in the U.S. and 93 other countries, Jensen et al. (2023) used innovative Bayesian methods and risk-adjusted anomalies returns captured by alphas in the CAPM to show that 82.4 percent of 153 anomalies could be replicated. They concluded that anomaly returns persist out of sample, in countries around the world, and can be grouped into a smaller number of themes for classification purposes.

Taken as a whole, the anomalies literature is mixed. Some studies argue that anomalies are disappearing over time due to statistical issues (e.g., in-sample versus out-of-sample differences), post-publication arbitrage by investors, and false discoveries (e.g., academic journal behavior and data mining by researchers). Other studies find that anomalies can be reliably reproduced, are present using accurate data, and persist in risk-adjusted returns (e.g., alphas based on the CAPM) as opposed to raw returns. In forthcoming chapters, we report empirical tests on the ability of asset pricing models to explain a large number of anomaly portfolios' returns. If no risk-adjusted anomaly returns exist, the models will fail as there is nothing for them to explain. On the other hand, consistent with the Jensen, Kelly, and Pedersen study, if the models' risk factors can explain anomaly returns, we can infer that anomaly returns exist but are explained by their systematic market risks. In this case, we can conclude that, after taking into account systematic risk factors that help to reduce or eliminate alpha mispricing error in the CAPM, stock market long/short portfolio anomalies do not exist.

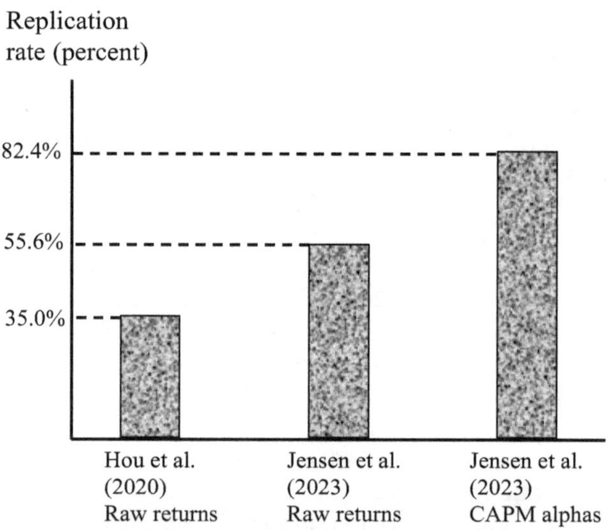

Fig. 2.1 Replication rates in finance studies

Appendix

Appendix A. 133 Anomaly Portfolios from Chen and Zimmermann (2022)

N	Abbreviation	Description
1	AbnormalAccruals ret	Abnormal accruals
2	Accruals ret	Accruals
3	AdExp ret	Advertisement expense
4	AM ret	Total assets to market
5	AnnouncementReturn ret	Earnings announcement return
6	AssetGrowth ret	Asset growth
7	Beta ret	CAPM beta
8	BetaFP ret	Frazzini-Pedersen beta
9	BetaTailRisk ret	Tail risk beta
10	BidAskSpread ret	Bid-ask spread
11	BM ret	Book to market using most recent ME
12	BMdec ret	Book to market using December ME
13	BookLeverage ret	Book leverage (annual)
14	BPEBM ret	Leverage component of BM
15	BrandInvest ret	Brand capital investment
16	Cash ret	Cash to assets
17	CashProd ret	Cash productivity
18	CBOperProf ret	Cash-based operating profitability
19	CF ret	Cash flow to market
20	Cfp ret	Operating cash flows to price
21	ChAssetTurnover ret	Change in asset turnover
22	ChEQ ret	Growth in book equity
23	ChInv ret	Inventory growth
24	ChInvIA ret	Change in capital investment (industry adjusted)
25	ChNNCOA ret	Change in net noncurrent operating assets
26	ChNWC ret	Change in net working capital
27	ChTax ret	Change in taxes
28	CompEquIss ret	Composite equity issuance
29	CompositeDebtIssuance ret	Composite debt issuance
30	Coskewness ret	Coskewness
31	DelCOA ret	Change in current operating assets
32	DelCOL ret	Change in current operating liabilities
33	DelEqu ret	Change in equity to assets
34	DelFINL ret	Change in financial liabilities
35	DelLTI ret	Change in long-term investment
36	DelNetFin ret	Change in net financial assets

N	Abbreviation	Description
37	DNoa ret	Change in net operating assets
38	DolVol ret	Past trading volume
39	EarningsConsistency ret	Earnings consistency
40	EarningsSurprise ret	Earnings surprise
41	EarnSupBig ret	Earnings surprise of big firms
42	EBM ret	Enterprise component of BM
43	EntMult ret	Enterprise multiple
44	EP ret	Earnings-to-Price ratio
45	EquityDuration ret	Equity duration
46	FirmAge ret	Firm age based on CRSP
47	Frontier ret	Efficient frontier index
48	GP ret	Gross profits/total assets
49	GrAdExp ret	Growth in advertising expenses
50	Grcapx ret	Change in capex (two years)
51	Grcapx3y ret	Change in capex (three years)
52	GrLTNOA ret	Growth in long-term operating assets
53	GrSaleToGrInv ret	Sales growth over inventory growth
54	GrSaleToGrOverhead ret	Sales growth over overhead growth
55	Herf ret	Industry concentration (sales)
56	HerfAsset ret	Industry concentration (assets)
57	HerfBE ret	Industry concentration (equity)
58	High52 ret	52 week high
59	Hire ret	Employment growth
60	IdioRisk ret	Idiosyncratic risk
61	IdioVol3F ret	Idiosyncratic risk (3 factor)
62	IdioVolAHT ret	Idiosyncratic risk (AHT)
63	Illiquidity ret	Amihud's illiquidity
64	IndMom ret	Industry momentum
65	IndRetBig ret	Industry return of big firms
66	IntanBM ret	Intangible return using BM
67	IntanCFP ret	Intangible return using CFtoP
68	IntanEP ret	Intangible return using EP
69	IntanSP ret	Intangible return using Sale2P
70	IntMom ret	Intermediate momentum
71	Investment ret	Investment to revenue
72	InvestPPEInv ret	Change in PPE and inventory/assets
73	InvGrowth ret	Inventory growth
74	Leverage ret	Market leverage
75	LRreversal ret	Long-run reversal
76	MaxRet ret	Maximum return over month
77	MeanRankRevGrowth ret	Revenue growth rank
78	Mom6m ret	Momentum (6 month)
79	Mom12m ret	Momentum (12 month)
80	Mom12mOffSeason ret	Momentum without the seasonal part

N	Abbreviation	Description
81	MomOffSeason ret	Off season long-term reversal
82	MomOffSeason06YrPlus ret	Off season reversal years 6 to 10
83	MomOffSeason11YrPlus ret	Off season reversal years 11 to 15
84	MomOffSeason16YrPlus ret	Off season reversal years 16 to 20
85	MomSeason ret	Return seasonality years 2 to 5
86	MomSeason06YrPlus ret	Return seasonality years 6 to 10
87	MomSeason11YrPlus ret	Return seasonality years 11 to 15
88	MomSeason16YrPlus ret	Return seasonality years 16 to 20
89	MomSeasonShort ret	Return seasonality last year
90	MRreversal ret	Medium-run reversal
91	NetDebtFinance ret	Net debt financing
92	NetDebtPrice ret	Net debt to price
93	NetEquityFinance ret	Net equity financing
94	NetPayoutYield ret	Net payout yield
95	NOA ret	Net operating asset
96	NumEarnIncrease ret	Earnings streak length
97	OperProf ret	Operating profits/book equity
98	OperProfRD ret	Operating profitability R&D adjusted
99	OPLeverage ret	Operating leverage
100	OrderBacklog ret	Order backlog
101	OrderBacklogChg ret	Change in order backlog
102	OrgCap ret	Organizational capital
103	PayoutYield ret	Payout yield
104	PctAcc ret	Percent operating accruals
105	Price ret	Price
106	PS ret	Piotroski F-score
107	RD ret	R&D over market cap
108	RDAbility ret	R&D ability
109	Realestate ret	Real estate holdings
110	ResidualMomentum ret	Momentum based on FF3 model residuals
111	ReturnSkew ret	Return skewness
112	ReturnSkew3F ret	Idiosyncratic skewness (3-factor model)
113	RevenueSurprise ret	Revenue surprise
114	Roaq ret	Return on assets (qtrly)
115	RoE ret	Net income/book equity
116	ShareIss1Y ret	Share issuance (1 year)
117	ShareIss5Y ret	Share issuance (5 year)
118	Size ret	Size
119	SP ret	Sales-to-price
120	Std turn ret	Share turnover volatility

N	Abbreviation	Description
121	STreversal ret	Short-term reversal
122	Tang ret	Tangibility
123	Tax ret	Taxable income to income
124	TotalAccruals ret	Total accruals
125	TrendFactor ret	Trend in the general stock market
126	VarCF ret	Cash flow to price variance
127	VolMkt ret	Volume to market equity
128	VolSD ret	Volume variance
129	VolumeTrend ret	Volume trend
130	XFIN ret	Net external financing
131	Zerotrade ret	Days with zero trades
132	ZerotradeAlt1 ret	Days with zero trades
133	ZerotradeAlt12 ret	Days with zero trades

Appendix B: 153 Anomaly Portfolios from Jensen et al. (2023)

N	Anomaly abbreviation	Description
1	capex abn	Abnormal corporate investment
2	z score	Altman Z-score
3	ami 126d	Amihud measure
4	at gr1	Asset growth
5	tangibility	Asset tangibility
6	sale bev	Assets turnover
7	at me	Assets-to-market
8	at be	Book leverage
9	bev mev	Book-to-market enterprise value
10	be me	Book-to-market equity
11	capx gr1	CAPEX growth (1 year)
12	capx gr2	CAPEX growth (2 years)
13	capx gr3	CAPEX growth (3 years)

N	Anomaly abbreviation	Description
14	at turnover	Capital turnover
15	ocfq saleq std	Cash flow volatility
16	cop at	Cash-based operating profits-to-book assets
17	cop atl1	Cash-based operating profits-to-lagged book assets
18	cash at	Cash to assets
19	dgp dsale	Change gross margin minus change sales
20	be gr1a	Change in common equity
21	coa gr1a	Change in current operating assets
22	col gr1a	Change in current operating liabilities
23	cowc gr1a	Change in current operating working capital
24	fnl gr1a	Change in financial liabilities
25	lti gr1a	Change in long-term investments
26	lnoa gr1a	Change in long-term net operating assets
27	nfna gr1a	Change in net financial assets
28	nncoa gr1a	Change in net noncurrent operating assets
29	noa gr1a	Change in net operating assets
30	ncoa gr1a	Change in noncurrent operating assets
31	ncol gr1a	Change in noncurrent operating liabilities
32	ocf at chg1	Change in operating cash flow to assets
33	niq at chg1	Change in quarterly return on assets
34	niq be chg1	Change in quarterly return on equity
35	sti gr1a	Change in short-term investments
36	ppeinv gr1a	Change PPE and Inventory
37	dsale dinv	Change sales minus change Inventory
38	dsale drec	Change sales minus change receivables
39	dsale dsga	Change sales minus change SG&A
40	dolvol var 126d	Coefficient of variation for dollar trading volume

N	Anomaly abbreviation	Description
41	turnover var 126d	Coefficient of variation for share turnover
42	coskew 21d	Coskewness
43	prc highprc 252d	Current price to high price over last year
44	debt me	Debt-to-market
45	beta dimson 21d	Dimson beta
46	div12m me	Dividend yield
47	dolvol 126d	Dollar trading volume
48	betadown 252d	Downside beta
49	ni ar1	Earnings persistence
50	earnings variability	Earnings variability
51	ni ivol	Earnings volatility
52	ni me	Earnings-to-price
53	ebitda mev	Ebitda-to-market enterprise value
54	eq dur	Equity duration
55	eqnpo 12m	Equity net payout
56	age	Firm age
57	betabab 1260d	Frazzini-Pedersen market beta
58	fcf me	Free cash flow to price
59	gp at	Gross profits-to-assets
60	gp atl1	Gross profits-to-lagged assets
61	debt gr3	Growth in book debt (3 years)
62	rmax5 21d	Highest 5 days of return
63	rmax5 rvol 21d	Highest 5 days of return scaled by volatility
64	emp gr1	Hiring rate
65	iskew capm 21d	Idiosyncratic skewness from the CAPM
66	iskew ff3 21d	Idiosyncratic skewness from the Fama-French 3-factor model
67	iskew hxz4 21d	Idiosyncratic skewness from the q-factor model
68	ivol capm 21d	Idiosyncratic volatility from the CAPM (21 days)
69	ivol capm 252d	Idiosyncratic volatility from the CAPM (252 days)
70	ivol ff3 21d	Idiosyncratic volatility from the Fama-French 3-factor model
71	ivol hxz4 21d	Idiosyncratic volatility from the q-factor model
72	ival me	Intrinsic value-to-market
73	inv gr1a	Inventory change
74	inv gr1	Inventory growth
75	kz index	Kaplan-Zingales index
76	sale emp gr1	Labor force efficiency
77	aliq at	Liquidity of book assets
78	aliq mat	Liquidity of market assets
79	ret 60 12	Long-term reversal
80	beta 60m	Market beta

N	Anomaly abbreviation	Description
81	corr 1260d	Market correlation
82	market equity	Market equity
83	rmax1 21d	Maximum daily return
84	mispricing mgmt	Mispricing factor: Management
85	mispricing perf	Mispricing factor: Performance
86	dbnetis at	Net debt issuance
87	netdebt me	Net debt to price
88	eqnetis at	Net equity issuance
89	noa at	Net operating assets
90	eqnpo me	Net payout yield
91	chcsho 12m	Net stock issues
92	netis at	Net total issuance
93	ni inc8q	Number of consecutive quarters with earnings increases
94	zero trades 21d	Number of zero trades with turnover as tiebreaker (1 month)
95	zero trades 252d	Number of zero trades with turnover as tiebreaker (12 months)
96	zero trades 126d	Number of zero trades with turnover as tiebreaker (6 months)
97	o score	Ohlson O-score
98	oaccruals at	Operating accruals
99	ocf at	Operating cash flow to assets
100	ocf me	Operating cash flow to market
101	opex at	Operating leverage
102	op at	Operating profits-to-book assets
103	ope be	Operating profits-to-book equity
104	op atl1	Operating profits-to-lagged book assets
105	ope bel1	Operating profits-to-lagged book equity
106	eqpo me	Payout yield
107	oaccruals ni	Percent operating accruals
108	taccruals ni	Percent total accruals
109	f score	Pitroski F-score
110	ret 12 1	Price momentum t-12 to t-1
111	ret 12 7	Price momentum t-12 to t-7
112	ret 3 1	Price momentum t-3 to t-1
113	ret 6 1	Price momentum t-6 to t-1
114	ret 9 1	Price momentum t-9 to t-1
115	prc	Price per share
116	ebit sale	Profit margin
117	qmj	Quality minus Junk: Composite
118	qmj growth	Quality minus Junk: Growth
119	qmj prof	Quality minus Junk: Profitability
120	qmj safety	Quality minus Junk: Safety

N	Anomaly abbreviation	Description
121	niq at	Change in quarterly return on assets
122	niq be	Quarterly return on equity
123	rd5 at	R&D capital-to-book assets
124	rd me	R&D-to-market
125	rd sale	R&D-to-sales
126	resff3 12 1	Residual momentum t-12 to t-1
127	resff3 6 1	Residual momentum t-6 to t-1
128	ni be	Return on equity
129	ebit bev	Return on net operating assets
130	rvol 21d	Return volatility
131	saleq gr1	Sales growth (1 quarter)
132	sale gr1	Sales growth (1 year)
133	sale gr3	Sales growth (3 years)
134	sale me	Sales-to-market
135	turnover 126d	Share turnover
136	ret 1 0	Short-term reversal
137	niq su	Standardized earnings surprise
138	saleq su	Standardized Revenue surprise
139	tax gr1a	Tax expense surprise
140	pi nix	Taxable income-to-book income
141	bidaskhl 21d	The high-low bid-ask spread
142	taccruals at	Total accruals
143	rskew 21d	Total skewness
144	seas 1 1an	Year 1-lagged return, annual
145	seas 1 1na	Year 1-lagged return, nonannual
146	seas 2 5an	Years 2-5 lagged returns, annual
147	seas 2 5na	Years 2-5 lagged returns, nonannual
148	seas 6 10an	Years 6-10 lagged returns, annual
149	seas 6 10na	Years 6-10 lagged returns, nonannual
150	seas 11 15an	Years 11-15 lagged returns, annual
151	seas 11 15na	Years 11-15 lagged returns, nonannual
152	seas 16 20an	Years 16-20 lagged returns, annual
153	seas 16 20na	Years 16-20 lagged returns, nonannual

References

Anginer, D., S. Ray, H. N. Seyhun, and L. Xu. 2024. Expensive anomalies. *Journal of Empirical Finance* 75: 101440.

Barbaris, N., and T. Thaler. 2003. A survey of behavioral finance: In *Handbook of Economics and Finance*, ed. Constantinides, G. M., M. Harris, and T. Stulz, 1051–1121. Amsterdam, Netherlands: Elsevier Science B. V.

Bowles, B., A. V. Reed, M. C. Ringgenberg, and J. R. Thornock. 2024. Anomaly time. *Journal of Finance* 79: 3543–3579.

Briere, M., C.-A. Lehalle, T. Nefedova, and A. Raboun. 2019. Stock market liquidity and the trading costs of asset pricing anomalies, Available at SSRN 3380239.

Cederburg, S., and M. S. O'Doherty. 2015. Asset-pricing anomalies at the firm level. *Journal of Econometrics* 186: 113–128.

Chen, A. Y., and M. Velikov. 2023. Zeroing in on the expected returns of anomalies. *Journal of Financial and Quantitative Analysis* 58: 968–1004.

Chen, A. Y., and T. Zimmermann. 2020. Publication bias and the cross-section of stock returns. *Review of Asset Pricing Studies* 10: 249–289.

Chen, A. Y., and T. Zimmerman. 2022. Open source cross-sectional asset pricing. *Critical Finance Review* 11: 207–264.

Cochrane, J. H. 1999. Portfolio advice for a multifactor world. *Economic Perspectives: Federal Reserve Bank of Chicago* 23: 59–78.

Cotter, R., and N. McGeever. 2018. Are equity market anomalies disappearing? Evidence from the U.K., Working paper, University College Dublin.

DeMiguel, V., A. Martin-Utrera, F. J. Nogales, and R. Uppal. 2020. A transaction-cost perspective on the multitude of firm characteristics. *Review of Financial Studies* 33: 2180–2222.

Fama, E. F., and K. R. French. 1993. Common risk factors in the returns on stocks and bonds. *Journal of Financial Economics* 33: 3–56.

Favero, C. A., A. Melone, and A. Tamoni. 2023. Anomaly predictability with the mean-variance portfolio, Working paper, Bocconi University, The Ohio State University, and Rutgers Business School.

Frazzini, A., R. Israel, and T. J. Moskowitz. 2015. Trading costs of asset pricing anomalies, Working paper.

Green, J., J. R. Hand, and X. F. Zhang. 2013. The supraview of return predictive signals. *Review of Accounting Studies* 18: 692–730.

Harvey, C. R. 2017. Presidential address: The scientific outlook in financial economics. *Journal of Finance* 72: 1399–1440.

Harvey, C. R., Y. Liu, and H. Zhu. 2016. and the cross-section of expected returns. *Review of Financial Studies* 29: 5–68.

Hou, K., C. Xue, and L. Zhang. 2020. Replicating anomalies. *Review of Financial Studies* 33: 2019–2133.

Jacobs, H., and S. Müller. 2020. Anomalies cross the globe: Once public, no longer existent? *Journal of Financial Economics* 135: 213–230.

Jensen, T. I., B. Kelly, and L. H. Pedersen. 2023. Is there a replication crisis in finance? *Journal of Finance* 78: 2465–2518.
Latif, M., S. Arshad, M. Fatima, and S. Farooq. 2011. Market efficiency, market anomalies, causes, evidences, and some behavioral aspects of market anomalies. *Research Journal of Finance and Accounting* 2: 1–13.
Lu, X., R. F. Stambaugh, and Y. Yuan. 2017. Anomalies abroad: Beyond data mining, NBER working paper 23809, Cambridge, MA.
McLean, R. D., and J. Pontiff. 1999. Does academic research destroy stock return predictability? *Journal of Finance* 71: 5–31.
McLean, R. D., and J. Pontiff. 2016. Does academic research destroy stock return predictability? *Journal of Finance* 87: 5–31.
Novy-Marx, R., and M. Velikov. 2016. A taxonomy of anomalies and their trading costs. *Review of Financial Studies* 29: 104–147.
Welch, I. 2019. Reproducing, extending, updating, replicating, reexamining, and reconciling. *Critical Finance Review* 8: 301–304.

PART II

Anomalies Literature and Asset Pricing Models

CHAPTER 3

Prominent Asset Pricing Models and Anomaly Portfolio Returns

Abstract The Capital Asset Pricing Model (CAPM) of Treynor (1961, 1962), Sharpe (1964), Lintner (1965), and Mossin (1966) established a new field in finance known as *asset pricing*. The first general equilibrium model of asset prices, it rapidly became popular with academics and spread to professionals in the financial markets. Even though early empirical evidence was weaker than predicted by theory in terms of the relation between market beta risk and real world stock returns, the CAPM dominated asset pricing for almost three decades and yielded a Nobel Prize in Economics for Sharpe in 1990. But in the 1990s, Fama and French (1992, 1993, 1995, 1996, 1998) published a series of papers that documented extensive empirical evidence using U.S. stock returns over decades that the CAPM did not work—that is, average stock returns were not related to beta. In its place, Fama and French proposed a three-factor model that augmented the market factor with size and value factors. These new factors were intended to explain market anomalies wherein small firms tended to have higher returns than big firms over time and value firms had higher returns than growth firms. To explain these anomalies, they developed innovative long/short portfolios of stocks with small market capitalization minus those with large market capitalization as well as value stocks' returns minus growth stocks' returns. Upon adding these long/short portfolios as factors in the three-factor model, the ability to explain stock returns of anomaly portfolios was much improved. Subsequently, as other market anomalies were identified by researchers, asset pricing models advanced to include more long/short portfolio factors. So-called emphmultifactor

J. W. Kolari et al., *Asset Pricing Models and Market Efficiency*,
https://doi.org/10.1007/978-3-031-92901-3_3

models appeared to be able to explain stock market anomalies. As discussed in Chapter 2, what happened next was surprising. The number of anomalies identified by researchers exploded into the hundreds and overwhelmed the ability of asset pricing models to keep up with them. While anomalies could be grouped into categories and then factors developed to explain different categories of anomalies, at the time of this writing, the large number of anomalies discovered by researchers are causing major gaps in asset pricing models. Behavioralists propose that psychological explanations can close these major gaps in asset pricing models. However, a fundamental rift is occurring in finance as behavioralists argue investors are not always rational and financial markets not always efficient, whereas asset pricing model researchers assume rational investors and efficient markets. In this chapter we review prominent asset pricing models that help to explain anomaly portfolio returns. In forthcoming chapters, we show that that widely accepted multifactor models do not explain hundreds of anomalies' returns. By contrast, a new model dubbed the ZCAPM by Kolari, Liu, and Zhang (2021) well explains virtually all of these anomalies.

3.1 Fama and French Three-Factor Model

Fama and French (1992, 1993) proposed the now-famous three-factor model to better explain the cross-section of average stock returns than the CAPM. Their 1992 paper used U.S. stock returns from 1963 to 1900. After sorting individual stocks into beta deciles, they documented that low beta decile stocks had average returns of 1.34 percent versus 1.14 percent for high beta decile stocks. CAPM theory predicts increasing expected returns as beta increases, not a decreasing relation. Citing previous literature, they observed that Banz (1981) documented small firms had higher returns than larger firms after taking into account their betas. Also, research by Statman (1980) and Rosenberg, Reid, and Lanstein (1985) showed that the ratio of book equity to market equity (hereafter BM) was related to stock returns. Other studies by Basu (1977), Lakonishok and Shapiro (1986), and Bhandari (1988) found that stock returns were related to financial leverage and earnings/price ratios. Upon sorting stocks by size and BM ratios into deciles, Fama and French (1992) discovered clear trends in average returns with low size decile small stocks outperforming large size decile big stocks and high BM decile value stocks earning higher returns than low BM decile growth stocks. These simple sorts on size and BM firm characteristics told a stunning story. Average stock returns are better explained by firm characteristics than market beta.

In 1993, Fama and French came out with their three-factor model. They specified their model as follows:

$$R_{it} - R_{ft} = \alpha_i + \beta_{im}(R_{mt} - R_{ft}) + \beta_{iS}SMB_t + \beta_{iV}HML_t + e_{it}, \quad (3.1)$$

where $R_{it} - R_{ft}$ is the excess return for the ith asset over the riskless rate proxied by U.S. Treasury bills, $R_{mt} - R_{ft}$ is the excess market return using the CRSP index to proxy the market portfolio, α_i is the intercept term, β_{im}, β_{iS} and β_{iV} are the beta risk parameters or loadings for market beta, size beta, and the value beta, respectively, and e_{it} is the error term. Long/short portfolio returns are defined as the: (1) size factor SMB computed as small stocks' returns minus big stocks' returns; and (2) value factor HML computed as high BM value stocks minus low BM growth portfolios. The latter *multifactors* were added to help explain the size and value anomalies.

Empirical evidence supported the three-factor model. Based on monthly U.S. stock returns in the period July 1963 to December 1991, the beta loadings for the market, size, and value factors were all statistically significant for test asset portfolios sorted into 25 size and BM portfolios (i.e., quintiles of size by quintiles of value). The size and value factors were generally uncorrelated with one another but had some correlation to the market factor that contains constituent stocks in these portfolios. More importantly, when the market model was augmented with their multifactors, the α_i estimates decreased substantially and were approximately zero for most of the 25 size and BM portfolios. Thus, the expected returns for size and value anomalies were explained by the three-factor model for the most part. In later work, Fama and French (1996) raised the question of the source of systematic risks related to the size and value factors. It is possible that some underlying state variables could be responsible for the variation in earnings and returns associated with these factors.

The three-factor model immediately became widely accepted in asset pricing circles. Even so, some controversy arose with respect to methodological issues in empirical tests of the CAPM. Kothari, Shanken, and Sloan (1995) re-tested the CAPM using annual returns rather than monthly returns. Using both equal- and value-weighted stock indexes to proxy the market portfolio and data spanning a long historical period from 1927 to 1990, they found that market beta loadings were significantly priced in cross-sectional regression tests based on the well-known Fama and MacBeth (1973) two-step procedure. We review this procedure in forthcoming Chapter 4. Further analyses of the period 1941 to 1990 produced similar results. Thus, they concluded that the CAPM is better supported by annual than monthly returns. Countering this criticism, Fama and French (1996, 1998) showed that the market factor needs to be supplemented with the size and value factors to more fully explain the cross-section of average stock returns. They conceded that the proxy market index (used in testing the CAPM) may well be a bad proxy for the true market portfolio as conjectured by Jensen (1968). In this case, the market model would yield diminished results for beta risk due to an inefficient market proxy.

3.2 Carhart Four-Factor Model

As recognized by Fama and French (2008), the momentum anomaly is the premier puzzle in financial economics. A long/short momentum portfolio is long high performing stock over the past year minus short low performing stocks. Jegadeesh and Titman (1993) published seminal work on momentum for U.S. stocks from 1965 to 1989. Abnormal returns of 1.3 percent to 1.5 percent per month, or about 16 or 17 percent per year, were achieved in their empirical tests. A large literature exists on the momentum anomaly that has been found in bonds, commodities, currencies, etc., in the U.S. and other countries. How could such a simple investment strategy continue to earn high returns? One possibility is that the returns are due to inherently high risks of these portfolios. Alternatively, behavioral explanations may provide the answer to this question.

Regardless of the source of the anomaly, Carhart (1997) added a momentum factor to the Fama and French three-factor model as follows:

$$R_{it} - R_{ft} = \alpha_i + \beta_{im}(R_{mt} - R_{ft}) + \beta_{iS}SMB_t + \beta_{iV}HML_t + \beta_{iMOM}MOM_t + e_{it}, \quad (3.2)$$

where MOM_t is the momentum factor, and other notation is as before. He estimated this four-factor model for mutual funds in the period 1963 to 1993 and found that the goodness-of-fit as measured by R^2 values was very high (i.e., 90 percent or higher), and α_i values were very low. Even so, like the size and value factors, the underlying state variables driving the momentum factor were unknown.

Closely related research by Aramov and Chordia (2006) conducted tests of the size, value, momentum, and liquidity anomalies across different asset pricing models. Unlike prior studies, stock level betas were allowed to vary with these anomalies and other macroeconomic variables. Their evidence suggested that time-varying betas in multifactor models improved their ability to explain anomalies, with the exception of momentum and liquidity. Further research on the developing a risk-based asset pricing model to explain the latter anomalies was suggested.[1]

3.3 Fama and French Five-Factor Model

Studies by Novy-Marx (2013), Titman, Wei, and Xie (2004), and others found that the three-factor model did not explain anomalies related to profitability and capital investment of firms. Due to this accumulating evidence in addition to traditional discount valuation of firm dividends modified to take into account expected profitability, expected investment, and BM ratios, Fama and French (2015) specified the following five-factor model:

$$\begin{aligned} R_{it} - R_{ft} = \alpha_i + \beta_{im}(R_{mt} - R_{ft}) + \beta_{iS}SMB_t + \beta_{iV}HML_t + \\ \beta_{iR}RMW_t + \beta_{iC}CMA_t + e_{it}, \end{aligned} \tag{3.3}$$

where RMW_t is the robust profit minus weak profitability factor, CMA_t is the conservative minus aggressive capital investment factor, and other notation is as before. These new multifactors were formed by using four sorts of stocks: two size groups, two B/M groups, two operating profit groups, and two capital investment groups. The intersection of these four sorts gives 16 value-weighted portfolios. For example, the size factor is long the eight small size portfolios and short the eight big portfolios. Similarly, value, profit, and investment factors are constructed. Empirical tests showed that five-factor model performance was similar to a four-factor model that drops the *HML* factor. For this reason, they trimmed the model down to four factors. They were careful to point out that, in the context of the intertemporal CAPM (ICAPM) of Merton (1973), the four multifactors measure sensitivities to unknown state variables. Despite not knowing the underlying state variables, the factors were attributed with capturing their respective effects on expected stock returns.

Fama and French (2016) examined the ability of the five-factor model and other models using subsets of its factors to explain a number of anomaly

[1] Barbaris, Jin, and Wang (2021) developed a new asset pricing model based on prospect theory. Their model was applied to predicting 23 well-known stock return anomalies. Despite being developed without specific attention to leading anomalies, they found that it performed similar to the Carhart four-factor model. Improving somewhat on the Carhart model, it was useful in explaining the momentum anomaly.

portfolios, including accruals, net share issues, momentum, volatility, and market beta. Their tests relied upon time-series regression model estimates of alpha (intercept) magnitudes as well as Gibbons, Ross, and Shanken (GRS) (1989) joint alpha tests. In general, they found that positive beta coefficients associated with RMW and CMA explain the high returns of low market β, share repurchases, and low stock return volatility stocks. Negative beta coefficients associated with RMW and CMA explained the low returns of high β, large share issues, and highly volatile returns. However, these factors did not explain the momentum anomaly.

3.4 Hou, Xue, and Zhang Four-Factor Model

Similar to Fama and French (2015), Hou, Xue, and Zhang (2015) proposed a four-factor q model that added profitability and capital investment factors to market and size factors. However, their conceptual framework was different. They relied upon the production CAPM of Cochrane (1991), which is grounded in the q-theory of investment. This theory predicts that higher stock returns are earned by firms with high investment/asset ratios (profit/assets ratios) compared to low investment/asset (profit/asset) ratios.

Their four-factor model was specified as:

$$R_{it} - R_{ft} = \alpha_i + \beta_{im}(R_{mt} - R_{ft}) + \beta_{iS} ME_t + \beta_{iR} ROE_t + \beta_{iC} IA_t + e_{it}, \tag{3.4}$$

where ME is equity market capitalization, ROE is return on equity, IA is the investment to total assets ratio of the firm, and other notation is as before.

To test their model, unlike Fama and French and other asset pricing studies, they substantially expanded the set of anomalies under investigation to include 80 long/short anomaly portfolios. Return series for these anomalies spanned the period 1972 to 2012. They found that about one-half of these anomalies were not significant in the cross section of stock returns, especially anomalies containing microcap stocks. Among 35 significant anomalies, upon comparing their model to the Fama and French three-factors model and Carhart four-factor model, their q-factor model had lower alphas on average—for example, 0.20 percent per month for the q-factor model versus 0.33 percent for the Carhart model and 0.55 percent for the Fama and French model. Also, it better captured momentum anomalies. They concluded that many anomalies are related to their profitability and investment factors; even so, they emphasized that the driving forces behind these factors (i.e., underlying state variables) were not fully understood.[2]

3.5 Stambaugh and Yuan Four-Factor Model

Stambaugh and Yuan (2017) specified another four-factor model as:

$$R_{it} - R_{ft} = \alpha_i + \beta_{im}(R_{mt} - R_{ft}) + \beta_{iS}SMB_t + \beta_{iMT}MGMT_t + \beta_{iP}PERF_t + e_{it}, \quad (3.5)$$

where *MGMT* is a management factor, *PERF* is a performance factor, and other notation is as before. Stocks' rankings with respect to a number of asset pricing anomalies were used to construct the *MGMT* and *PERF* factors. They grouped 11 well-known anomalies[3] into two clusters. These clusters were used to define two long/short zero-investment portfolios (viz., $MGMT$ and $PERF$), which they called *mispricing factors.* A small-minus-big size factor was created that excluded stocks in these two mispricing clusters. Similar to Fama and French (2015), the value factor (HML) was dropped as it did not boost the performance of the model.

They employed the same large dataset of anomalies in Hou, Xue, and Zhang. Again in-sample GRS tests of the joint equality of alphas were used to compare their model to other models, including the Fama and French three- and four-factor models as well as Hou, Xue, and Zhang four-factor model. Their four-factor model outperformed other models in terms of smaller and less significant mispricing error. Additionally, they found that their model better explained factors in the other models. In these tests, the factors in other models were used as anomaly or test asset portfolios. They concluded that parsimonious asset pricing models can be developed from the anomalies themselves. In so doing, the number of multifactors in time-series regression asset pricing models can be reduced to explain large numbers of anomalies.

[2] A recent working paper by Sakemoto (2024) sought to investigate groups of factors identified by Hou, Xue, and Zhang. They found that these so-called *group common factors* better explain anomaly returns than a common risk factor.

[3] The 11 anomalies are: net stock issues, equity issuance, accruals, net operating assets, asset growth, investment to assets, financial distress, O-score of distress, momentum, gross profitability, and return on assets.

3.6 Fama and French Six-Factor Model

Given issues with pricing momentum anomalies, following Carhart's four-factor model, Fama and French (2018) modified their five-factor model to include a momentum factor (MOM). The resultant six-factor model is:

$$\begin{aligned} R_{it} - R_{ft} = \alpha_i + \beta_{im}(R_{mt} - R_{ft}) + \beta_{iS} SMB_t + \beta_{iV} HML_t \\ + \beta_{iR} RMW_t + \beta_{iC} CMA_t + \beta_{iM} MOM_t + e_{it}, \end{aligned} \quad (3.6)$$

where notation is as before. Experimenting with different factors, they constructed a total of 48 variations or multifactors. U.S. stock returns from 1963 to 2016 were employed. To compare different versions of their three-, five- and six-factor models, they used a metric based on work in Barillas and Shanken (2018) defined as the smallest squared Sharpe ratio of the intercepts. The winner was a six-factor model using market and size factors plus small stock factors for the value, profitability, capital investment, and momentum factors. Tests rejected the CAPM and other multifactor models. Fama and French cautioned that theory should be used to guide the development OLS asset pricing models. Also, out-of-sample tests of models were advised to check their robustness. In the present book, consistent with their recommendation, we emphasize out-of-sample tests to evaluate the validity of different asset pricing models. Additionally, we add tests of the ZCAPM by Kolari, Liu, and Huang (2021) that is theoretically derived as a general equilibrium CAPM model based on the zero-beta CAPM of Black (1972).

In another paper, Fama and French (2020) developed alternative versions of their models using long/short mimicking portfolios in place of their multifactors. To construct these portfolios, they used the estimated market prices of risk associated with beta loadings in the cross-sectional regression in the second step of the Fama-MacBeth procedure. This approach employs the test asset portfolio returns themselves to estimate long/short portfolios rather than ad hoc researcher judgment to form long/short portfolios as factors. We review this procedure in forthcoming Chapter 4. Referring to the new long/short portfolios as *cross-section factors*, for U.S. stock returns in the period from 1963 to 2018, they found that these factors yielded lower in-sample average alphas than their original factors. No out-of-sample tests were reported to check robustness. Another asset pricing model was specified as a simple mathematical relation as opposed to time-series regression model. This model relied upon firm characteristic variables as factors instead of long/short portfolios. Moreover, it allowed the factor loadings to vary from month-to-month over time rather than being fixed in typical time-series models using (for example) a five-year estimation window. They found that the mathematical relation tended to outperform the cross-section factor models. While these results are interesting, a major disadvantage of the mathematical relation is that it can only be tested in sample, such that no robustness checks on its validity are possible on an out-of-sample basis.

3.7 Lettau and Pelger Latent Five-Factor Model

Lettau and Pelger (2020) implemented the well-known statistical method of Principal Component Analysis (PCA) to identify asset pricing factors. PCA lets the test asset portfolios returns select a smaller number of components that summarize their information. Factor components are derived that correspond to different dimensions of the data. These so-called *latent or hidden* factors are generated in order of importance such that the number of factors can be limited at some point. Unfortunately, there is no clear economic meaning for the factors.

Using U.S. stock returns in the period 1963 to 2017, the authors tested PCA models using 370 portfolios sorted on size, BM, accruals, investment, profitability, momentum, volatility measures, and other characteristics of firms. Most of their tests focused on in-sample alphas or mispricing errors. Comparative analyses were conducted for different PCA models as well as Fama and French three- and five-factor models. They found smaller mispricing errors for a five-factor PCA model than for other models—for example, 0.16 percent percent per month for the five-factor PCA model compared to 0.26 percent per month for the Fama and French five-factor model. Out-of-sample alpha tests confirmed their findings. They inferred that PCA offers a statistical approach for developing asset pricing models that can outperform traditional models based on potentially redundant firm characteristics or factors. A drawback of PCS models is that there is no clear interpretation of the economic risk associated with latent factors. Hence, a deeper understanding of asset pricing in the context of risk and return in financial markets is not possible.

3.8 Summary

Fama and French (1992, 1993) introduced their now-famous three-factor model augmenting the market factor with long/short size and value factors to help explain size and value anomalies in stock returns. The success of their model led to a new branch of asset pricing that incorporates long/short multifactors to better explain for anomaly portfolios' returns.

For example, Carhart (1997) added a momentum factor due to momentum stock returns. Extending their three-factor model, Fama and French (2015, 2016) added profitability and capital investment factors in view of related anomalies in addition to accruals, net share issues, volatility, and market beta anomalies. Hou, Xue, and Zhang (2015) proposed a similar model to the five-factor model and showed that it was able to explain a much larger set of anomaly portfolio returns. Relatedly, Stambaugh, and Yuan (2017) augmented the market factor with size, management, and performance factors to explain anomaly portfolios in the Hou et al. study. Continuing to expand their models, Fama and French (2018; 2020) included momentum in the five-factor model and experimented with new cross-section market factors of original factors in addition to a mathematical model using firm characteristics themselves. Finally, Lettau and Pelger (2020) used the statistical method of Principal Components Analysis (PCA) to derive latent or hidden factors in an effort to explain a large set of anomaly portfolios' returns.

In the years ahead, no doubt more factors will be added to these multifactor models. How many more factors will researchers incorporate to take into account the growing number of anomalies? Can anomalies be clustered as Stambaugh and Yuan proposed to enable more parsimonious asset pricing models? Or, should asset pricing models be developed with potentially large numbers of factors? At the present time, asset pricing models are facing some difficult challenges. If models cannot be developed to explain the growing list of anomalies, are behavioralists' views about irrational investors and inefficient markets warranted? As we will see in forthcoming chapters, a new two-factor model dubbed the ZCAPM by Kolari, Liu, and Zhang (2021) goes a long way in resolving these issues.

References

Avramov, D., and T. Chordia. 2006. Asset pricing models and financial market anomalies. *Review of Financial Studies* 19: 1001–1040.

Banz, R. W. 1981. The relationship between return and market value of common stocks. *Journal of Financial Economics* 9: 3–18.

Barberis, N., L. J. Jin, and B. Wang. 2021. Prospect theory and stock market anomalies. *Journal of Finance* 56: 2639–2687.

Barillas, F., and J. Shanken. 2018. Comparing asset pricing models. *Journal of Finance*, 715–754.

Basu, S. 1977. Investment performance of common stocks in relation to their price-earnings ratios: A test of the efficient market hypothesis. *Journal of Finance* 12: 129–156.

Bhandari, L. C. 1988. Debt/equity ratio and expected common stock returns: Empirical evidence. *Journal of Finance* 43: 507–528.

Black, F. 1972. Capital market equilibrium with restricted borrowing. *Journal of Business* 45: 444–454.

Black, F. 1993. Beta and return. *Journal of Portfolio Management* 20: 8–18.

Black, F. 1995. Estimating expected return. *Financial Analysts Journal* 49: 36–38.

Black, F., M. C. Jensen, and M. Scholes. 1972. The capital asset pricing model: Some empirical tests. In *Studies in the Theory of Capital Markets*, ed. M. C. Jensen. New York, NY: Praeger.

Carhart, M. M. 1997. On persistence in mutual fund performance. *Journal of Finance* 52: 57–82.

Clare, A. D., R. Priestley, and S. H. Thomas. 1998. Reports of beta's death are premature: Evidence from the UK. *Journal of Banking and Finance* 22: 1207–1229.

Daniel, K., and S. Titman. 2012. Testing factor-model explanations of market anomalies. *Critical Finance Review* 1: 103–139.

Fama, E. F., and K. R. French. 1992. The cross-section of expected stock returns. *Journal of Finance* 47: 427–465.

Fama, E. F., and K. R. French. 1993. The cross-section of expected returns. *Journal of Financial Economics* 33: 3–56.

Fama, E. F., and K. R. French. 1995. Size and book-to-market factors in earnings and returns. *Journal of Finance* 50: 131–156.

Fama, E. F., and K. R. French. 1996. The CAPM is wanted, dead or alive. *Journal of Finance* 51: 1947–1958.

Fama, E. F., and K. R. French. 1998. Value versus growth: The international evidence. *Journal of Finance* 53: 1975–1999.

Fama, E. F., and K. R. French. 2004. The Capital Asset Pricing Model: Theory and evidence. *Journal of Economic Perspectives* 18: 25–46.

Fama, E. F., and K. R. French. 2008. Dissecting anomalies. *Journal of Finance* 63: 1653–1678.

Fama, E. F., and K. R. French. 2015. A five-factor asset pricing model. *Journal of Financial Economics* 116: 1–22.
Fama, E. F., and K. R. French. 2016. Dissecting anomalies with a five-factor model. *Review of Financial Studies* 29: 69–103.
Fama, E. F., and K. R. French. 2018. Choosing factors. *Journal of Financial Economics* 128: 234–252.
Fama, E. F., and K. R. French. 2020. Comparing cross-section and time-series factor models. *Review of Financial Studies* 33: 1891–1926.
Fama, E. F., and J. D. MacBeth. 1973. Risk, return, and equilibrium: Empirical tests. *Journal of Political Economy* 81: 607–636.
Gibbons, M. R., S. A. Ross, and J. Shanken. 1989. A test of the efficiency of a given portfolio. *Econometrica* 57: 1121–1152.
Hou, K., C. Xue, and L. Zhang. 2015. Digesting anomalies: An investment approach. *Review of Financial Studies* 28: 650–705.
Jegadeesh, N., and S. Titman. 1993. Returns to buying winners and selling losers: Implications for stock market efficiency. *Journal of Finance* 48: 65–91.
Jensen, M. C. 1968. The performance of mutual funds in the period 1945–1964. *Journal of Finance* 23: 389–416.
Kolari, J. W., W. Liu, and J. Huang. 2021. *A New Capital Asset Pricing Model: Theory and Evidence*. New York, NY: Palgrave Macmillan.
Kothari, S. P., J. Shanken, and R. G. Sloan. 1995. Another look at the cross-section of expected stock returns. *Journal of Finance* 50: 185–224.
Lakonishok, J., and A. C. Shapiro. 1986. Systematic risk, total risk, and size as determinants of stock market returns. *Journal of Banking and Finance* 10: 115–132.
Lakonishok, J., and A. Shleifer. 1984. Stock returns, beta, variance and size: An empirical analysis. *Financial Analysts Journal* 40: 36–41.
Lettau, M., and M. Pelger. 2020. Factors that fit the time series and cross-section of stock returns. *Review of Financial Studies* 33: 2274–2325.
Lintner, J. 1965. The valuation of risk assets and the selection of risky investments in stock portfolios and capital budgets. *Review of Economics and Statistics* 47: 13–37.
Markowitz, H. M. 1959. *Portfolio Selection: Efficient Diversification of Investments*. New York, NY: John Wiley & Sons.
Merton, R. C. 1973. An intertemporal capital asset pricing model. *Econometrica* 41: 867–887.
Mossin, J. 1966. Equilibrium in a capital asset market. *Econometrica* 34: 768–783.
Novy-Marx, R. 2013. The other side of value: The gross profitability premium. *Journal of Financial Economics* 108: 1–28.
Rosenberg, B., K. Reid, and R. Lanstein. 1985. Persuasive evidence of market inefficiency. *Journal of Portfolio Management* 11: 9–17.

Sakemoto, R. 2024. Time-varying group common factors in the stock market anomalies, Working paper, Hokkaidio University, Japan.

Sharpe, W. F. 1964. Capital asset prices: A theory of market equilibrium under conditions of risk. *Journal of Finance* 19: 425–442.

Stambaugh, R. F., and Y. Yuan. 2017. Mispricing factors. *Review of Financial Studies* 30: 1270–1315.

Statman, D. 1980. Book values and stock returns. *The Chicago MBA: A Journal of Selected Papers* 4: 25–45.

Titman, S., K. Wei, and F. Xie. 2004. Capital investments and stock returns. *Journal of Financial and Quantitative Analysis* 39: 677–700.

Treynor, J. L. 1961. Market value, time, and risk, Unpublished manuscript.

Treynor, J. L. 1962. Toward a theory of market value of risky assets, Unpublished manuscript.

CHAPTER 4

The ZCAPM and Previous Tests of Anomaly Portfolio Returns

Abstract Black (1972) proposed the zero-beta CAPM in an effort to reconcile empirical evidence on tests of the famed Capital Asset Pricing Model (CAPM) by Treynor (1961, 1962), Sharpe (1964), Lintner (1965), and Mossin (1966). The CAPM is a general equilibrium model that can be graphically represented by the Security Market Line (SML) defined by excess expected returns over the riskless rate of assets on the Y-axis and associated estimated betas on the X-axis. A positive linear relationship is hypothesized between expected returns and beta risk. Using U.S. stock market returns, early evidence by Black, Jensen, and Scholes (1972) showed that the SML was flatter with a higher intercept (or α parameter) than predicted by the CAPM. More specifically, low beta stocks had higher returns than theorized by the CAPM and vice versa for high beta stocks. They inferred that, instead of using the riskless rate as in the CAPM, a higher borrowing rate should be used in line with investor practice in financial markets. Black extended this potential solution by proposing the possible existence of a zero-beta portfolio uncorrelated with the market portfolio in the CAPM. In effect, there are two factors—namely, a market factor and zero-beta factor. Unfortunately, he did not provide any guidance on how to construct a zero-beta portfolio in the real world. For this reason, no empirical model of the zero-beta CAPM is available.

A recent book by Kolari, Liu, and Huang (KLH) (2012) derived an alternative theoretical form of Black's zero-beta CAPM dubbed the ZCAPM. Importantly, they proposed an empirical ZCAPM that can be tested with readily available market data. The ZCAPM is comprised of two factors:

J. W. Kolari et al., *Asset Pricing Models and Market Efficiency*,
https://doi.org/10.1007/978-3-031-92901-4_4

(1) a market factor and (2) a cross-sectional market volatility factor. On any given day (for example) these two factors coincide with the first and second moments of stock returns of all stocks in the market. The market factor is associated with beta risk, and the cross-sectional market factor is related to so-called *zeta risk*. Both factors use value-weighted daily refOut-of-sample Fama-MacBethturns of all stocks in the market. Unlike the zero-beta CAPM, both ZCAPM factors can be computed using daily stock market returns. Also, departing from prominent multifactor models reviewed in Chapter 3, the ZCAPM uses machine learning to estimate a hidden or latent variable that indicates the direction of zeta risk effects on security.

Empirical tests of the ZCAPM by KLH were impressive. Mispricing errors computed on an out-of-sample basis were considerable lower for the ZCAPM compared to well-known multifactor models. In standard Fama and MacBeth (1973) out-of-sample cross-sectional regression test comparisons to often-cited multifactor models discussed in Chapter 3, based on commonly used anomaly portfolios as well as individual stocks, the ZCAPM always outperformed these prominent models by sizable margins at times. The goodness-of-fit in terms of R^2 values were much higher than other models. Also, the t-statistics associated with zeta risk loadings were more significant than those for multifactor beta loadings. The consistency of these out-of-sample predictive results across different test assets provided compelling support for the ZCAPM as a valid asset pricing model with strong machine learning capabilities due to its ability to predict out-of-sample returns.

In this chapter, we review the theoretical and empirical ZCAPM and present selected stock return tests by KLH. We apply the ZCAPM to large datasets of anomaly portfolios in the next chapter. As we will see, the ZCAPM does a good job of explaining the cross-section of average anomaly returns; by contrast, commonly used multifactor models perform poorly in explaining the cross-section of average anomaly returns.

4.1 The ZCAPM

The ZCAPM of Kolari, Liu, and Huang (KLH) (2021) breaks new ground in asset pricing models. This lesser known model augments the market model with a cross-sectional market return dispersion factor that is measured in percent return terms. Different from typical multifactor models, the theoretically justified return dispersion factor is not tradable by investors. Also, unlike most asset pricing models, the return dispersion factor implies a nonlinear model.

In the present context using stock market returns, market dispersion is the cross-sectional standard deviation of returns across all stocks in the market on day t, as opposed to the time-series standard deviation of returns in the market.[1] We compute market dispersion using the value-weighted CRSP index return (denoted R_{at}) on each day t as follows:

$$\sigma_{at} = \sqrt{\frac{n}{n-1}\sum_{i=1}^{n} w_{it-1}(R_{it} - R_{at})^2}, \tag{4.1}$$

where n is the total number of stocks, w_{it-1} is the previous day's market value weight for the ith stock (i.e., market capitalization of the stock divided by the market capitalization of all n stocks), R_{it} is the return of the ith stock on day t, and R_{at} is value-weighted average return of all available stocks in the CRSP database on day t. All common stocks in the CRSP database are included in the above computation.

In their empirical tests of the ZCAPM, KLH found that market return dispersion should be measured on a daily basis, as opposed to monthly or lower frequency estimation, to more fully capture pricing information associated with changes in cross-sectional market volatility over time. Previous studies provide justification for this market risk factor. Numerous studies have shown that stock market return dispersion is related to macroeconomic shocks, including unemployment rates, economic uncertainty, economic restructuring, business cycles, and market volatility.[2] Garcia, Mantilla-Garcia, and Martellini (2014) and others have argued that market return dispersion is related to aggregate idiosyncratic risk. Moreover, Cooper, Gulen, and Ion (2024) showed that macroeconomic shocks associated with market return dispersion help to explain the asset growth

[1] Numerous asset pricing studies investigate time-series market volatility (e.g., the Chicago Board Options Exchange's (CBOE) Volatility Index, or VIX), including Ang, Hodrick, Xing, and Zhang (2006), Bekaert, Engstrom, and Ermolov (2023), Detzel, Duarte, Kamara, and Siegel (2024), and citations therein. This time-series measure of market return dispersion is much different than the cross-sectional market return dispersion in the ZCAPM.

[2] See Loungani, Rush, and Tave (1990), Christie and Huang (1994), and Bekaert and Harvey (1997, 2000), Connolly and Stivers (2003), Gomes, Kogan, and Zhang (2003), Stivers (2003), Bansal and Yaron (2004), Zhang (2005), Pastor and Veronesi (2009), Bansal, Kiku, Shaliastovich, and Yaron (2014), Angelidis, Sakkas, and Tessaromatis (2015), among others.

factor in the Hou, Xue, and Zhang (2015) and Fama and French (2015) five-factor models. We next review the theoretical and empirical versions of the ZCAPM. Readers seeking additional information on the ZCAPM are referred to Kolari, Liu, and Huang (2021) as well as publications and presentations by Liu, Kolari, and Huang (2012), Liu (2013), Liu, Kolari, and Huang (2019), Liu, Kolari, and Huang (2020), Kolari, Huang, Butt, and Liao (2022), Kolari, Huang, Liu, and Liao (2022, 2025), Kolari and Pynnonen (2023), Kolari, Liu, and Pynnonen (2024), and Kolari, Huang, Liu, and Liao (2024, 2025).

Theoretical ZCAPM

Based on the celebrated Markowitz (1952; 1959) mean-variance investment parabola, KLH derived the theoretical ZCAPM as a special case of Black's zero-beta CAPM. An important insight mathematically proven by the authors is that the width of the mean-variance parabola is largely determined by the cross-sectional standard deviation of expected returns of all assets in the market (i.e., market return dispersion). Figure 4.1 illustrate this concept. In the right-hand margin of this figure, we show the frequency distribution of assets' expected returns. This cross-sectional return distribution contains all assets' expected returns within the parabola and therefore corresponds to the width of the parabola. Given this new perspective, the expected average return of all assets in the market, or $E(R_a)$, lies approximately on the axis of symmetry that splits the parabola into two halves.

To reach the upper efficient frontier of the parabola, rather than using a ray from the riskless rate on the Y-axis to the tangent portfolio on the efficient frontier as in the CAPM of Sharpe and others, the ZCAPM posits that investors move along the axis of symmetry at the expected market return and then upwards to the frontier via positive cross-sectional dispersion of expected returns. Figure 4.1 marks this geometry with arrows. Likewise, the lower boundary of the parabola can be geometrically reached by moving along the axis of symmetry and then downwards via negative cross-sectional dispersion of expected returns.

Using this mean-variance parabola framework, as shown in Fig. 4.1, KLH identify a unique pair of portfolios labeled as efficient portfolio I^* and orthogonal inefficient zero-beta portfolio ZI^*. These two unique Black

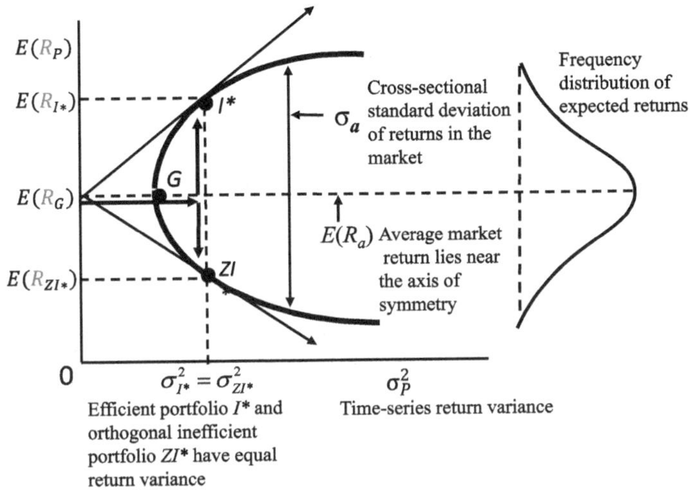

Fig. 4.1 Locating orthogonal portfolios I^* and ZI^* on the mean-variance parabola (*Source* Adapted from Kolari, Liu, and Huang (2021, Fig. 3.2, p. 59))

zero-beta CAPM portfolios distinctively have equal return variance.[3] Consistent with the geometry indicated by arrows drawn in Fig. 4.1, their expected returns can be written simply as:[4]

$$E(R_{I^*}) \approx E(R_a) + \sigma_a \tag{4.2}$$

$$E(R_{ZI^*}) \approx E(R_a) - \sigma_a, \tag{4.3}$$

where $E(R_a)$ is the expected return of the portfolio of all assets in the market, and σ_{at} is the cross-sectional dispersion of the expected returns of all asset returns in the market. It is important to note that portfolio a is not the market portfolio as in the CAPM; instead, it is simply a portfolio containing all assets in the market with well diversified weights. The portfolio a has an expected return approximately equal to that of the global minimum variance portfolio G denoted $E(R_G)$ in Fig. 4.1.

[3] In Black's model, there are an infinite number of efficient portfolios matched with their orthogonal inefficient (or zero-beta) portfolios. The ZCAPM is a special case that focuses on one unique pair of portfolios with equal return variance.

[4] In their book, the authors use $f(\theta)\sigma_a$ instead of simply σ_a in these equations, where $f(\theta) > 0$ is a complex function of other terms.

The CAPM assumes perfect capital markets, homogeneous investor expectations, two-parameter probability distributions of returns, investor risk aversion, no short selling, and a riskless rate. Black (1972) relaxed the last two assumptions to allow short selling and borrowing at a rate greater than the riskless rate. According to Black, the general market equilibrium expected return for the ith asset can be specified as follows:

$$E(R_i) = E(R_{ZM}) + \beta_{iM}[E(R_M) - E(R_{ZM})], \tag{4.4}$$

where $E(R_M)$ is the expected market portfolio return, $E(R_{ZM})$ is the expected zero-beta portfolio return that is uncorrelated (orthogonal) to the market portfolio, and β_{iM} is beta risk associated with excess expected market returns. Referencing Roll (1977) in their popular finance textbook, Copeland and Weston (1980) noted: "Roll points out that there is nothing unique about the market portfolio. The zero-beta relationship applies to *any* efficient portfolio. It is always possible to choose an efficient portfolio as an index, then find the minimum variance portfolio which is uncorrelated with the selected efficient index." (Copeland and Weston 1980, p. 184) Subsequently, they re-wrote Black's zero-beta CAPM in the following more general form:

$$E(R_i) = E(R_{ZI}) + \beta_{iI}[E(R_I) - E(R_{ZI})], \tag{4.5}$$

where I and ZI are any efficient index and its orthogonal zero-beta counterpart, respectively, located on the minimum variance boundary of the parabola.

Black (1972, pp. 452–454) extended the zero-beta CAM to the existence of a riskless asset. In this case, investors can buy the riskless asset but cannot short (borrow) this asset. Investors can only take short positions in risky assets (i.e., the zero-beta portfolio). It is straightforward to derive the zero-beta CAPM with a riskless asset. Rearranging Eq. (4.5), we get:

$$E(R_i) = \beta_{iI}E(R_I) + (1 - \beta_{iI})E(R_{ZI}). \tag{4.6}$$

Adding a riskless asset, we invest proportion α in risky assets I and ZI and proportion (1-α) in the riskless asset:

$$(E(r_i) = \alpha[\beta_{iI}E(R_I) + (1 - \beta_{iI})E(R_{ZI}] + (1 - \alpha)R_f. \tag{4.7}$$

Rearranging terms, we can re-write the zero-beta CAPM with a riskless asset as:

$$\begin{aligned} E(R_i) - R_f &= \alpha\beta_{iI}[E(R_I) - R_f] + \alpha(1 - \beta_{iI})[E(R_{ZI}) - R_f] \\ &= \beta'_{i,I}[E(R_I) - R_f] + \beta'_{i,ZI}[E(R_{ZI}) - R_f], \end{aligned} \tag{4.8}$$

where $\beta'_{i,I}$ and $\beta'_{i,ZI}$ represent the sensitivities or beta risks of asset i with respect to efficient portfolio I and its zero-beta portfolio counterpart ZI, respectively.

To derive the ZCAPM, KLH substituted the expected returns for unique efficient portfolio I^* and zero-beta counterpart portfolio ZI^* in Eqs. (4.2) and (4.3), respectively, into zero-beta CAPM relation (4.5). Upon doing so, the theoretical ZCAPM can be specified as:

$$\begin{aligned} E(R_i) &= E(R_{ZI^*}) + \beta_{iI^*}[E(R_{I^*}) - E(R_{ZI^*})] \\ &= E(R_a) - \sigma_a + \beta_{iI^*}\{[E(R_a) + \sigma_a] - [E(R_a) - \sigma_a]\} \\ &= E(R_a) + (2\beta_{iI^*} - 1)\sigma_a \\ E(R_i) &= E(R_a) + Z^*_{ia}\sigma_a, \end{aligned} \tag{4.9}$$

where $Z^*_{ia} = 2\beta_{iI^*} - 1$ (i.e., the systematic risk of asset i associated with σ_{at}) . Notice that the theoretical ZCAPM is an alternative equivalent form of the zero-beta CAPM with respect to portfolios I^* and ZI^*. Assuming a riskless asset exists, the final form of the theoretical ZCAPM is[5]:

$$E(R_i) - R_f = \beta_{ia}[E(R_a) - R_f] + Z^*_{ia}\sigma_a, \tag{4.10}$$

where $\beta_{i,a}$ measures beta risk related to expected market excess returns, and Z^*_{ia} measures zeta risk associated with cross-sectional dispersion of expected returns. Crucially, zeta risk is positive or negative in sign with respect to the expected returns of portfolios I^* and ZI^*, respectively. Of course, if we set the expected return on the zero-beta portfolio equal to the riskless rate, or $E(R_{ZI^*}) = R_f$ in Eq. (4.7), then the ZCAPM (like Black's zero-beta CAPM) collapses to the CAPM of Sharpe and others.

An interesting aspect of the ZCAPM is that, as the width of the parabola changes with increases or decreases in σ_a, assets located in the top and bottom halves of the parabola are differentially affected. For example, ceteris paribus, as σ_a increases (decreases), all assets above the axis of symmetry of

[5] See Kolari, Liu, and Huang (2021, p. 71) for the proof of this derivation.

the parabola including portfolio I^* will experience increasing (decreasing) expected returns. Conversely, as σ_a increases (decreases), all assets below the axis of symmetry of the parabola including portfolio ZI^* will experience decreasing (increasing) expected returns. Thus, comparing assets located above or below the axis of symmetry of the parabola, σ_a has opposite effects on their expected returns.

Empirical ZCAPM

How can the theoretically different positive and negative effects of the cross-sectional dispersion of expected returns on asset returns be modeled in the real world? Replacing expected returns with realized returns, KLH proposed the following novel empirical form of the ZCAPM:

$$R_{it} - R_{ft} = \alpha_i + \beta_{ia}(R_{at} - R_{ft}) + Z_{ia} D_{it} \sigma_{at} + u_{it}, \quad t = 1, \ldots, T, \quad (4.11)$$

where Z_{ia} measures the sensitivity of excess stock returns to the cross-sectional standard deviation of returns of all assets (i.e., market return dispersion) σ_{at}, D_{it} is a hidden signal variable[6] with values +1 and −1 representing positive and negative market return dispersion effects on stock returns at time t, respectively, α_i is the intercept related to mispricing errors, $u_{it} \sim$ iid $N(0, \sigma_i^2)$, and other notation is as before. In the present study of anomalous stock market returns, as already mentioned, we proxy the average of the expected returns of all assets in the market, or $E(R_a)$, with the value-weighted CRSP index return (i.e., an average market return based on stock market capitalization weights[7]) denoted R_a. Similarly, we proxy the market return dispersion of the expected returns of all assets, or σ_{at}, using all stock returns in the CRSP index per Eq. (4.1). Hidden signal variable D_{it} is introduced to take into account the potential positive ($D_{it} = +1$) versus negative ($D_{it} = -1$) effects of market return dispersion (σ_{at}) on asset returns theoretically posited by Eqs. (4.2) and (4.3) with respect to orthogonal portfolios I^* and ZI^*.

[6] The introduction of a hidden or latent variable in an asset pricing model is not new. Principal component analysis (PCA) and factor analysis have been utilized in numerous asset pricing studies to identify hidden factors in asset pricing models. See, for example, Roll and Ross (1980), Chen (1983), Lettau and Pelger (2020), and others.

[7] Some researchers use the equal-weighted CRSP index return, which is another way to compute average market returns that tends to give more weight to small stocks relative to big stocks.

Departing from other asset pricing models that typically rely upon ordinary least squares (OLS) regression, because signal variable D_{it} is unknown, KLH employ well-known expectation-maximization (EM) regression methods to estimate the probability of positive versus negative market return dispersion effects on stock returns.[8] In the EM algorithm, hidden signal variable D_{it} is an independent random variable with the following two-point distribution:

$$D_{it} = \begin{cases} +1 & \text{with probability } p_i \\ -1 & \text{with probability } 1 - p_i, \end{cases} \tag{4.12}$$

where p_i (or $1 - p_i$) is the probability of a positive (or negative) market return dispersion effect, and D_{it} are independent of u_{it}. The EM algorithm estimates probability p_i using available in-sample information about the dependent and independent variables in the model.

In empirical ZCAPM relation (4.11), $Z_{ia}D_{it}$ is an interaction term with two possible values equal to $+Z_{ia}$ or $-Z_{ia}$ due to the sign of signal variable D_{it}. Given that the mean of binary signal variable $D_{i,t}$ equals $2p_i - 1$, the zeta risk coefficient can be defined as $Z^*_{ia} = Z_{ia}(2p_i - 1)$, which is a systematic risk coefficient associated with stock market return dispersion σ_{at}. Consequently, the empirical ZCAPM can be re-specified as:

$$R_{it} - R_{ft} = \alpha_i + \beta_{ia}(R_{at} - R_{ft}) + Z^*_{ia}\sigma_{at} + u_{it}, \quad t = 1, \ldots, T, \tag{4.13}$$

where beta risk coefficient β_{ia} and zeta risk coefficient Z^*_{ia} proxy these respective risk parameters in theoretical ZCAPM relation (4.10). Notice that the positive or negative sign of Z^*_{ia} is determined by the estimated probability p_i of hidden signal variable D_{it} in-sample period $t = 1, \ldots, T$. In this respect, if $p_i > 1/2$ (or $< 1/2$), Z^*_{ia} is positive (or negative) in sign.

Zeta risk as measured by Z^*_{ia} can be interpreted as the average increase or decrease of asset returns in response to a one unit change in market

[8] See original work by Dempster, Laird, and Rubin (1977) as well studies by Jones and McLachlan (1990), McLachlan and Peel (2000), McLachlan and Krishnan (2008), among others. While the EM algorithm and its usage in regression analyses is well known in scientific studies due to fairly common missing data issues, its application in finance has been limited (e.g., see Asquith, Jones, and Kieschnick 1998; McLachlan and Krishnan 2008; Harvey and Liu 2016; Chen, Cliff, and Zhao 2017, and others). Bo and Batzoglou (2008) provide a good primer on the EM algorithm with some applications to computational biology. Wikipedia gives an excellent discussion of the EM algorithm and further literature citations.

return dispersion σ_{at} measured in percent returns (i.e., the span or width of the parabola in the stock market). Unlike OLS models, the empirical ZCAPM is a probabilistic mixture model with two components, wherein each component is a two-factor model with either positive or negative sensitivity to cross-sectional market return dispersion.

Some studies have augmented the market factor with a cross-sectional market return dispersion factor, including Jiang (2010), Demirer and Jategaonkar (2013), and Garcia, Mantilla-Garcia, and Martellini (2014). However, in contrast to the ZCAPM, they employ OLS regression that does not model the positive and negative effects of market return dispersion on asset returns. These studies report mixed and less significant findings on the market return dispersion factor than in KLH.[9] By contrast, KLH show that zeta risk coefficient Z^*_{ia} is very significantly and linearly related to out-of-sample average returns for anomaly portfolios sorted on size, value, momentum, and other characteristics.

The empirical ZCAPM in Eq. (4.11) differs from OLS asset pricing models in two fundamental ways. First, the variance of error terms u_{it} in Eq. (4.11) depends on market return dispersion (Kolari, Liu, and Huang, 2021, p. 98). This heterogeneity of error variance is a distinctive feature of the ZCAPM that separates it from OLS models in asset pricing. Also, it invalidates previously cited OLS models that augment the market factor with a market return dispersion factor. Second, almost all extant asset pricing models contain an intercept parameter. However, there is no intercept in the empirical ZCAPM. KLH found that residual error variance was not reduced by nonzero intercepts. Relevant to this discussion, Fama and French (2020) specified a mathematical asset pricing model (not estimated via OLS) without an intercept term. To obtain an economic estimate of mispricing error for this model, they computed the mean of residual errors as a proxy for the intercept. In the present book, forthcoming Chapter 7 follows this approach by estimating the intercept for the empirical ZCAPM using mean residual errors.

[9] As recognized by Garcia, Mantilla-Garcia, and Martellini, an econometric problem in using cross-sectional market return dispersion, or σ_{at}, as an asset pricing factor is that it is highly skewed. While they nonetheless augment the Fama and French three-factor model with a market return dispersion factor, it is well known that the tail region of the distribution can introduce outlier effects that severely diminish the performance of the model (i.e., the distribution has larger variances than mean values which affect parameter estimates and related statistical tests). By contrast, in the ZCAPM as shown in Eq. (4.9), market return dispersion is multiplied by hidden signal variable D_{it}. Since D_{it} has +1 and −1 values, the interaction variable $D_{it}\sigma_{at}$ has a symmetric distribution.

Additionally, unlike traditional OLS regression methods, the EM algorithm estimates the probability of a positive or negative sign for the zeta risk coefficient based on latent information contained in observed data, which determines which two-factor regression model is operative. This estimation procedure is *machine learning* (ML) in the sense that the mathematical optimization algorithm benefits from large amounts of daily return data, identifies patterns in the data, and makes inferences about the unknown direction of market return dispersion effects on security returns in the future. The predictive ability of EM machine learning to boost the significance of information about cross-sectional return volatility in the market is crucial to the out-of-sample performance of the empirical ZCAPM, which is consistent with the predictive nature of artificial intelligence.

Concerning the evaluation of models, Breiman (2001) has observed that:

> More publication of predictive accuracy estimates would establish standards for comparison of models, a practice that is common in machine learning. (Breiman, 2001, p. 204)

In the next section, based on out-of-sample results in the next month after estimating a model, we compare the predictive accuracy of a wide variety of asset pricing models. As we shall see, the ZCAPM well outperforms other models in terms of predicting out-of-sample anomaly portfolio returns.

Finally, for readers interested in running the empirical ZCAPM themselves, KLH make available open source empirical ZCAPM software using Matlab, R, and Python programs on the internet at GitHub (https://Github.com/zcapm). The Appendix gives the details of their step-by-step procedure for estimating the empirical ZCAPM based on the EM algorithm. Programs for running Fama-MacBeth cross-sectional regression tests are available at their GitHub website also.

4.2 Empirical Evidence

KLH reported the results of extensive empirical tests of the ZCAPM compared to prominent multifactor models. We review some of their evidence in the discussion below.

Predicted Versus Actual Excess Returns of Anomaly Portfolios

A well-known method of measuring mispricing error in asset pricing models is to compare predicted returns to actual returns of anomaly portfolios (i.e., test assets). Predicted returns are typically measured as the out-of-sample returns in the next month. Using one year of daily returns, KLH run the time-series *EM regression* for the empirical ZCAPM to estimate factor loadings. Here we define EM regression as the implementation of the EM algorithm in regression analysis. This expression is similar to the common usage of OLS regression to describe the application of OLS in regression analysis.

Next, cross-sectional regression models are estimated for anomaly portfolios using one-month-ahead excess returns. This process is rolled forward one month at a time to generate $t = 1, \cdots, 648$ cross-sectional regressions in the analysis period January 1965 to December 2018. Using these cross-sectional regressions, fitted one-month-ahead excess returns are computed for each portfolio for all months in the analysis period. Finally, average excess returns over all sample months are computed for each portfolio. These average fitted one-month-ahead excess returns are compared to each portfolio's one-month-ahead average actual (or realized) excess returns.

Based on Table 6.7 in KLH (2021, p. 146), Fig. 4.2 compares the mispricing errors of the Fama and French (1992, 1993) three-factor model to the empirical ZCAPM. The anomaly portfolios are from the online French database for 25 size and book-to-market (BM) sorted portfolios. These portfolios are used by Fama and French to test their three-factor model. Casual inspection of this graph shows that the ZCAPM provides a closer relation between average predicted and actual excess returns than the three-factor model in the sample period. This result is surprising due to the fact that size and BM firm characteristics are closely related to the size and value factors in the three-factor model but are unrelated to the market factor and cross-sectional return dispersion factor in the ZCAPM.

Many researchers have complained that the three-factor model should be tested using exogenous portfolios unrelated to their size and value factors. Following this recommendation, KLH compared the three-factor model and empirical ZCAPM using anomaly portfolios comprised of 25 size and BM portfolios plus 47 industry portfolios. As shown in Fig. 4.3 based on Table 6.8 in KLH (2021, p. 147), the three-factor model fails this test. By contrast, the ZCAPM continues to perform quite well in terms

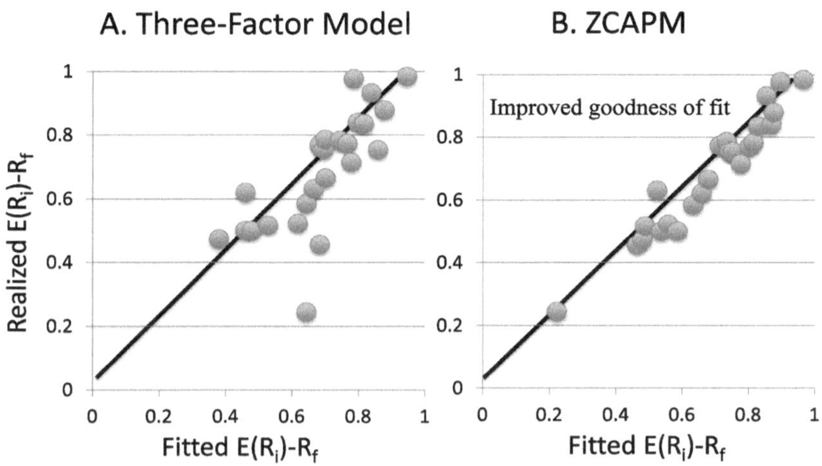

Fig. 4.2 Out-of-sample cross-sectional relationship between average one-month-ahead realized excess returns in percent (Y-axis) and average one-month-ahead predicted (fitted) excess returns in percent (X-axis) for 25 size-BM sorted portfolios: Fama and French three-factor model in Panel A and empirical ZCAPM in Panel B. The analysis period is January 1965 to December 2018 (*Source* Kolari, Liu, and Huang 2021, p. 146))

of predicting average excess returns that are close to actual average excess returns.

KLH continued to make mispricing error comparisons of different multifactor models to the empirical ZCAPM. In Figs. 4.4 and 4.5 based on Tables 6.11 and 6.12, respectively, in KLH (2021, pp. 151–151), they compared the Fama and French (2018) six-factor model to the ZCAPM. Anomaly portfolios include 25 size and profit-investment sorted portfolios in Fig. 4.4. The six-factor model performs fairly well in this figure. However, it is important to recognize that the anomaly portfolios are endogenously related to the profit and capital investment factors included in their model. Despite this advantage, the ZCAPM performs somewhat better than the six-factor model. A more reliable comparison is shown in Fig. 4.5 based on adding 47 exogenous industry portfolios to the 25 profit and investment portfolios. It is apparent that average mispricing errors increase in both models but noticeably more in the six-factor model than the ZCAPM.

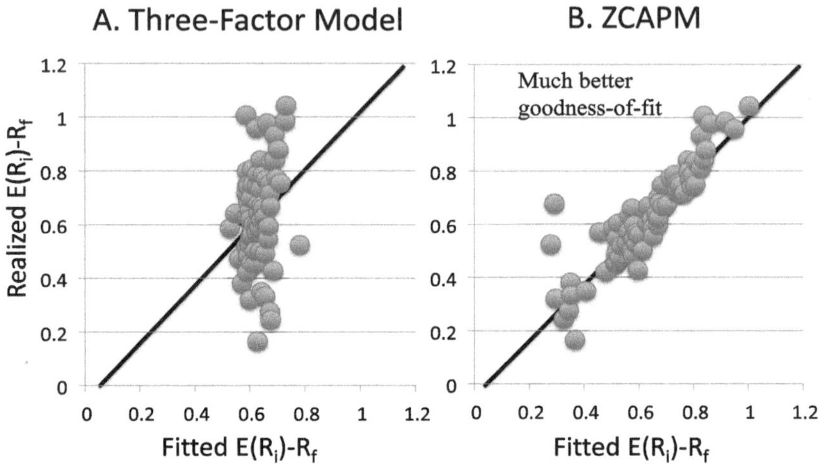

Fig. 4.3 Out-of-sample cross-sectional relationship between average one-month-ahead realized excess returns in percent (Y-axis) and average one-month-ahead predicted (fitted) excess returns in percent (X-axis) for 25 size-BM sorted plus 47 industry portfolios: Fama and French Fama and French three-factor model in Panel A and empirical ZCAPM in Panel B. The analysis period is January 1965 to December 2018 (*Source* Kolari, Liu, and Huang (2021, p. 147))

In general, average mispricing errors were smaller for the empirical ZCAPM than popular multifactor models. At times the differences were large when they incorporated exogenous industry portfolios in the test asset portfolios. The outperformance of the ZCAPM is readily observed in graphs of out-of-sample predicted versus actual excess returns.

Fama and MacBeth Cross-Sectional Tests

Based on standard Fama and MacBeth (1973) cross-sectional regression analyses, KLH reported out-of-sample, predictive test results of the ZCAPM. Other asset pricing models in their tests included the CAPM, Carhart (1997) four-factor model, and Fama and French (1992, 1993, 2015, 2018) three-, five-, and six-factor models. First, these models were estimated using time-series regression analyses of anomaly portfolios. The resultant factor loadings were retained. In the next step, they estimated a cross-sectional regression of one-month-ahead (out-of-sample) excess re-

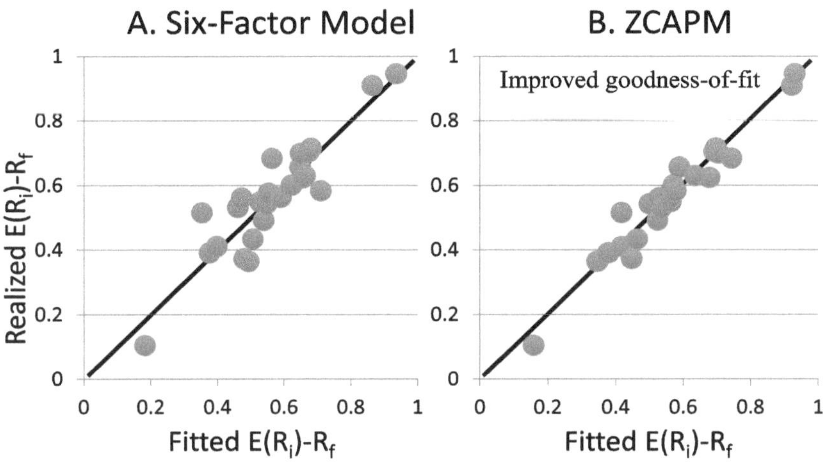

Fig. 4.4 Out-of-sample cross-sectional relationship between average one-month-ahead realized excess returns in percent (Y-axis) and average one-month-ahead predicted (fitted) excess returns in percent (X-axis) for 25 profit-investment sorted portfolios: Fama and French six-factor model in Panel A and empirical ZCAPM in Panel B. The analysis period is January 1965 to December 2018 (*Source* Kolari, Liu, and Huang (2021, p. 150))

turns on previously estimated factor loadings using the anomalies. These steps were repeated by rolling forward one month at a time until the last month of the sample period. This process generated a monthly time series of 648 market prices of risk, denoted λ_k for the kth factor, from January 1965 to December 2018. Lastly, averages of these λ_ks and t-statistics are computed.

For the empirical ZCAPM, the following cross-sectional regression was run using the $\hat{\beta}_{i,a}$ and $\hat{Z}^*_{i,a}$ loadings from estimating the empirical ZCAPM with one year of daily returns prior to month $T+1$:

$$R_{i,T+1} - R_{fT+1} = \lambda_0 + \lambda_a \hat{\beta}_{i,a} + \lambda_{RD} \hat{Z}^*_{i,a} + u_{it}, i = 1, ..., N, \quad (4.14)$$

where λ_0 is the intercept term, λ_a and λ_{RD} are coefficient estimates of the market prices of the beta risk and zeta risk loadings in percent terms, respectively, and other notation is as before. In this regression, the dependent variable is one-month ahead excess returns for the ith anomaly test asset portfolio. Because zeta risk loadings are estimated in the empirical ZCAPM

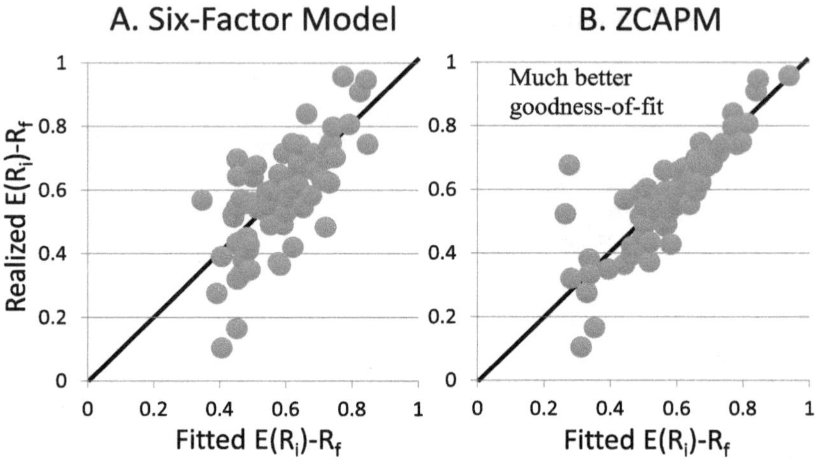

Fig. 4.5 Out-of-sample cross-sectional relationship between average one-month-ahead realized excess returns in percent (Y-axis) and average one-month-ahead predicted (fitted) excess returns in percent (X-axis) for 25 profit-investment sorted plus 47 industry portfolios: Fama and French Fama and French six-factor model in Panel A and empirical ZCAPM in Panel B. The analysis period is January 1965 to December 2018 (*Source* Kolari, Liu, and Huang (2021, p. 151))

using daily returns, the estimated zeta risk coefficient $\hat{Z}^*_{i,a}$ was rescaled from a daily to monthly basis as follows:

$$R_{i,T+1} - R_{fT+1} = \lambda_0 + \lambda_M \hat{\beta}_{i,a} + \lambda_{RD} \hat{Z}^*_{i,a} N_{T+1} + +u_{it}, i = 1, \ldots., N, \quad (4.15)$$

where N_{T+1} is the number of trading days in month $T + 1$ (i.e., 21 days), $Z^*_{i,a} N_{T+1}$ is the monthly estimated zeta risk, and λ_{RD} is the monthly risk premium associated with zeta risk. Notice that risk premium $\hat{\lambda}_{RD}$ per unit zeta risk is not changed by this rescaling. Since $Z^*_{i,T}$ is rescaled to a monthly basis, its market price of zeta risk estimates, or λ_{RD}, can be compared to λ_a estimates associated with beta risk loadings.

Table 4.1 reproduces Table 7.1 in KLH (2021, p. 166). Anomaly portfolios include 25 size-BM (Panel A), 47 industry (Panel B), 25 beta-zeta sorted (Panel C), and 97 combined (Panel D) portfolios. Goodness-of-fit as measured by R^2 values is consistently higher for the ZCAPM compared

Table 4.1 Out-of-sample Fama-MacBeth cross-sectional tests for ZCAPM regression factor loadings compared to other asset pricing models in the period January 1965 to December 2018: 12-month rolling windows

Panel A: 25 size-BM sorted portfolios

Model	$\hat{\alpha}$	$\hat{\lambda}_m$	$\hat{\lambda}_{RD}$	$\hat{\lambda}_{SMB}$	$\hat{\lambda}_{HML}$	$\hat{\lambda}_{MOM}$	$\hat{\lambda}_{RMW}$	$\hat{\lambda}_{CMA}$	R^2
CAPM	0.98	−0.35							0.48
	(4.03)	(−0.35)							
ZCAPM	0.78	−0.19	0.46						0.94
	(3.26)	(−0.77)	(4.22)						
Three-factor	0.93	−0.41		0.17	0.31				0.63
	(4.98)	(−1.96)		(1.27)	(2.64)				
Four-factor	1.12	−0.60		0.16	0.29	0.08			0.69
	(5.84)	(−2.83)		(1.29)	(2.57)	(0.35)			
Five-factor	0.98	−0.45		0.21	0.28		0.13	0.11	0.75
	(4.94)	(−2.06)		(1.73)	(2.49)		(1.10)	(0.84)	
Six-factor	1.07	−0.55		0.22	0.30	0.16	0.12	0.06	0.80
	(5.39)	(−2.52)		(1.80)	(2.69)	(0.68)	(1.03)	(0.45)	

Panel B: 47 industry portfolios

Model	$\hat{\alpha}$	$\hat{\lambda}_m$	$\hat{\lambda}_{RD}$	$\hat{\lambda}_{SMB}$	$\hat{\lambda}_{HML}$	$\hat{\lambda}_{MOM}$	$\hat{\lambda}_{RMW}$	$\hat{\lambda}_{CMA}$	R^2
CAPM	0.57	0.03							0.00
	(2.95)	(0.15)							
ZCAPM	0.49	0.11	0.32						0.70
	(2.71)	(0.53)	(4.07)						
Three-factor	0.43	0.11		0.02	0.14				0.15
	(2.21)	(0.48)		(0.14)	(1.17)				
Four-factor	0.46	0.08		0.04	0.08	0.43			0.39
	(2.31)	(0.37)		(0.31)	(0.73)	(2.09)			
Five-factor	0.36	0.19		0.07	0.09		0.20	0.24	0.18
	(1.78)	(0.83)		(0.51)	(0.76)		(2.03)	(2.48)	
Six-factor	0.51	0.04		0.04	0.06	0.39	0.20	0.17	0.50
	(2.53)	(0.16)		(0.32)	(0.52)	(1.92)	(2.05)	(1.78)	

Panel C: 25 beta-zeta sorted portfolios

Model	$\hat{\alpha}$	$\hat{\lambda}_m$	$\hat{\lambda}_{RD}$	$\hat{\lambda}_{SMB}$	$\hat{\lambda}_{HML}$	$\hat{\lambda}_{MOM}$	$\hat{\lambda}_{RMW}$	$\hat{\lambda}_{CMA}$	R^2
CAPM	0.49	−0.06							0.11
	(3.23)	(−0.26)							
ZCAPM	0.29	0.17	0.35					0.96	
	(1.91)	(0.83)	(4.03)						
Three-factor	0.66	−0.05		−0.28	0.14				0.65
	(3.34)	(−0.24)		(−1.49)	(1.00)				
Four-factor	0.54	−0.03		−0.25	0.25	0.28			0.70
	(3.50)	(−0.15)		(−1.51)	(1.76)	(1.61)			
Five-factor	0.52	−0.03		−0.19	0.25		0.17	0.09	0.67
	(3.06)	(−0.13)		(−1.11)	(1.56)		(1.18)	(0.77)	
Six-factor	0.62	−0.11		−0.14	0.30	0.26	0.17	0.02	0.76
	(3.86)	(−0.54)		(−0.88)	(1.90)	(1.50)	(1.30)	(0.14)	

(continued)

Table 4.1 (continued)

Panel D: 97 combined portfolios

Model	$\hat{\alpha}$	$\hat{\lambda}_m$	$\hat{\lambda}_{RD}$	$\hat{\lambda}_{SMB}$	$\hat{\lambda}_{HML}$	$\hat{\lambda}_{MOM}$	$\hat{\lambda}_{RMW}$	$\hat{\lambda}_{CMA}$	R^2
CAPM	0.64	−0.06							0.05
	(3.93)	(−0.31)							
ZCAPM	0.48	0.09	0.38					0.83	
	(3.24)	(0.47)	(5.42)						
Three-factor	0.52	0.002		0.06	0.18				0.06
	(3.55)	(0.01)		(0.49)	(1.64)				
Four-factor	0.53	−0.01		0.09	0.17	0.43			0.28
	(3.75)	(−0.06)		(0.75)	(1.64)	(2.54)			
Five-factor	0.44	0.09		0.12	0.14		0.21	0.21	0.22
	(2.97)	(0.45)		(1.02)	(1.35)		(1.99)	(2.36)	
Six-factor	0.57	-0.04		0.14	0.17	0.40	0.19	0.16	0.35
	(4.02)	(-0.24)		(1.20)	(1.68)	(2.40)	(1.94)	(1.84)	

[1] In the ZCAPM, the price of beta risk associated with CRSP index excess returns is denoted $\hat{\lambda}_a$ rather than $\hat{\lambda}_m$ in the other models.

to the other models. This difference is largest in the 97 combined portfolios, wherein the ZCAPM had an R^2 equal to 83 percent compared to at best 35 percent for the six-factor model and at worst 5 percent for the CAPM. The poor performance of the CAPM was not much improved by the three-factor model with only a 6 percent R^2. Even for the 25 size and BM sorted portfolios of Fama and French, the ZCAPM outperformed all the multifactor models with R^2 at best 80 percent compared to the ZCAPM at 94 percent. Since these are predictive, out-of-sample tests, no possible manipulation is possible to somehow favor the ZCAPM over other models.

Another useful metric for comparing different models is the significance of market prices of risk (denoted λ_k). We see in Table 4.1 that the t-statistics associated with the market price of zeta risk loadings, or λ_{RD}, range from 4.03 to 5.42 across Panels A to D. The market prices of size factor loadings., or λ_{SMB}, are insignificant in all models and anomalies. At times the market prices of loadings for value (λ_{HML}), momentum (λ_{MOM}), profit (λ_{RMW}), and capital investment (λ_{CMA}) are significant in different tests but do not exceed 3 in any model or sample anomalies. Also, the market price of market beta risk loadings, or λ_m, are insignificant in Panels B to D but negatively significant in Panel A for the three- to six-factor models. Because the CAPM predicts a positive relationship between beta risk and expected returns, these results are contrary to theory and therefore difficult to interpret.

Taken as a whole, the cross-sectional regression results in Table 4.1 provide compelling evidence in favor of the empirical ZCAPM over widely used multifactor models. The dominance of the ZCAPM in terms of predictive goodness-of-fit and factor loading significance, especially zeta risk loadings, is manifested in the consistency of the results across different models and anomaly portfolios. Can the ZCAPM be employed to explain large numbers of anomaly portfolio returns on an out-of-sample basis? Forthcoming chapters turn to this difficult challenge.

4.3 Summary

Recently, Kolari, Liu, and Zhang (KLH) (2021) introduced a new asset pricing model dubbed the ZCAPM. They derived the model as a special case of Black's (1972) zero-beta CAPM. Unlike Black's model, the ZCAPM contains market factors that are readily estimable from daily market prices—namely, the first and second moments of the returns for all stocks in the market on a given day (for example). These moments coincide with the market factor and cross-sectional standard deviation of stock returns in the market (or market dispersion), which are associated with beta risk and zeta risk, respectively.

The theoretical ZCAPM implies a new geometry for reaching the efficient frontier of Markowitz (1959). Rather than a ray from the riskless rate to the tangent point on the efficient frontier (i.e., the market portfolio denoted M) as in the CAPM, investors can move horizontally along the axis of symmetry of the mean-variance investment parabola at the average market return (or first moment) and then vertically upward to the efficient frontier using the market dispersion of stock returns (second moment). The inefficient minimum variance boundary of the mean-variance parabola can be reached using the average market return and then moving vertically downward by means of the market dispersion of stocks returns. KLH applied this geometry to identifying an efficient portfolio I and its inefficient zero-beta counterpart portfolio ZI with equal return variance. By substituting the expected returns of these portfolios into Black's zero-beta CAPM, they derived an alternative form in the ZCAPM.

Due to the fact that zeta risk related to market dispersion can have positive or negative effects on asset prices, the authors proposed an innovative empirical ZCAPM. Since positive and negative sensitivity to market dispersion is not known a priori for any asset at time t, a hidden dummy variable was specified that can take values of $+1$ or -1. To estimate the probability that the sign of the latent dummy variable is positive or negative, they employed the expectation-maximization (EM) algorithm in a regression analysis. The empirical ZCAPM is a probabilistic mixture model with two mixture components. Each component is by itself a two-factor regression model with a market factor and market dispersion factor. The latter market dispersion factor can have either positive or negative effects on asset returns which results in two mixture components. The operative EM regression model is determined by the hidden dummy variable. To our knowledge, no previous empirical asset pricing model is based on a mixture model EM framework.

Unlike most other asset pricing models that are linear regressions of tradable factors using ordinary least squared (OLS) regression, the empirical ZCAPM is a nonlinear model containing a nontradable factor (viz., market dispersion) that is estimated via EM regression. Also, it relies upon machine learning via the EM algorithm to estimate a hidden or latent variable related to the direction of a security's return sensitivity to market return dispersion or volatility in the future. No previous models in asset pricing are similar to the ZCAPM.

Empirical tests of the empirical ZCAPM by KLH provided strong support of this new asset pricing model. In out-of-sample tests, which are consistent with the application of machine learning to artificial intelligence and its emphasis on predictability, comparisons of predicted and actual excess returns for different sets of test assets comprised of anomaly stock portfolios showed that the ZCAPM has markedly lower mispricing errors than other prominent asset pricing models. Also, out-of-sample cross-sectional regression tests documented that the ZCAPM had higher goodness-of-fit and factor loading significance compared to the CAPM as well as a variety of often-cited multifactor models. In these tests, the dominance of the ZCAPM over multifactor models at times was by large margins. In no test did any other model outperform the ZCAPM. KLH concluded that the ZCAPM is a valid asset pricing model worthy of further attention in the finance literature and profession.

Can the ZCAPM explain anomaly portfolio returns on an out-of-sample (predictive) basis? Anomalies represent a major challenge for any asset pricing model. Researchers expend considerable resources scouring stock return databases for abnormal return patterns that can be exploited to build high yielding long/short stock portfolios. Behavioralists argue that these abnormal returns are attributable to irrational investors influenced by natural psychological biases. Efficient markets proponents counterargue that anomaly returns are determined by their inherent risks. In forthcoming chapters, we present stock market evidence on the ability of risk factors in asset pricing models to explain anomaly returns. In general, in out-of-sample tests consistent with machine learning and artificial intelligence, we find that the ZCAPM consistently does a good job of explaining hundreds of anomaly portfolio returns but not well-known multifactor models. Our ZCAPM empirical evidence, therefore, is most consistent with the efficient market hypothesis.

Appendix. Expectation-Maximization (EM) Algorithm for Empirical ZCAPM

This appendix gives the step-by-step procedure for estimating the empirical ZCAPM by means of the EM algorithm (see Kolari, Huang, and Liu (2021, Chapter 4). For the empirical ZCAPM in Eqs. (4.12) and (4.13), the parameters for the ith asset are represented as $\theta_i = (\beta_{i,a}, Z_{i,a}, \sigma_i^2, p_i)$. The complete data set for the ith asset is denoted as $\{R_{it}, D_{it}\}$, the (incomplete) observed data set as $\{R_{it}\}$, and the unobservable latent data set as $\{D_{it}\}$. The complete data likelihood of the model is:

$$\mathcal{L}(\theta_i; \{R_{it}, D_{it}\}) = \prod_{t=1}^{T} P_{\theta_i}(R_{it}|D_{it}) P_{\theta_i}(D_{it}), \tag{4.16}$$

where

$$\begin{aligned} P_{\theta_i}(D_{it}) &= p_i^{I(D_{it}=1)}(1-p_i)^{I(D_{it}=-1)}, \\ P_{\theta_i}(R_{it}|D_{it}) &= \frac{1}{\sqrt{2\pi\sigma_i^2}} \exp\left\{-\frac{(R_{it}-R_{ft}-\beta_{i,a}(R_{at}-R_{ft})-Z_{i,a}D_{it}\sigma_{at})^2}{2\sigma_i^2}\right\}. \end{aligned} \tag{4.17}$$

When estimating model parameters, the maximum likelihood method seeks to maximize the following observed data likelihood:

$$\mathcal{L}(\theta_i; \{R_{it}\}) = \sum_{D_{it}=\pm 1; t=1,\ldots,T} \mathcal{L}(\theta_i; \{R_{it}, D_{it}\}), \tag{4.18}$$

where the summation is over 2^T possible combinations of values for $\{D_{it}\}$. Because the calculation of this summation is difficult for even moderate large T, direct maximization of equation (4.18) is not computationally feasible.

The EM algorithm iteratively applies the following two steps in an effort to converge on the maximum likelihood estimator:

(1) *Expectation step (E-step)*. Compute the expected value of the log complete data likelihood function conditional on the observed data, i.e., the expected log likelihood:

$$Q_i(\theta_i, \theta_i') = E_{\theta_i'}\left[\log \mathcal{L}(\theta_i; \{R_{it}, D_{it}\}) | \{R_{it}\}\right], \tag{4.19}$$

where $\theta_i' = (\beta_{i,a}', Z_{i,a}', (\sigma_i')^2, p_i')$ is the current guess of the parameter vector θ_i.

(2) *Maximization step (M-step)*. Use the following optimization problem to update the estimate of θ_i:

$$M(\theta_i) = \underset{\theta_i}{\text{Max}}\ Q_i(\theta_i, \theta_i'). \tag{4.20}$$

Next, the details of these two steps are worked out. Using Eqs. (4.16) and (4.17), the log complete data likelihood can be written as

$$\log \mathcal{L}(\theta_i; \{R_{it}, D_{it}\}) = \sum_{t=1}^{T}\Bigg\{[I(D_{it} = 1)\log p_i + I(D_{it} = -1)\log(1 - p_i)]$$

$$-\frac{1}{2}\log[2\pi\sigma_i^2] - \frac{1}{2\sigma_i^2}[R_{it} - R_{ft} - \beta_{i,a}(R_{at} - R_{ft}) - Z_{i,a}D_{it}\sigma_{at}]^2\Bigg\}, \tag{4.21}$$

where $I(\cdot)$ denotes the indicator function. To compute the expected log likelihood in Eq. (4.19), we need to compute $\hat{p}_{it}(\theta_i') \equiv P_{\theta_i'}(D_{it} = 1|R_{it})$ and

$$\widehat{RSS}(\theta_i') \equiv E_{\theta_i'}\{[R_{it} - R_{ft} - \beta_{i,a}(R_{at} - R_{ft}) - Z_{i,a}D_{it}\sigma_{at}]^2|R_{it}\}. \tag{4.22}$$

Upon convergence of the EM algorithm with respect to θ_i' values, $\hat{p}_{it}$ estimates the probability of a positive return dispersion effect for the ith asset at time t.

Bayes' rule is applied to compute $\hat{p}_{it}(\theta_i') = P_{\theta_i'}(D_{it} = 1|R_{it})$:

$$\hat{p}_{it} = \frac{P_{\theta_i'}(R_{it}|D_{it} = 1)\cdot P_{\theta_i'}(D_{it} = 1)}{P_{\theta_i'}(R_{it}|D_{it} = 1)\cdot P_{\theta_i'}(D_{it} = 1) + P_{\theta_i'}(R_{it}|D_{it} = -1)\cdot P_{\theta_i'}(D_{it} = -1)}, \tag{4.23}$$

where

$$P_{\theta_i'}(D_{it}=1)=p_i', \qquad P_{\theta_i'}(D_{it}=-1)=1-p_i' \tag{4.24}$$

$$P_{\theta_i'}(R_{it}|D_{it}=\pm 1)=\frac{1}{\sqrt{2\pi(\sigma_i')^2}}\exp\left\{-\frac{(R_{it}-R_{ft}-\beta_{i,a}'(R_{at}-R_{ft})\mp Z_{i,a}'\sigma_{at})^2}{2(\sigma_i')^2}\right\}. \tag{4.25}$$

It readily follows that

$$E_{\theta_i'}(I(D_{it}=1)|R_{it})=P_{\theta_i'}(D_{it}=1|R_{it})=\hat{p}_{it}(\theta_i'), \tag{4.26}$$

$$E_{\theta_i'}(I(D_{it}=-1)|R_{it})=P_{\theta_i'}(D_{it}=-1|R_{it})=1-\hat{p}_{it}(\theta_i'), \tag{4.27}$$

and

$$\hat{D}_{it}\equiv E_{\theta_i'}(D_{it}|R_{it})=P_{\theta_i'}(D_{it}=1|R_{it})-P_{\theta_i'}(D_{it}=-1|R_{it}) \tag{4.28}$$

$$=\hat{p}_{it}-(1-\hat{p}_{it})$$

$$\hat{D}_{it}\equiv 2\hat{p}_{it}-1. \tag{4.29}$$

On the other hand, using Eq. (4.29) and the fact that $D_{it}^2=1$, we have

$$\begin{aligned}\widehat{RSS}(\theta_i') &= E_{\theta_i'}\{[R_{it}-R_{ft}-\beta_{i,a}(R_{at}-R_{ft})]^2\\ &\quad -2[R_{it}-R_{ft}-\beta_{i,a}(R_{at}-R_{ft})]Z_{i,a}D_{it}\sigma_{at}+Z_{i,a}^2D_{it}^2\sigma_{at}^2|R_{it}\}\\ &=[R_{it}-R_{ft}-\beta_{i,a}(R_{at}-R_{ft})]^2\\ &\quad -2[R_{it}-R_{ft}-\beta_{i,a}(R_{at}-R_{ft})]Z_{i,a}\hat{D}_{it}\sigma_{at}+Z_{i,a}^2\sigma_{at}^2\\ &=[R_{it}-R_{ft}-\beta_{i,a}(R_{at}-R_{ft})-Z_{i,a}\hat{D}_{it}\sigma_{at}]^2+Z_{i,a}^2(1-\hat{D}_{it}^2)\sigma_{at}^2.\end{aligned} \tag{4.30}$$

Combining Eqs. (4.21) and (4.22) as well as Eqs. (4.26) to (4.30), we obtain

$$\begin{aligned}Q_i(\theta_i,\theta_i') = \sum_{t=1}^{T}\Bigg\{&[\hat{p}_{it}\log p_i+(1-\hat{p}_{it})\log(1-p_i)]-\frac{1}{2}\log[2\pi\sigma_i^2]\\ &-\frac{(R_{it}-R_{ft}-\beta_{i,a}(R_{at}-R_{ft})-Z_{i,a}\hat{D}_{it}\sigma_{at})^2}{2\sigma_i^2}\\ &-\frac{Z_{i,a}^2(1-\hat{D}_{it}^2)\sigma_{at}^2}{2\sigma_i^2}\Bigg\}.\end{aligned} \tag{4.31}$$

This expression is the expected log likelihood from Eq. (4.19) needed in the E-step of the EM algorithm.

The M-step of the EM algorithm optimizes θ_i in the $Q_i(\theta_i, \theta_i')$ function where θ_i' is the current guess of θ_i. Inspection of expression $Q_i(\theta, \theta_i')$ in Eq. (4.31) indicates that the parameters $(\beta_{i,a}, Z_{i,a}, \sigma_i^2, p_i)$ are well-separated such that each parameter can be optimized with a closed-form solution when other parameters are fixed. This condition suggests the M-step of the EM algorithm can be implemented by iteratively optimizing the parameters. The simplicity of this iterative procedure is the main rationale for using the EM algorithm, as opposed to directly maximizing the observed data likelihood.

The steps of the whole EM algorithm are provided below.

(1) Initialize the set of parameters $\hat{\theta}_i^0 = (\hat{\beta}_{i,a}^0, \hat{Z}_{i,a}^0, (\hat{\sigma}_i^0)^2, \hat{p}_i^0)$ for the ith asset. First, estimate the simple OLS regression for the CAPM market model with no mispricing error:

$$R_{it} - R_{ft} = \beta_{i,a}(R_{at} - R_{ft}) + \epsilon_{it}, \quad t = 1, \cdots, T \tag{4.32}$$

and set $D_{it}^0 = +1$ when $\epsilon_{it} > 0$ or $D_{it}^0 = -1$ when $\epsilon_{it} < 0$ to compute the initial probability $\hat{p}_i^0 = \frac{1}{T}\sum_{t=1}^{T} I(D_{it}^0 = +1)$. Next, run the following regression:

$$R_{it} - R_{ft} = \beta_{i,a}(R_{at} - R_{ft}) + Z_{i,a} D_{it}^0 \sigma_{at} + \varepsilon_{it}, \quad t = 1, \cdots, T \tag{4.33}$$

to obtain $\hat{\beta}_{i,a}^0$, $\hat{Z}_{i,a}^0$, and the initial variance $(\hat{\sigma}_i^0)^2 = \frac{1}{T}\sum_{t=1}^{T} \varepsilon_{it}^2$. Set these initials as the current estimates of the parameters; that is, set $\theta_i' = \hat{\theta}_i^0$.

(2) Compute:

$$\hat{p}_{it} = \frac{\eta_{it}^{+} p_i'}{\eta_{it}^{+} p_i' + \eta_{it}^{-}(1 - p_i')} \tag{4.34}$$

with

$$\eta_{it}^{\pm} = \exp\left\{-\frac{(R_{it} - R_{ft} - \beta_{i,a}'(R_{at} - R_{ft}) \mp Z_{i,a}'\sigma_{at})^2}{2(\sigma_i')^2}\right\}, \tag{4.35}$$

and $\hat{D}_{it} = 2\hat{p}_{it} - 1$.

(3) Solve the following linear equations to get updated estimates of $\hat{\beta}_{i,a}$ and $\hat{Z}_{i,a}$:

$$\left(\sum_{t=1}^{T}(R_{at} - R_{ft})^2\right)\beta_{i,a} + \left(\sum_{t=1}^{T}\hat{D}_{it}(R_{at} - R_{ft})\sigma_{at}\right)Z_{i,a}$$
$$= \sum_{t=1}^{T}(R_{it} - R_{ft})(R_{at} - R_{ft}),$$
$$\left(\sum_{t=1}^{T}\hat{D}_{it}(R_{at} - R_{ft})\sigma_{at}\right)\beta_{i,a} + \left(\sum_{t=1}^{T}\sigma_{at}^2\right)Z_{i,a}$$
$$\sum_{t=1}^{T}\hat{D}_{it}(R_{it} - R_{ft})\sigma_{at}. \tag{4.36}$$

If $\hat{Z}_{i,a} < 0$, let $\hat{Z}_{i,a} \leftarrow -\hat{Z}_{i,a}$.

(4) Compute the updated variance:

$$\hat{\sigma}_i^2 = \frac{1}{T}\sum_{t=1}^{T}\Big\{(R_{it} - R_{ft} - \hat{\beta}_{i,a}(R_{at} - R_{ft}) - \hat{Z}_{i,a}\hat{D}_{it}\sigma_{at})^2$$
$$+\hat{Z}_{i,a}^2(1 - \hat{D}_{it}^2)\sigma_{at}^2\Big\}. \tag{4.37}$$

(5) Compute the updated probability:

$$\hat{p}_i = \frac{1}{T}\sum_{t=1}^{T}\hat{p}_{it}. \tag{4.38}$$

(6) Define the vector

$$\Delta\theta = \left(\frac{|\hat{\beta}_{i,a} - \beta'_{i,a}|}{|\beta'_{i,a}| + 1}, \frac{|\hat{Z}_{i,a} - Z'_{i,a}|}{|Z'_{i,a}| + 1}, \frac{|(\hat{\sigma}_i)^2 - (\sigma'_i)^2|}{|(\sigma'_i)^2| + 1}, \frac{|\hat{p}_i - p'_i|}{|p'_i| + 1}\right), \tag{4.39}$$

where convergence is achieved when $\mathrm{Max}(\Delta\theta) < 0.1\%$. If convergence is not achieved, then update θ'_i to the recent values of $\hat{\theta}_i$ obtained from steps (3) to (5) and repeat steps (2) to (5).

References

Asquith, D., J. Jones, and R. Kieschnick. 1998. Evidence on price stabilization and underpricing in early IPO returns. *Journal of Finance* 53: 1759–1773.

Bekaert, G., and C. Harvey. 1997. Emerging equity market volatility. *Journal of Financial Economics* 43: 29–77.

Black, F. 1972. Capital market equilibrium with restricted borrowing. *Journal of Business* 45: 444–454.

Black, F. 1993. Beta and return. *Journal of Portfolio Management* 20: 8–18.

Black, F. 1995. Estimating expected return. *Financial Analysts Journal* 49: 36–38.

Black, F., M. C. Jensen, and M. Scholes. 1972. The capital asset pricing model: Some empirical tests. In *Studies in the Theory of Capital Markets*, ed. M. C. Jensen. New York, NY: Praeger.

Bo, C. B., and S. Batzoglou. 2008. What is the expectation maximization algorithm? *Nature Biotechnology* 26: 897–899.

Breiman, L. 2001. Statistical modeling: The two cultures. *Statistical Science* 16: 199–231.

Carhart, M. M. 1997. On persistence in mutual fund performance. *Journal of Finance* 52: 57–82.

Chen, Y., M. Cliff, and H. Zhao. 2017. Hedge funds: The good, the bad, and the lucky. *Journal of Financial and Quantitative Analysis* 52: 1081–1109.

Christie, W., and R. Huang. 1994. The changing functional relation between stock returns and dividend yields. *Journal of Empirical Finance* 1: 161–191.

Demirer, R., and S. P. Jategaonkar. 2013. The conditional relation between dispersion and return. *Review of Financial Economics* 22: 125–134.

Dempster, A. P., N. M. Laird, and D. B. Rubin. 1977. Maximum likelihood from incomplete data via the EM algorithm. *Journal of the Royal Statistical Society* 39: 1–38.

Fama, E. F., and K. R. French. 1992. The cross-section of expected stock returns. *Journal of Finance* 47: 427–465.

Fama, E. F., and K. R. French. 1993. The cross-section of expected returns. *Journal of Financial Economics* 33: 3–56.

Fama, E. F., and K. R. French. 2015. A five-factor asset pricing model. *Journal of Financial Economics* 116: 1–22.

Fama, E. F., and K. R. French. 2018. Choosing factors. *Journal of Financial Economics* 128: 234–252.

Fama, E. F., and J. D. MacBeth. 1973. Risk, return, and equilibrium: Empirical tests. *Journal of Political Economy* 81: 607–636.

Harvey, C. R., and Y. Liu. 2016. Rethinking performance evaluation, Working paper no. 22134, National Bureau of Economic Research, Cambridge, MA.

Hou, K., C. Xue, and L. Zhang. 2015. Digesting anomalies: An investment approach. *Review of Financial Studies* 28: 650–705.

Garcia, R., D. Mantilla-Garcia, and L. Martellini. 2014. A model-free measure of aggregate idiosyncractic volatility and the prediction of market returns. *Journal of Financial and Quantitative Analysis* 49: 1133–1165.

Jiang, X. 2010. Return dispersion and expected returns. *Financial Markets and Portfolio Management* 24: 107–135.

Jones, P. N., and G. J. McLachlan. 1990. Algorithm AS 254: Maximum likelihood estimation from grouped and truncated data with finite normal mixture models. *Applied Statistics* 39: 273–282.

Kolari, J. W., J. Z. Huang, H. A. Butt, and H. Liao. 2022. International tests of the ZCAPM asset pricing model. Journal of International Financial Markets. *Institutions & Money* 79: 101607.

Kolari, J. W., J. Z. Huang, W. Liu, and H. Liao. 2022. Further tests of the ZCAPM asset pricing model. *Journal of Risk and Financial Management* 15, 1-23. Reprinted in Kolari, J. W., and S. Pynnonen, 2022, eds., *Frontiers of Asset Pricing* (MDPI, Basel, Switzerland).

Kolari, J. W., J. Z. Huang, W. Liu, and H. Liao. 2023. The alpha force: Testing missing asset pricing factors, Presented at the annual conference meetings of the Western Economic Association International, San Diego, CA.

Kolari, J. W., J. Z. Huang, W. Liu, and H. Liao. 2023. A cross-sectional asset pricing test of model validity, Presented at the annual conference meetings of the Southwestern Finance Association, Las Vegas, NV. Available on SSRN at https://papers.ssrn.com/sol3/papers.cfm?abstract_id=4203990

Kolari, J. W., J. Z. Huang, W. Liu, and H. Liao. 2024. *A quantum leap in asset pricing: Explaining anomalous returns.* Palm Beach Gardens, FL: Presented at the annual conference meetings of the Southern Finance Association.

Kolari, J. W., J. Z. Huang, W. Liu, and H. Liao. 2025. A quantum leap in asset pricing: Explaining anomalous returns, Presented at the annual conference meetings of the Southwestern Finance Association, San Antonio, TX. Awarded the Best Paper in Investments.

Kolari, J. W., W. Liu, and J. Z. Huang. 2012. A new asset pricing model based on the zero-beta CAPM, Presented at the at the annual conference meetings of the Financial Management Association, Atlanta. Awarded the Best Paper in Investments.

Kolari, J. W., W. Liu, and J. Z. Huang. 2021. *A New Model of Capital Asset Prices: Theory and Evidence.* Cham, Switzerland: Palgrave Macmillan.

Kolari, J. W., W. Liu, and S. Pynnonen. 2024. *Professional Investment Portfolio Management: Boosting Performance with Machine-Made Portfolios and Stock Market Evidence.* Cham, Switzerland: Palgrave Macmillan.

Kolari, J. W., and S. Pynnonen. 2023. *Investment Valuation and Asset Pricing: Models and Methods.* Cham, Switzerland: Palgrave Macmillan.

Kothari, S. P., J. Shanken, and R. G. Sloan. 1995. Another look at the cross-section of expected stock returns. *Journal of Finance* 50: 185–224.

Lintner, J. 1965. The valuation of risk assets and the selection of risky investments in stock portfolios and capital budgets. *Review of Economics and Statistics* 47: 13–37.
Liu, W. 2013. *A New Asset Pricing Model Based on the Zero-Beta CAPM: Theory and Evidence*, Doctoral dissertation, Texas A&M University.
Liu, W., J. W. Kolari, and J. Z. Huang. 2012. *A new asset pricing model based on the zero-beta CAPM, Best paper award in investments at the 2012 annual meetings of the Financial Management Association*. GA (October): Atlanta.
Liu, W., J. W. Kolari, and J. Z. Huang. 2019. Creating superior investment portfolios, Working paper, Texas A&M University.
Liu, W., J. W. Kolari, and J. Z. Huang. 2020. *Return dispersion and the cross-section of stock returns*. Palm Springs, CA: Presented at the annual meetings of the Southern Finance Association.
Loungani, P., M. Rush, and W. Tave. 1990. Stock market dispersion and unemployment. *Journal of Monetary Economics* 25: 367–388.
Markowitz, H. M. 1952. Portfolio selection. *Journal of Finance* 7: 77–91.
Markowitz, H. M. 1959. *Portfolio Selection: Efficient Diversification of Investments*. New York, NY: Wiley.
McLachlan, G. J., and T. Krishnan. 2008. *The EM Algorithm and Extensions*, 2nd ed. New York, NY: Wiley.
McLachlan, G., and D. Peel. 2000. *Finite Mixture Models*. New York, NY: Wiley Interscience.
Mossin, J. 1966. Equilibrium in a capital asset market. *Econometrica* 34: 768–783.
Sharpe, W. F. 1964. Capital asset prices: A theory of market equilibrium under conditions of risk. *Journal of Finance* 19: 425–442.
Treynor, J. L. 1961. Market value, time, and risk, Unpublished manuscript.
Treynor, J. L. 1962. Toward a theory of market value of risky assets, Unpublished manuscript.

PART III

Explaining Anomaly Portfolio Returns

CHAPTER 5

The ZCAPM and Large Online Datasets of Anomaly Portfolio Returns

Abstract This chapter utilizes open source datasets with over 250 anomaly portfolios constructed by Chen and Zimmerman (2022) and Jensen, Kelly, and Pedersen (2023) to conduct out-of-sample tests of prominent asset pricing models. Chen and Zimmerman found that 161-out-of-319 long-short anomalies are "clear predictors" in terms of the statistical significance of cross-sectional return predictability on an out-of-sample basis. Jensen, Kelly, and Pedersen documented that 153 long-short factors across 93 countries can be replicated over time, survive joint modeling of all factors, hold up out-of-sample after their original publication, are strengthened by the large number of factors including global evidence, and can be grouped into a smaller number of anomaly clusters. Unlike previous studies, the authors employed alphas from the CAPM to measure anomaly returns. These risk-adjusted returns yielded results different from those of raw returns – unlike declining raw returns, alphas have not decreased over time. An important inference from the Jensen et al. study is that anomaly returns contain mispricing errors that likely arise from premiums associated with their risks. As we will see in this chapter, confirming this conjecture, risk premiums associated with systematic risk factors in the ZCAPM well explain large datasets of anomaly portfolio returns. The ZCAPM is a new asset pricing model by Kolari, Liu, and Huang (2021). Because large numbers of anomalies can be explained by ZCAPM systematic risk factors (viz., market returns and market return dispersion), the market efficiency hypothesis is supported. Also, we infer that hundreds of long-short portfolio anomalies

J. W. Kolari et al., *Asset Pricing Models and Market Efficiency*,
https://doi.org/10.1007/978-3-031-92901-3_5

yielding relatively high abnormal returns are no longer anomalous or unexplained. If previously published anomalies are explained by the ZCAPM, further research is needed to find long-short portfolios not explained by the ZCAPM. Finally, the consistent outperformance of the ZCAPM compared to prominent multifactor models in our out-of-sample empirical tests, in many cases by large margins, suggests that the ZCAPM is a valid asset pricing model worthy of further study by researchers. Can multifactor models be enhanced to match the out-of-sample performance of the ZCAPM? Or, should extant multifactor models be scrapped by researchers to make way for future progress in the development of the ZCAPM?

5.1 Methodology

Data

Daily returns for large datasets[1] of long-short anomalies are generously made available by both Chen and Zimmerman (2022) and Jensen, Kelly, and Pedersen (2023) on the internet. Out of a total of 172 portfolios in the Chen and Zimmerman dataset, we retain 133 anomaly portfolios with complete daily return data in the full sample period July 3, 1972 to December 31, 2021 (see Appendix A in Chapter 2).[2] We download daily factors for the Fama and French and Carhart models from Kenneth French's website. Daily factors for the Hou, Xue, and Zhang as well as Stambaugh and Yuan models are obtained from online databases provided by the authors, which are available for the restricted sample period July 1972 to December 2016. In robustness tests, we replicate the analyses using 153 anomaly portfolios available online based on the Jensen, Kelly, and Pedersen dataset (see Appendix B in Chapter 2).

[1] Empirical results in this chapter were presented by Kolari, Huang, Liu, and Liao (2024) at the 2024 Southern Finance Association Conference in Palm Beach Gardens, FL and 2025 Southwestern Finance Association Conference in San Antonio, TX (Best Paper Award in Investments).

[2] As mentioned by Chen and Velikov (2021), this database contains most if not all anomalies studied by Harvey, Liu, and Zhu (2016), McLean and Pontiff (2016), Green, Hand, and Zhang (2017), and Hou, Xue, and Zhang (2020).

Cross-Sectional Regression Analyses

We follow the standard two-step Fama and MacBeth (1973) procedure in our cross-sectional regression analyses. It is important to note that we use out-of-sample rather than in-sample tests. Many researchers have argued that out-of-sample tests are more reliable than in-sample tests due to the inability to tamper with the results via data mining. Also, we believe that out-of-sample tests are consistent with an investable strategy wherein investors buy stocks based on their current risks and then observe their return performance in the future. If you obtained good investment performance within some in-sample period, it does not mean that you will continue to earn high returns per unit risk in the future. Practitioners are well aware of this problem in evaluating investment strategies. Any strategy is unproven until it can perform well on an out-of-sample basis.

In the first step of the Fama-MaBeth procedure, for each asset pricing model, a time-series OLS regression is estimated using 1 year of daily returns (i.e., 252 trading days). While most studies utilize monthly returns in this step, we employ daily returns in line with our database of anomaly returns.[3] Furthermore, using daily returns allows comparisons to the recent ZCAPM of Kolari, Liu, and Huang (2021) (to be discussed shortly) which is normally estimated using daily returns. For the ith anomaly portfolio, in the one-year estimation window from July 1972 to June 1973, we begin by estimating the following time-series regression:

$$R_{it} - R_{ft} = \alpha_i + \sum_{k=1}^{K} b_{ik} F_{kt} + e_{it}, t = 1, \ldots, T, \tag{5.1}$$

where $R_{it} - R_{ft}$ is the realized excess return on the ith test asset for day t, R_{ft} is the riskless rate proxied by the Treasury bill rate, α_i is the intercept term or alpha, F_{kt} are asset pricing factors for $k = 1, \ldots, K$ factors, b_{ik} are corresponding K beta risk loadings for the ith portfolio, $i = 1, \ldots, N$ correspond to the number of portfolios, $t = 1, \ldots, T$ is the estimation period, and $e_{it} \sim \text{iid}\,(0, \sigma_i^2)$. A number of researchers, including Ferson, Sarkissian, and Simin (1999), Lewellen, Nagel, and Shanken (2010), Daniel and Titman (2012), and others, have cautioned against using test asset portfolios

[3] Some authors have used daily returns in cross-sectional regression tests of models, such as Bali, Engle, and Tang (2017).

that are closely related to attribute-based factors in asset pricing models. In the present case, while some anomalies are attribute-sorted portfolios related to factors in models under consideration, the large number of anomaly portfolios in our sample data effectively dilutes this problem for the most part.

In the second step, we estimate an out-of-sample cross-sectional regression in the next month. In this regard, Simin (2008), Ferson, Nallareddy, and Xie (2013), Barillas and Shanken (2018), Fama and French (2018), and others have contended that out-of-sample tests are important in order to avoid data snooping issues and other econometric problems in explaining stock returns using in-sample tests. Due to the fact that investors are faced with many possible predictors of equilibrium price changes, Martin and Nagel (2021) asserted that out-of-sample tests are favored over in-sample tests.[4] Using one-month-ahead July 1973 returns for anomaly portfolios, we estimate the following OLS cross-sectional regression:

$$R_{iT+1} - R_{fT+1} = \hat{\alpha} + \lambda_1 \hat{b}_{i1} + \lambda_2 \hat{b}_{i2} + \ldots + \lambda_K \hat{b}_{iK} + u_{iT+1}, \quad i = 1, \ldots, N, \tag{5.2}$$

where $R_{iT+1} - R_{fT+1}$ is the realized excess return on the ith portfolio in out-of-sample (one-month-ahead) month $T + 1$, $\hat{\alpha}$ is the intercept,[5] $\hat{b}_{ik}$, $k = 1, \ldots, K$ are K beta risk loadings estimated for N anomaly portfolios in the estimation period $t = 1, \ldots, T$, λ_k are corresponding estimated market prices of beta risk loadings, and u_{iT+1} are zero mean and independent of the explanatory variables. As discussed by Ferson, Sarkissian, and Simon (1999), Cochrane (2005), Back, Kapadia, Ostdiek (2013, 2015), Ferson (2019), and others, the estimated market prices of risk are long-short mimicking portfolios of stock portfolios' factor loadings.

We roll forward the above regression equations 1 month at a time and repeat the analyses until December 2021. The average of the cross-sectional λ_k parameters are estimated for the full analysis period from July 1973

[4] For further discussion of problems related to data snooping and model mining, see Lo and MacKinlay (1990) and Tian (2021).

[5] Fama and French (2020) defined the intercept as a level return that equals the common return to all test assets not captured by the explanatory variables in the cross-sectional regression (i.e., the excess return on a standard portfolio of N test assets with weights that sum to one and zero out each explanatory variable).

to December 2021 (i.e., 582 λ_ks).[6] Based on average λ_ks over time, we compute t-statistics to evaluate their significance. After evaluating different econometric methods for estimating linear beta pricing models, including OLS, weighted least squares (WLS), generalized least squares (GLS), general method of moments (GMM), and maximum likelihood (ML) estimation, Giglio and Xiu (2021) concluded that the asymptotic efficiency of OLS estimates is not improved to a first order by these alternative methods. Like their study, we report results for cross-sectional OLS regressions.[7]

Additionally, as cross-sectional regressions are rolled forward 1 month at a time, we generate a monthly time series of realized and predicted returns[8] for each portfolio from July 1973 to December 2021. These monthly series of realized and predicted returns are averaged for each of the 133 anomaly portfolios. Subsequently, following Jagannathan and Wang (1996) and Lettau and Ludwigson (2001, footnote 17, p. 1254), we run a single equation cross-sectional regression of average realized returns on average predicted returns to obtain an estimate of the R^2 value. These average realized and predicted returns are plotted in forthcoming empirical results to graphically display mispricing errors for anomaly portfolios.

Asset Pricing Models

Prominent asset pricing models

The following leading or renowned asset pricing models are studied:

- CAPM market model with CRSP value-weighted index minus the Treasury bill rate as the market factor, or R_m;
- Fama and French (1992, 1993) three-factor model (FF3) based on augmenting the market model with a size factor (small minus large firms' stock returns, or *SMB*) and value factor (high book-to-market equity minus low book-to-market equity firms' stock returns, or *HML*);

[6] This 1-month rolling method allows the risk parameters in models to change over time and, therefore, captures the dynamic risk structure of assets in the market. Also, Cochrane (2005, p. 246) has pointed out that the cross-sectional regression for each period generates independent estimates of λ_k that are averaged over time to deduce their variance.

[7] For further discussion of the statistical properties of the two-step Fama and MacBeth regression procedure, see MacKinlay and Richardson (1991), Shanken (1992), Cochrane (2005), Shanken and Zhou (2007), Jagannathan, Skoulakis, and Wang (2010), among others.

[8] Predicted or fitted returns are computed using the estimated regression relation in Eq. (5.2).

- Carhart (1997) four-factor model (C4) based on augmenting the three-factor model with a momentum factor (firms with high past return stock returns minus low past stock returns, or *MOM*);
- Fama and French (2015) five-factor model (FF5) based on augmenting their three-factor model with a profitability factor (robust operating profitability minus weak operating profitability returns, *RMW*) and capital investment factor (conservative investment minus aggressive investment returns, or *CMA*);
- Fama and French (2018) six-factor model (FF6) based on augmenting their five-factor model with a momentum factor;
- Hou, Xue, and Zhang (2015) four-factor *q* model (HXZ4) based on augmenting the market model with a size factor (equity market capitalization, *ME*), profitability factor (return on equity, *ROE*), and capital investments factor (investment to assets ratio of the firm, *IA*); and
- Stambaugh and Yuan (2017) four-factor model (SY4) based on augmenting the market model with a size factor (*SMB*), management factor (derived from rankings of stocks' returns with respect to 6 anomaly portfolios, *MGMT*), and a performance factor (derived from rankings of stocks' returns with respect to 5 anomaly portfolios, *PERF*).

Due to data limitations, the latter two models have a restricted sample period from July 1972 to December 2016. For comparison purposes, we repeat the estimations of all models in this subperiod.

The ZCAPM

In Chapter 4, we reviewed the recent asset pricing model by Kolari, Liu, and Huang (2021) dubbed the ZCAPM. An interesting aspect of the ZCAPM is that, as the width of the parabola changes with increases or decreases in market return dispersion as measured by σ_{at} at any time t, assets located in the top and bottom halves of the Markowitz (1952, 1959) mean-variance investment parabola are differentially affected. For example, holding all else the same, as σ_{at} increases (decreases), all assets above the axis of symmetry of the parabola will experience increasing (decreasing) expected returns. Conversely, as σ_{at} increases (decreases), all assets below the axis of symmetry of the parabola will experience decreasing (increasing) expected returns. Thus, comparing assets located above or below the axis of symmetry of the parabola, a change in σ_{at} (i.e., the width or span of the parabola) has opposite effects on their expected returns.

To take into account positive versus negative effects of σ_{at} on asset returns, the empirical ZCAPM introduces a hidden dummy or signal variable, viz., $D_{it} = +1$ or -1. Departing from other asset pricing models that typically rely upon ordinary least squares (OLS) regression, because signal variable D_{it} is unknown, the empirical ZCAPM employs the well-known expectation-maximization (EM) algorithm in a regression model. EM regression estimates the probability (p_i) that the dummy variable for the ith stock or stock portfolio is positive versus negative related to market return dispersion effects on stock returns.[9]

Wikipedia defines machine learning (ML) as "... a field of study in artificial intelligence concerned with the development and study of statistical algorithms that can learn from data and generalize to unseen data, and thus perform tasks without explicit instructions."[10] ML allows the empirical ZCAPM to do ***predictive analytics.*** As reviewed in Chapter 4, the empirical ZCAPM contains a beta risk coefficient β_{ia} related to average excess market returns and a zeta risk coefficient Z^*_{ia} associated with market return dispersion σ_{at}. The positive or negative sign of Z^*_{ia} is determined by the estimated probability p_i of hidden or latent signal variable D_{it} in sample period $t = 1, \ldots, T$. In this respect, if $p_i > 1/2$ (or $< 1/2$), Z^*_{ia} is positive (or negative) in sign. This kind of probability analysis is considered by ML to be ***probability approximately correct (PAC) learning.***

The empirical ZCAPM regresses excess stock returns for the ith stock or portfolio ($R_{it} - R_{ft}$) on average excess market returns ($R_{at} - R_{ft}$) and market return dispersion (σ_{at}) as follows:

$$R_{it} - R_{ft} = \beta_{ia}(R_{at} - R_{ft}) + Z^*_{ia}\sigma_{at} + u_{it}, \quad t = 1, \ldots, T. \tag{5.3}$$

In line with the OLS cross-sectional regression in Eq. (5.2) using one-month-ahead returns in month $T+1$ for $i = 1, \ldots, N$ assets, the second step in the Fama-MacBeth procedure estimates the following standard ordinary least squares (OLS) cross-sectional regression:

$$R_{i,T+1} - R_{fT+1} = \lambda_0 + \lambda_a\hat{\beta}_{ia} + \lambda_{RD}\hat{Z}^*_{ia} + u_{it}, \tag{5.4}$$

where λ_a and λ_{RD} are estimated coefficients that represent the market price of beta risk and market price of zeta risk, respectively. The estimated risk premiums λ_a and λ_{RD} approximate mimicking portfolio returns. In

[9] EM regression was developed by Dempster, Laird, and Rubin (1977), Jones and McLachlan (1990), McLachlan and Peel (2000), McLachlan and Krishnan (2008), and others. See Wikipedia for an excellent discussion of EM regression and literature citations.

[10] See https://en.wikipedia.org/wiki/Machine_learning.

Table 5.1 Descriptive statistics for asset pricing factors This table summarizes the descriptive statistics for the asset pricing factors. Daily factor returns (in percent) corresponding to different asset pricing models are denoted as follows: $R_m - R_f$ (CRSP index return minus Treasury bill rate, see footnote 1), *SMB* (size), *HML* (value), *MOM* (momentum), *RMW* (profitability), *CMA* (capital investment), *RD* (market return dispersion), *ME* (equity market capitalization), *IA* (investments-to-asset ratio), *ROE* (return on equity), *MGMT* (management), and *PERF* (performance). Panel A (B) contains results for the full sample period, July 1972 to December 2021 (restricted sample period July 1972 to December 2016)

Panel A: Full sample period July 1972 to December 2021

Statistic	$R_m - R_f$	*SMB*	*HML*	*MOM*	*RMW*	*CMA*	*RD*
Mean	0.03	0.005	0.01	0.03	0.01	0.01	1.86
Standard deviation	1.07	0.57	0.59	0.79	0.41	0.37	0.66
Maximum	11.35	6.17	6.74	7.12	4.52	2.53	10.77
Minimum	–17.44	–11.19	–5.00	–14.37	–3.01	–5.87	0.68

Panel B: Restricted subperiod July 1972 to December 2016

Statistic	$R_m - R_f$	*ME*	*IA*	*ROE*	*MGMT*	*PERF*	*RD*
Mean	0.03	0.01	0.02	0.03	0.03	0.03	1.88
Standard deviation	1.05	0.56	0.37	0.42	0.52	0.80	0.64
Maximum	11.35	6.49	2.75	3.26	5.72	8.10	10.77
Minimum	–17.44	–10.81	–6.88	–3.96	–6.38	–13.49	0.75

[1]In the ZCAPM, due to using average market excess returns rather than a proxy for market portfolio excess returns, the market factor associated with CRSP index excess returns is denoted $R_a - R_f$ instead of $R_m - R_f$ per other models

effect, λ_a portfolio returns are long relatively high beta stocks and short relatively low beta stocks with respect to average market returns. Likewise, λ_{RD} portfolio returns are long relatively high zeta risk stocks and short relatively low zeta risk stocks with respect to market return dispersion.

It is known that beta risk loadings ($\hat{\beta}_{ia}$) are generally invariant to using daily, monthly, or annual returns in their time-series regression estimation. By contrast, zeta risk loadings ($\hat{Z}^*_{ia}$) are time variant. Because zeta risk loadings are estimated in the EM time-series regression via daily returns and then used in the above OLS cross-sectional regression with one-month-ahead returns on the left-hand-side, $\hat{Z}^*_{ia}$ can be rescaled from a daily to monthly basis as follows:

$$R_{i,T+1} - R_{fT+1} = \lambda_0 + \lambda_a \hat{\beta}_{ia} + \lambda_{RD} \hat{Z}^*_{ia} N_{T+1} + u_{it}, \tag{5.5}$$

where N_{T+1} is the number of trading days in month $T + 1$ (i.e., 21 days), $Z^*_{ia} N_{T+1}$ is the monthly estimated zeta risk, and λ_{RD} is the monthly risk premium associated with zeta risk. This rescaling does not change the per unit zeta risk return premium $\hat{\lambda}_{RD}$. Conveniently, rescaling Z^*_{ia} to a monthly basis enables us to compare λ_{RD} estimates with monthly λ_a estimates related to beta loadings.

5.2 Empirical Evidence

Descriptive statistics for asset pricing factors in different models are summarized in Table 5.1 Panel A (B) covers the full sample period (restricted sample period). The market return dispersion factor σ_{at} in equation (3) is denoted as *RD*.

To illustrate the relationship between average daily returns and zeta risk as well as beta risk, we construct Fig. 5.1. For the 133 anomaly portfolios, we estimate parameters $\hat{\beta}$ and $\hat{Z}^*$ for the empirical ZCAPM using 1 year of daily returns (e.g., estimates begin for the estimation period July 1972 to June 1973). This estimation window is rolled forward 1 month at a time (e.g., August 1972 to July 1973), and the empirical ZCAPM is re-estimated. Averages of $\hat{\beta}$ and $\hat{Z}^*$ estimates are computed for the full sample period, i.e., 594 1-month rolling regressions from July 1972 to December 2021. Next, we sort the 133 anomaly portfolios into beta quintiles as well as zeta risk quintiles. For each quintile, we plot the average daily returns for anomaly portfolios against their average zeta risk coefficients denoted Z^* and average beta risk coefficients denoted β, respectively.

Casual inspection of the graphs in Fig. 5.1 shows that, conditional on beta risk in the left-hand column of the graphs, average daily returns for anomalies are positively and linearly related to average zeta risk coefficients. While low beta quintile portfolios exhibit a weak relationship, the other four beta quintiles exhibit a strong relationship between average daily returns and zeta risk coefficients in support of the empirical ZCAPM. In the right-hand column of Fig. 5.1, consistent with prior literature, with the exception of the fourth zeta risk quintile, we find no relationship between average daily returns and average beta risk (sorted into zeta risk quintiles).[11]

[11] In Chapter 6 of their book, Kolari, Liu, and Huang (2021) generated similar graphs of average portfolio returns with respect to both zeta risk and beta risk using quintile sorts for different test asset portfolios. The results were similar to those for anomaly portfolios in Fig. 5.1.

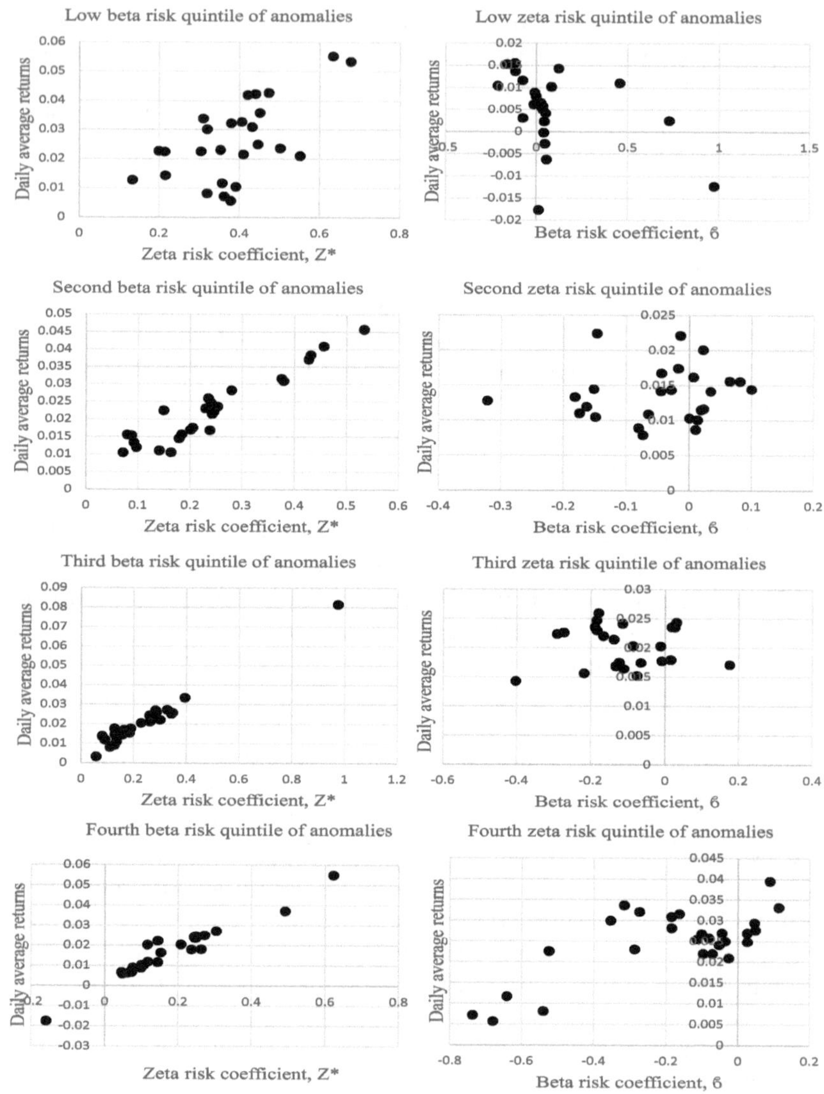

Fig. 5.1 Average daily returns (Y-axis) for the 133 anomaly portfolios plotted against both average zeta risk coefficients, or Z^* and average beta risk coefficients. or β, (X-axis) based on quintile sorts of beta risk and zeta risk, respectively. Results for the low, second, and third beta quintiles and zeta quintiles are shown. The full sample period is July 1972 to December 2021

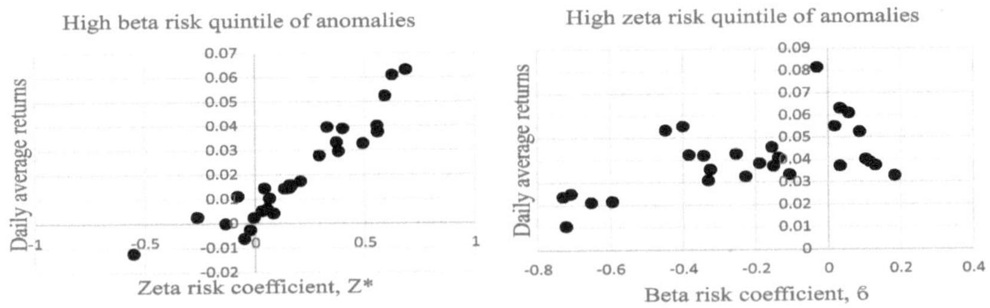

Fig. 5.1 (continued)

Cross-Sectional Regression Results: Full Analysis Period

Using value-weighted daily returns for 133 anomaly portfolios in the full analysis period July 1973 to December 2021, cross-sectional tests for the CAPM and leading multifactor models are shown in Table 5.2. All tests are out-of-sample on a 1-month rolling basis over time. That is, a model is estimated using daily returns for 1 year, and beta risk loadings from the estimated model are used in a one-month-ahead cross-sectional regression of excess portfolio returns on the previously estimated risk loadings. The latter cross-sectional regression yields estimates of the market prices of risk for different risk loadings (i.e., $\hat{\lambda}_k$). This two-step, Fama-MacBeth process is rolled forward 1 month and repeated. Lastly, averages of the monthly generated market prices of risk over time and t-statistics are computed.

In Panel A of Table 5.2, the CAPM in the first row has almost no explanatory power, and the market price of market beta risk (denoted $\hat{\lambda}_m$) is zero. The Fama and French three-factor model (FF3) performs better with an estimated R^2 value of 11% and a marginally significant market price of value loadings ($\hat{\lambda}_{HML}$) at the 10% level (in a two-tailed t-test).[12] The

[12] Kolari, Liu, and Huang (2021, Table 7.1, p. 166) reported fairly strong out-of-sample cross-sectional regression results for the FF3 model using Fama and French's (1992, 1993) 25 size and book-to-market test asset portfolios. In the analysis period January 1965 to December 2018, the R^2 was 63%, and the market price of value loadings ($\hat{\lambda}_{HML}$) was significant at the 1% level with a t-statistic of 2.64. While these results supported the FF3 model, the ZCAPM had an R^2 of 94%, and the t-statistic for the market price of return dispersion loadings ($\hat{\lambda}_{RD}$) was 4.22. Surprisingly, the ZCAPM outperformed the FF3 model even with test asset portfolios that were based on firm characteristics endogenous to the long-short size and value factors in FF3 but exogenous to the average market excess return and market return dispersion factors in the ZCAPM.

Carhart four-factor model (C4) boosts R^2 to 17%, and again the market price of value loadings are marginally significant at the 10% level. The Fama and French five-factor model (FF5) has similar explanatory power to C4 with significant capital investment loadings ($\hat{\lambda}_{CMA}$) at the 5% level. Capital investment loadings are again significant at the 5% level in the Fama and French six-factor model (FF6), and R^2 increases to 19%.

Table 5.2 Out-of-sample Fama-MacBeth cross-sectional tests of 133 anomaly portfolios for asset pricing models in the full sample period July 1972 to December 2021. Using 133 anomalous portfolios from Chen and Zimmerman (2020), this table contains results for the full sample period July 1972 to December 2021. Based on standard two-step Fama-MacBeth cross-sectional tests, we report out-of-sample (one-month-ahead) estimated market prices of risk denoted $\hat{\lambda}_k$ for the kth factor for the analysis period July 1973 to December 2021. Associated t-statistics are shown below estimated prices of risk. The asset pricing models are: CAPM, Fama and French three-factor model (FF3), Carhart four-factor model (C4), Fama and French five-factor model (FF5), Fama and French six-factor model (FF6), and ZCAPM. Factors in these models are denoted as m (CRSP index excess return, see footnote 1), *RD* (market return dispersion), *SMB* (size), *HML* (value), *MOM* (momentum), *RMW* (profitability), and *CMA* (capital investment). Results are shown for the full analysis period (Panel A) in addition to analysis subperiods July 1973 to December 2000 (Panel B) and January 2001 to December 2021 (Panel C)

Panel A: Full analysis period July 1973 to December 2021

Model	$\hat{\alpha}$	$\hat{\lambda}_m$	$\hat{\lambda}_{RD}$	$\hat{\lambda}_{SMB}$	$\hat{\lambda}_{HML}$	$\hat{\lambda}_{MOM}$	$\hat{\lambda}_{RMW}$	$\hat{\lambda}_{CMA}$	R^2
CAPM	0.44	−0.00							0.01
	17.77	−0.01							
FF3	0.42	0.07		−0.09	0.27				0.11
	19.37	0.39		−0.37	1.82				
C4	0.40	−0.04		−0.13	0.26	0.31			0.17
	18.52	−0.23		−0.61	1.84	1.29			
FF5	0.40	0.12		0.04	0.12		0.18	0.32	0.15
	20.33	0.7		0.17	0.77		1.25	2.76	
FF6	0.38	−0.04		0.03	0.18	0.40	0.19	0.26	0.19
	19.00	−0.26		0.16	1.19	1.64	1.54	2.31	
ZCAPM	0.28	0.30	0.72						0.84
	9.96	1.43	6.69						

condt.

Table 5.2 continued

Panel B: Analysis subperiod July 1973 to December 2000									
Model	$\hat{\alpha}$	$\hat{\lambda}_m$	$\hat{\lambda}_{RD}$	$\hat{\lambda}_{SMB}$	$\hat{\lambda}_{HML}$	$\hat{\lambda}_{MOM}$	$\hat{\lambda}_{RMW}$	$\hat{\lambda}_{CMA}$	R^2
CAPM	0.56	−0.07							0
	17.53	−0.22							
FF3	0.54	0.06		−0.24	0.31				0.11
	18.54	0.26		−0.86	1.74				
C4	0.49	−0.11		−0.18	0.41	0.76			0.21
	17.77	−0.45		−0.65	2.26	2.72			
FF5	0.50	0.08		−0.19	0.22		0.08	0.29	0.13
	19.13	0.33		−0.73	1.04		0.48	1.76	
FF6	0.47	−0.07		−0.26	0.34	0.85	−0.05	0.25	0.22
	18.19	−0.32		−0.98	1.73	3.10	−0.33	1.51	
ZCAPM	0.30	0.24	0.96						0.94
	8.04	0.87	7.09						
Panel C: Analysis subperiod January 2001 to December 2021									
Model	$\hat{\alpha}$	$\hat{\lambda}_m$	$\hat{\lambda}_{RD}$	$\hat{\lambda}_{SMB}$	$\hat{\lambda}_{HML}$	$\hat{\lambda}_{MOM}$	$\hat{\lambda}_{RMW}$	$\hat{\lambda}_{CMA}$	R^2
CAPM	0.25	0.16							0.01
	6.94	0.45							
FF3	0.24	0.15		0.08	0.16				0.09
	8.20	0.57		0.21	0.68				
C4	0.24	0.14		−0.13	−0.01	−0.13			0.12
	8.00	0.52		−0.41	−0.03	−0.37			
FF5	0.23	0.24		0.38	−0.11		0.34	0.28	0.18
	8.94	0.97		1.26	−0.48		1.45	1.87	
FF6	0.22	0.09		0.32	−0.09	−0.02	0.47	0.24	0.21
	8.32	0.36		1.19	−0.45	−0.06	2.44	1.61	
ZCAPM	0.22	0.46	0.46						0.61
	5.83	1.38	2.95						

[1] In the ZCAPM, due to using average market excess returns rather than a proxy for market portfolio excess returns, the price of beta risk associated with CRSP index excess returns is denoted $\hat{\lambda}_a$ instead of $\hat{\lambda}_m$ in the other models

Among the different models in Panel A of Table 5.2, the ZCAPM results stand out with an estimated R^2 value equal to 84%, which demonstrates much stronger out-of-sample goodness-of-fit than other models. Also, the market price of return dispersion loadings ($\hat{\lambda}_{RD}$) is highly significant at below the 1% level; indeed, the t-statistic of 6.69 well exceeds any market prices of risk in the other models. With a relatively high estimated risk premium of 0.72% per month per unit of zeta risk (denoted Z^*), the magnitude of zeta risk premiums materially exceeds the estimated risk premiums of other factors and therefore is economically important in explaining anomaly portfolio returns.

We infer from these results that, among the six asset pricing models tested in Panel A, only the ZCAPM explains the cross-section of average returns for the 133 anomaly portfolios. Also, applying the 3 t-statistic threshold recommended by Harvey, Liu, and Zhu (2016) and Chordia, Goyal, and Saretto (2020) for the significance of factor loadings, only zeta risk loadings associated with market return dispersion pass these authors' hurdle to avoid false discoveries.[13]

In Panels B and C of Table 5.2, we report the subperiod cross-sectional regression results. Prior studies using anomaly portfolios as test assets do not conduct subperiod analyses.[14] In the present analyses, for the subperiod July 1972 to December 2000 (i.e., analysis period beginning July 1973), the results in Panel B show that explanatory power for the multifactor models ranges from 11% (FF3) to 22% (FF6), but the ZCAPM is much higher with an R^2 equal to 94%. To the authors' knowledge, this goodness-of-fit exceeds published studies of out-of-sample cross-sectional tests of asset pricing models and is strong evidence that the ZCAPM can price the anomaly portfolios. Again the market price of value loadings ($\hat{\lambda}_{HML}$) is significant at the 5 and 10% levels in some multifactor models, and capital investment loadings ($\hat{\lambda}_{CMA}$) are significant but now only marginally so at the 10% level in FF5. Also, momentum factor loadings ($\hat{\lambda}_{MOM}$) are now highly significant with t-statistics at 2.72 and 3.10 in the FF4 and FF6 models, respectively. As in the full analysis period, the market price of return dispersion loadings in the ZCAPM ($\hat{\lambda}_{RD}$) is very significant with a t-statistic equal to 7.09, which far exceeds those of other factors' loadings as well as the recommended 3 threshold.

In the analysis subperiod January 2001 to December 2021 in Panel C of Table 5.2, the cross-sectional results weaken to some extent compared to

[13] We re-ran the analyses using an in-sample full sample period regression analysis, rather than a out-of-sample approach using 1-month rolling regressions. Using the full period from July 1972 to December 2021, we estimated the empirical ZCAPM. Then we estimated cross-sectional regressions in each month and averaged the monthly results. We found that the results are unchanged for the most part. The market prices of beta and zeta risk loadings were 0.45% and 1.32% with t-statistics equal to 2.21 and 8.62. The R^2 value was estimated at 86%. Interestingly, when we ran daily cross-sectional regressions and average the results, the t-statistic on the market price of zeta risk loadings jumped to 13.69, which is extremely significant. It is clear that zeta risk is important to explaining the cross-section of average anomaly portfolio returns.

[14] Hou, Xue, and Zhang (2015) and Stambaugh and Yuan (2017) studied anomaly portfolio returns in the sample periods 1972 to 2012 and 1967 to 2013, respectively.

Panels A and B. Only two multifactors' loadings are significant: profitability ($\hat{\lambda}_{RMW}$) at the 5% level (FF6) and capital investment ($\hat{\lambda}_{CMA}$) at the marginal 10% level (FF5). Moreover, the results for the ZCAPM are significant but not as strong as in the other sample periods. The estimated R^2 value equals 61%, which is somewhat lower than before. Also, the t-statistic associated with the market price of return dispersion loadings ($\hat{\lambda}_{RD}$) is 2.95, which passes the 3 threshold after rounding up.[15]

In sum, the ZCAPM does a good job of explaining the cross-section of average anomaly portfolio returns. However, the CAPM is virtually useless, and commonly used multifactor models do a poor job with respect to exogenous anomaly returns.

Cross-Sectional Regression Results: Restricted Analysis Period

Due to data availability that restricts the analyses to the sample period July 1972 to December 2016 in studies by Hou, Xue, and Zhang (HXZ4) and Stambaugh and Yuan (SY4), we run out-of-sample cross-sectional regression tests for their multifactor models in this sample period. Using the 133 anomaly portfolios, for comparison purposes, we re-run the previous models in Table 5.2. As shown in Panel A of Table 5.3, these two models have R^2 estimates close to those for the multifactor models (i.e., 18% for HXZ4 and 13% for SY4), but some of their factor loadings have higher significance—namely, capital investments factor loadings ($\hat{\lambda}_{IA}$) and management factor loadings ($\hat{\lambda}_{MGMT}$) with t-statistics exceeding the 3 threshold at 3.93 and 3.36, respectively. Also, profitability factor loadings ($\hat{\lambda}_{ROE}$) and performance factor loadings ($\hat{\lambda}_{PERF}$) are significant at the 5% level, and momentum factor loadings ($\hat{\lambda}_{MOM}$) now reach the 10% marginal significance level (C4).

The results for the multifactor models in the top portion of Panel A in Table 5.3 are similar to those for the full analysis period in Panel A of Table 5.2, with the exception that value factor loadings ($\hat{\lambda}_{HML}$) are more significant at the 1 and 5% levels for C4 and FF3, respectively, instead of 10% level. Additionally, the ZCAPM continues to do comparatively well with a relatively high R^2 equal to 88% and very high t-statistic on the market price of return dispersion loadings (λ_{RD}) at 6.67 with a relatively high average magnitude of 0.56% per month per unit zeta risk.

[15] Harvey, Liu, and Zhu (2016) have contended that theory-based factors should have a lower t-statistic threshold than empirical-based factors. In this respect, the market return dispersion factor in the ZCAPM is theory-based rather than empirically determined.

Table 5.3 Out-of-sample Fama-MacBeth cross-sectional tests of 133 anomaly portfolios for asset pricing models in the restricted sample period July 1972 to December 2016. Using 133 anomalous portfolios from Chen and Zimmerman (2020), this table contains the results for the restricted sample period July 1972 to December 2016. Based on standard two-step Fama-MacBeth cross-sectional tests, we report out-of-sample (one-month-ahead) estimated market prices of risk denoted $\hat{\lambda}_k$ for the kth factor for the analysis period July 1973 to December 2021. Associated t-statistics are shown below estimated prices of risk. The asset pricing models are: CAPM, Fama and French three-factor model (FF3), Carhart four-factor model (C4), Fama and French five-factor model (FF5), Fama and French six-factor model (FF6), ZCAPM, Hou, Xue, and Zhang four-factor q model (HXZ4), and Stambaugh and Yuan four-factor model (SY4). Factors in these models are denoted as m (CRSP index excess return, see footnote 1), RD (market return dispersion), SMB (size), HML (value), MOM (momentum), RMW (profitability), CMA (capital investment), ME (equity market capitalization), IA (investments-to-asset ratio), ROE (return on equity), $MGMT$ (management), and $PERF$ (performance). Results are shown for the restricted analysis period (Panel A) in addition to the analysis subperiods July 1973 to December 2000 (Panel B) and January 2001 to December 2016 (Panel C)

Panel A: Restricted analysis period July 1973 to December 2016

Model	$\hat{\alpha}$	$\hat{\lambda}_m$	$\hat{\lambda}_{RD}$	$\hat{\lambda}_{SMB}$	$\hat{\lambda}_{HML}$	$\hat{\lambda}_{MOM}$	$\hat{\lambda}_{RMW}$	$\hat{\lambda}_{CMA}$		R^2
CAPM	0.48	−0.03								0.02
	18.57	−0.13								
FF3	0.45	0.04		−0.15	0.35					0.14
	19.53	0.21		−0.65	2.25					
C4	0.43	−0.08		−0.14	0.34	0.34				0.21
	18.98	−0.39		−0.66	2.38	1.33				
FF5	0.42	0.08		−0.05	0.2		0.14	0.36		0.16
	20.75	0.44		−0.23	1.20		0.90	2.93		
FF6	0.41	−0.09		0.00	0.24	0.44	0.17	0.31		0.22
	19.79	−0.51		0.00	1.59	1.67	1.26	2.54		
ZCAPM	0.30	0.23	0.75							0.88
	9.65	1.05	6.67							
Model	$\hat{\alpha}$	$\hat{\lambda}_m$	$\hat{\lambda}_{RD}$	$\hat{\lambda}_{SMB}$	$\hat{\lambda}_{ME}$	$\hat{\lambda}_{IA}$	$\hat{\lambda}_{ROE}$	$\hat{\lambda}_{MGMT}$	$\hat{\lambda}_{PERF}$	R^2
HXZ4	0.41	0.02			0.09	0.56	0.49			0.18
	16.83	0.12			0.45	3.93	2.24			
SY4	0.41	−0.02		0.03				0.01	0.01	0.13
	18.29	−0.12		0.12				3.36	2.01	

condt.

Table 5.3 continued

Panel B: Analysis subperiod July 1973 to December 2000										
Model	$\hat{\alpha}$	$\hat{\lambda}_m$	$\hat{\lambda}_{RD}$	$\hat{\lambda}_{SMB}$	$\hat{\lambda}_{HML}$	$\hat{\lambda}_{MOM}$	$\hat{\lambda}_{RMW}$	$\hat{\lambda}_{CMA}$		R^2
CAPM	0.56	–0.07								0
	17.53	–0.22								
FF3	0.54	0.06		–0.24	0.31					0.11
	18.54	0.26		–0.86	1.74					
C4	0.49	–0.11		–0.18	0.41	0.76				0.21
	17.77	–0.45		–0.65	2.26	2.72				
FF5	0.50	0.08		–0.19	0.22		0.08	0.29		0.13
	19.13	0.33		–0.73	1.04		0.48	1.76		
FF6	0.47	–0.07		–0.26	0.34	0.85	–0.05	0.25		0.22
	18.19	–0.32		–0.98	1.73	3.10	–0.33	1.51		
ZCAPM	0.30	0.24	0.96							0.94
	8.04	0.87	7.09							
Model	$\hat{\alpha}$	$\hat{\lambda}_m$	$\hat{\lambda}_{RD}$	$\hat{\lambda}_{SMB}$	$\hat{\lambda}_{ME}$	$\hat{\lambda}_{IA}$	$\hat{\lambda}_{ROE}$	$\hat{\lambda}_{MGMT}$	$\hat{\lambda}_{PERF}$	R^2
HXZ4	0.49	0.09			–0.02	0.69	0.62			0.19
	15.34	0.37			–0.08	3.58	2.42			
SY4	0.48	0.04		–0.10				0.01	0.01	0.14
	17.75	0.19		–0.34				2.84	2.55	
Panel C: Analysis subperiod July 2001 to December 2016										
Model	$\hat{\alpha}$	$\hat{\lambda}_m$	$\hat{\lambda}_{RD}$	$\hat{\lambda}_{SMB}$	$\hat{\lambda}_{HML}$	$\hat{\lambda}_{MOM}$	$\hat{\lambda}_{RMW}$	$\hat{\lambda}_{CMA}$		R^2
CAPM	0.30	0.13								0
	7.32	0.32								
FF3	0.26	0.09		–0.05	0.34					0.16
	7.72	0.30		–0.12	1.33					
C4	0.27	0.10		–0.18	0.13	–0.20				0.21
	8.05	0.32		–0.51	0.59	–0.48				
FF5	0.25	0.16		0.26	0.05		0.28	0.39		0.19
	8.90	0.57		0.87	0.18		0.95	2.31		
FF6	0.25	–0.01		0.32	0.01	–0.06	0.50	0.37		0.25
	9.11	–0.05		1.17	0.06	–0.14	2.14	2.15		
ZCAPM	0.23	0.30	0.46							0.74
	5.24	0.81	2.72							
Model	$\hat{\alpha}$	$\hat{\lambda}_m$	$\hat{\lambda}_{RD}$	$\hat{\lambda}_{SMB}$	$\hat{\lambda}_{ME}$	$\hat{\lambda}_{IA}$	$\hat{\lambda}_{ROE}$	$\hat{\lambda}_{MGMT}$	$\hat{\lambda}_{PERF}$	R^2
HXZ4	0.22	–0.00			0.29	0.23	0.41			0.17
	7.14	–0.01			1.03	1.21	1.20			
SY4	0.24	–0.04		0.20				0.00	0.01	0.07
	6.92	–0.12		0.58				1.55	1.06	

[1] In the ZCAPM, due to using average market excess returns rather than a proxy for market portfolio excess returns, the price of beta risk associated with CRSP index excess returns is denoted $\hat{\lambda}_a$ instead of $\hat{\lambda}_m$ in the other models

We next turn to the cross-sectional regression results for the analysis subperiods July 1973 to December 2000 and January 2001 to December 2016 in Panels B and C of Table 5.3, respectively. In Panel B, we reprint the multifactor model results in Panel B of Table 5.2 to better enable comparisons to the HXZ4 and SY4 models. As before in these two models, capital investments factor loadings ($\hat{\lambda}_{IA}$) and management factor loadings ($\hat{\lambda}_{MGMT}$) have relatively high t-statistics equal to 3.58 and 2.84, respectively. Additionally, profitability factor loadings ($\hat{\lambda}_{ROE}$) and performance factor loadings ($\hat{\lambda}_{PERF}$) increase in significance from the 5% to 1% level.

Finally, the results in the later analysis subperiod in Panel C of Table 5.3, like those for the full analysis period in Panel C of Table 5.2, indicate that the models' performance weakens to some extent. Now only capital investment loadings ($\hat{\lambda}_{CMA}$) in FF5 and FF6 as well as profitability factor loadings ($\hat{\lambda}_{RMW}$) in FF6 are significant at the 5% level. None of the multifactors' loadings in HXZ4 and SY4 is significant. Also, the ZCAPM's performance diminishes somewhat with R^2 equal to 74% and t-statistic for the market price of return dispersion loadings ($\hat{\lambda}_{RD}$) at 2.72, which is significant at the 1% level. The fact that the goodness-of-fit remains relatively high for the ZCAPM in this later subperiod bodes well for its ability to explain anomaly portfolio returns.

Summarizing the findings, the ZCAPM dominates other widely accepted models in out-of-sample cross-sectional regression tests. Similar to the full analysis period results in the prior subsection, all models experience diminished performance in the post-2000 subperiod compared to full analysis period and the prior analysis subperiod from July 1973 to December 2000. In forthcoming graphical results of realized and predicted returns, we return to this issue.

Graphical Cross-Sectional Results: Full Analysis Period

Fama and MacBeth (1973) posit that *normative models* seeking to help investors make better decisions are only valid to the extent that past information is related to future returns. In this respect, Cochrane (1996) and Lettau and Ludvigson (2001) have recommended comparative analyses of predicted versus realized (actual) returns to evaluate mispricing errors in asset pricing models. According to Cochrane, "Expected return pricing errors ... are a useful characterization of a model's performance" (Cochrane, 1996, p. 596). In this respect, he cautions that "... it is important to examine a model's ability to explain the expected returns of economically interesting portfolios" (Cochrane, 1996, p. 598). Since asset pricing models strive to explain anomaly portfolio returns, analyses of mispricing errors for these compelling portfolios should be useful for evaluating different models.

As discussed in the previous section, mispricing errors are computed on an out-of-sample basis using one-month-ahead cross-sectional regressions. Using 1 year of daily returns for the 133 anomaly portfolios, we estimate the time-series regression for each asset pricing model to obtain factor loadings. Next, cross-sectional regression models are estimated for test asset portfolios using one-month-ahead excess returns. Rolling forward the process 1 month at a time to generate $t = 1, \cdots, 582$ cross-sectional regressions from July 1973 to December 2021, averages of the estimated alpha intercepts, factor prices of risk $\hat{\lambda}_k$, and estimated loadings for the ith portfolio are used to compute average fitted excess returns in the next month for each portfolio. These average fitted excess returns are compared to each portfolio's one-month-ahead average realized (or actual) excess returns. Upon plotting these two average return series, we obtain a graph of mispricing errors for the 133 anomaly portfolios.

In Fig. 5.2, using the 133 anomaly portfolios in the full analysis period from July 1973 to December 2021, we compare the average pricing errors of the CAPM in Panel A to those of the Fama and French three-factor model in Panel B. If no pricing errors exist, all anomaly portfolios should line up on the 45 degree line. However, it is apparent that the CAPM performs poorly in these out-of-sample (one-month-ahead) comparisons of average realized and fitted anomaly portfolio returns. That is, predicted market risk premiums related to market beta are essentially zero. The Fama and French three-factor model (FF3) in Panel B performs better but large mispricing errors are still evident, particularly for portfolios with the highest realized returns located distantly to the left of the 45 degree line. In Fig. 5.3, the results for the Carhart four-factor model (C4) in Panel A and Fama and French five-factor model (FF5) in Panel B look slightly better but similar to those for the FF3 model.

In Panel A of Fig. 5.4, we see that the Fama and French six-factor model nominally improves upon the other multifactor models with somewhat smaller pricing errors. It still has problems pricing the high-return portfolios far off the 45 degree line. By contrast, the ZCAPM in Panel B of Fig. 5.4 has noticeably smaller mispricing errors than FF6 as well as other models in Figs. 5.2 and 5.3 with a greater density of anomaly portfolio points around the 45 degree line. Also notice that, for the ZCAPM, the

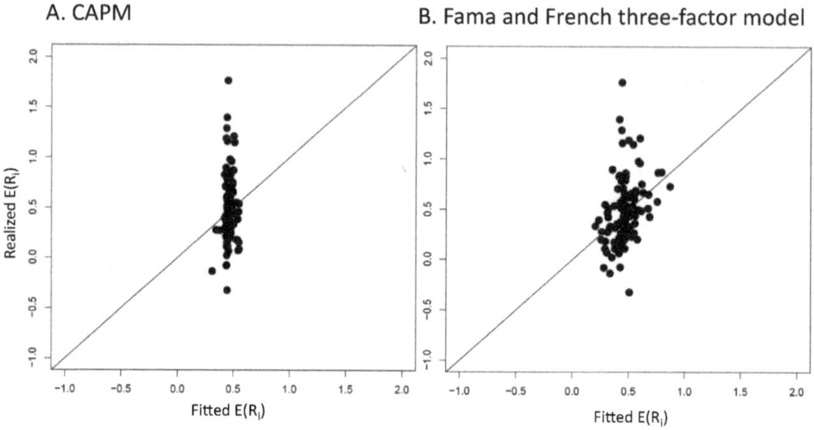

Fig. 5.2 Out-of-sample cross-sectional CAPM (Panel A) and Fama and French three-factor model (Panel B) mispricing errors comparing average one-month-ahead realized excess returns in percent (Y-axis) to average one-month-ahead predicted (fitted) excess returns in percent (X-axis) for 133 portfolios. The full analysis period is July 1973 to December 2021

portfolios with the highest realized returns are now much closer to the line with pricing errors similar to other portfolios. We infer that the ZCAPM markedly outperforms the other models with respect to mispricing errors.

Referring back to cross-sectional regression tests in Table 5.2, the R^2 value for the ZCAPM in Panel A for the full analysis period was computed (as discussed earlier) using the average realized and one-month-ahead fitted returns for anomaly portfolios. There we see that the ZCAPM has an estimated R^2 equal to 84% compared to only 19% for the FF6 model. These goodness-of-fit statistics quantify the smaller mispricing errors of the ZCAPM compared to other models. Interestingly, our results imply that momentum portfolios' returns in our sample (i.e., 12 portfolios) are largely explained by the ZCAPM. Momentum portfolios are notoriously anomalous in terms of being difficult to explain. Indeed, Fama and French (1998, p. 1653) refer to momentum as the premier anomaly in asset pricing. It appears that the mystery of momentum returns is solved to a large extent.

Graphical analyses for the 133 anomaly portfolios in subperiods July 1973 to December 2000 and January 2001 to December 2021 are shown in Figs. 5.5 and 5.6, respectively. For these analyses, we only report results

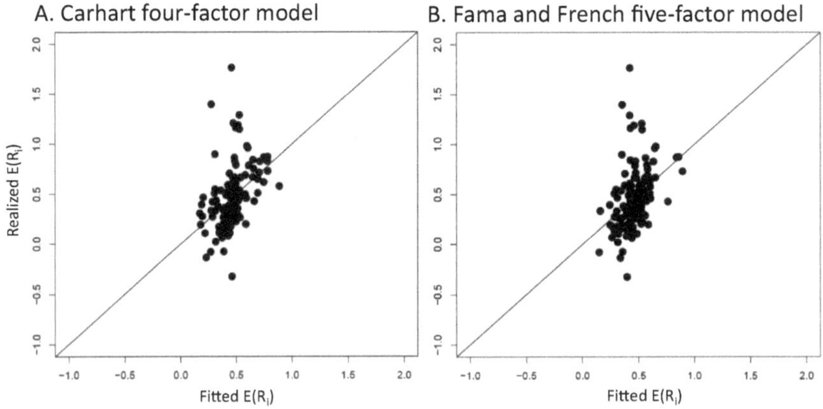

Fig. 5.3 Out-of-sample cross-sectional Carhart four-factor model (Panel A) and Fama and French five-factor model (Panel B) mispricing errors comparing average one-month-ahead realized excess returns in percent (Y-axis) to average one-month-ahead predicted (fitted) excess returns in percent (X-axis) for 133 portfolios. The full analysis period is July 1973 to December 2021

for FF6 and the ZCAPM. Graphs for other models are available upon request from the authors. Looking at the comparative results in Panels A and B of Fig. 5.5 in the earlier subperiod, FF6 mispricing errors are slightly improved compared to the full analysis period in Fig. 5.4. However, in our opinion, the ZCAPM exhibits outstanding performance in this earlier subperiod. The pricing ability of the ZCAPM well exceeds the FF6 model (i.e., from Panel B of Table 5.2, their respective R^2 values are 94% and 22%). Moreover, in the later post-2000 subperiod results displayed in Fig. 5.6, consistent with the cross-sectional regression results in Panel C of Table 5.2 (i.e., R^2 values of 61% for the ZCAPM and 21% for the FF6 model), both models experience somewhat diminished performance.

One possible explanation for the decreased pricing ability of models in the post-2000 subperiod is market turmoil, especially during the 2008-2009 financial crisis. It is reasonable to believe that asset pricing models would be less useful in a market experiencing chaos and panic selling. To investigate this conjecture, we dropped the years 2008 and 2009 from

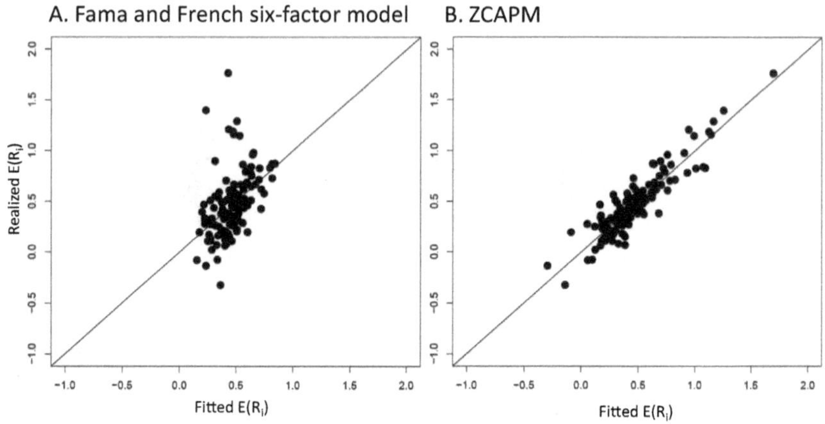

Fig. 5.4 Out-of-sample cross-sectional Fama and French six-factor model (Panel A) and ZCAPM (Panel B) mispricing errors comparing average one-month-ahead realized excess returns in percent (Y-axis) to average one-month-ahead predicted (fitted) excess returns in percent (X-axis) for 133 portfolios. The full analysis period is July 1973 to December 2021

the post-2000 subperiod.[16] In unreported results to conserve space, the cross-sectional regression results are little changed.

Another potential explanation for increased pricing errors in models over time is that, in line with previous research, anomaly portfolio returns decreased in the post-2000 subperiod. As anomaly returns decreased or even disappeared in some portfolios over time, the pricing ability of asset pricing models would be diminished due to their reduced economic significance. Comparing Figs. 5.5 and 5.6, in the earlier subperiod the range of average mispricing errors is from –0.5% to 1.8% per month, whereas the range decreases in the later subperiod to –0.3% to 1.0% . As a further check, we compute the daily cross-sectional average return for the 133 anomalies on each day t in our sample period. Five-year moving averages of this daily cross-sectional average return are computed by rolling forward 1 year at a time. Plotting the 5-year average on the last day for each five-year period over time, Panel A of Fig. 5.7 shows that average anomaly returns

[16] Now the analysis subperiods for cross-sectional regression tests consist of July 1973 to December 2007 and January 2010 to December 2021.

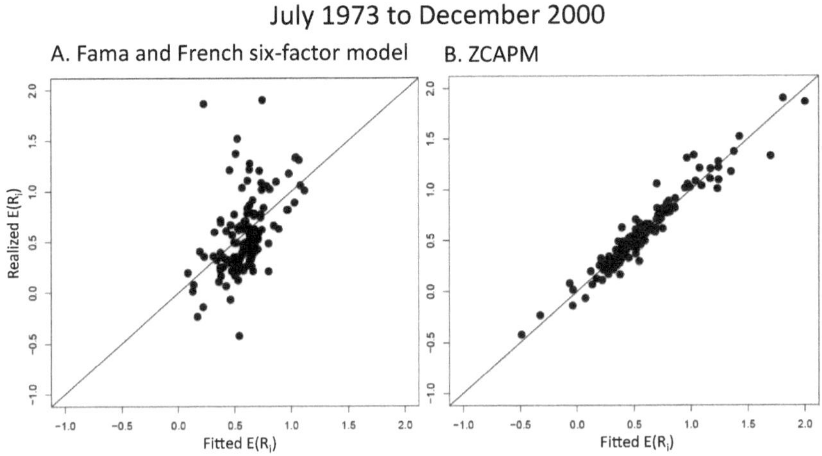

Fig. 5.5 Out-of-sample cross-sectional Fama and French six-factor model (Panel A) and ZCAPM (Panel B) mispricing errors comparing average 1-month-ahead realized excess returns in percent (Y-axis) to average one-month-ahead predicted (fitted) excess returns in percent (X-axis) for 133 portfolios. The analysis subperiod is July 1973 to December 2000

(in percent returns per day) decreased over time. A distinct break in average returns occurred around the mid-2000s with decidedly lower returns thereafter. By 2020, anomaly returns had almost entirely vanished on average. In Panel B of Fig. 5.7, we graph the 5-year moving averages of the cross-sectional standard deviation of daily returns. As before, the analyses roll forward 1 year at a time. Between 2001 and 2005, we see a jump in the cross-sectional dispersion of anomaly returns that is permanent for the most part. We infer from these findings that anomaly returns decreased and became more volatile over time, which has tended to diminish asset pricing model performance.

Lastly, Bowles, Reed, Ringgenberg, and Thornock (2023) documented that the informativeness of anomaly returns degraded over time due to stale information in their computation. Technological innovations in information processing, trading, and data access may well have affected the time patterns of anomalies after the release of event information related to anomalies. For these reasons, to more precisely measure anomaly returns for 28 portfolios, they utilized real-time data available from the Compustat

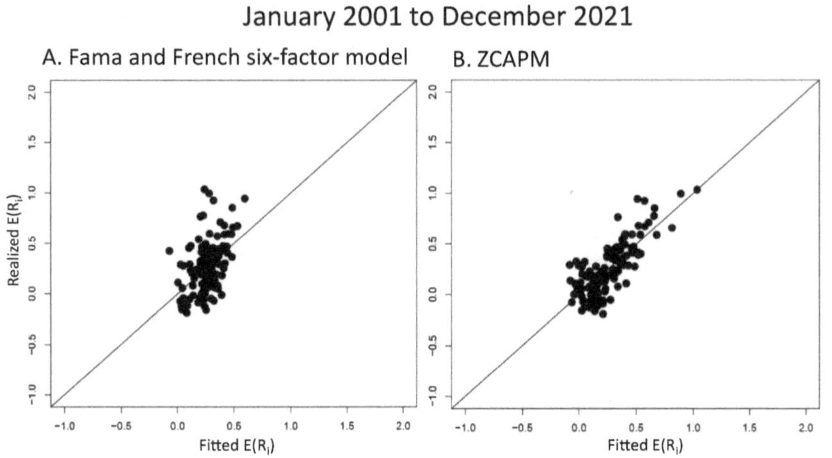

Fig. 5.6 Out-of-sample cross-sectional Fama and French six-factor model (Panel A) and ZCAPM (Panel B) mispricing errors comparing average one-month-ahead realized excess returns in percent (Y-axis) to average one-month-ahead predicted (fitted) excess returns in percent (X-axis) for 133 portfolios. The analysis subperiod is January 2001 to December 2021

Snapshot database. Upon constructing panel data series around anomaly event dates from 1990 to 2019, they showed that anomaly returns did not decline as much as previously believed.[17] Anomaly portfolio returns were economically and statistically significant after news announcements but decayed rapidly thereafter. In the context of our findings in the subperiod 2001 to 2021, we infer that declining anomaly return informativeness plausibly reduced asset pricing model performance.

In sum, in the post-2000 subperiod, declining intertemporal patterns of anomaly returns and decreasing anomaly return informativeness are likely explanations for the weakened pricing ability of asset pricing models compared to the earlier subperiod July 1973 to December 2000. Despite these trends, the ZCAPM continues to dominate other asset pricing models under study and does a good job of pricing anomaly portfolios. Also, other models continue to have difficulty pricing anomaly portfolios.

[17] Citing numerous supporting studies, Chen and Velikov (2023) found that stale historical data tended to bias upward expected anomaly returns.

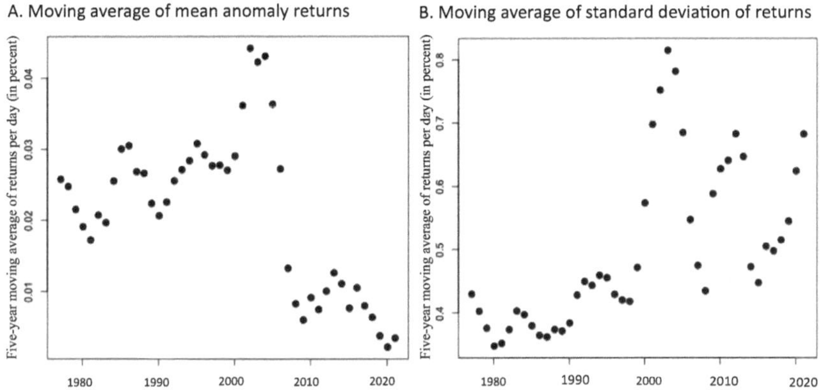

Fig. 5.7 5-year moving of mean daily returns in percent (Panel A) and 5-year moving average of standard deviation of returns (Panel B) for 133 anomaly portfolios rolling forward 1 year at a time. The full analysis period is July 1973 to December 2021

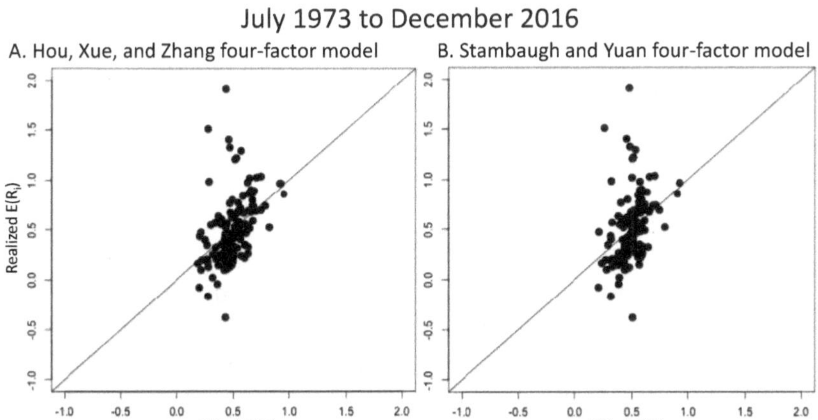

Fig. 5.8 Out-of-sample cross-sectional Hou, Xue, and Zhang four-factor model (Panel A) and Stambaugh and Yuan four-factor model (Panel B) mispricing errors comparing average one-month-ahead realized excess returns in percent (Y-axis) to average one-month-ahead predicted (fitted) excess returns in percent (X-axis) for 133 portfolios. The restricted analysis period is July 1973 to December 2016

Graphical Cross-Sectional Results: Restricted Analysis Period

Using the 133 anomaly portfolios in the sample period July 1972 to December 2016, we graphically compare average mispricing errors for the four-factor models of Hou, Xue, and Zhang (HXZ4) and Stambaugh and Yuan (SY4) in addition to the ZCAPM. Taking into account for the first 1-year estimation period for the models, the full analysis period for out-of-sample returns is July 1973 to December 2016. Figure 5.8 illustrates the findings for these models, which look similar to the FF3, C4, FF5, and FF6 models. Consistent with their estimated R^2 statistics in Panel A of Table 5.3, the HXZ4 model in Panel A appears to have somewhat lower pricing errors than the SY4 model in Panel B. Pricing errors for the ZCAPM are plotted in Fig. 5.9, which are much smaller than those for the HXZ4 and YS4 models (i.e., the ZCAPM has an R^2 value of 88% compared to at most 18% for these two models). As before, the ZCAPM does a good job of pricing the anomaly portfolios.

We graph the analysis subperiod results for the HXZ4 and SY4 models as well as ZCAPM in Figs. 5.10, 5.11 and 5.12, respectively. The takeaways from these graphs are: (1) pricing errors clearly increase in the post-2000 subperiod for all three models; and (2) the ZCAPM well outperforms the HXZ4 and SY4 models in terms of smaller pricing errors. Even in the post-2000 subperiod, despite increased pricing errors, the ZCAPM has markedly lower pricing errors than the other models (i.e., a relatively good R^2 value equal to 74%).

Robustness Tests

As cited earlier, the recent study by Jensen, Kelly, and Pedersen (2023) examined the replicability of anomaly portfolios for 153 factors across 93 countries. The authors make available online datasets for these portfolios (https://jkpfactors.com). [18] Their analyses revealed that pre- and post-publication alphas for anomaly portfolios were similar with some attenuation over time only among the strongest factors. As a robustness test of our results using the 133 anomaly portfolios in the Chen and Zimmerman study, this section employs their 153 capped value-weighted daily returns

[18] Accounting data were lagged 4 months to create tercile spreads among portfolio returns, whereas other authors have utilized different updating procedures that mix quarterly, annual, and other schemes. By comparison, Chen and Zimmerman (2022, p. 215) used 6-month lags to standardize annual accounting data to compute raw long-short portfolio returns, which they recognized are less timely than some papers and thereby tends to reduce mean returns.

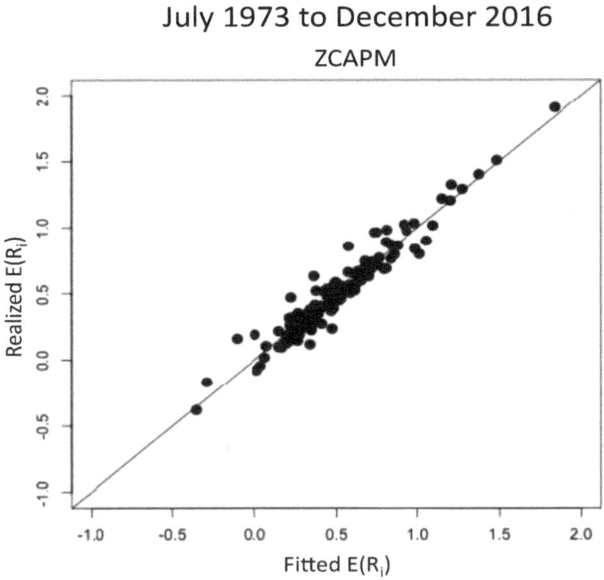

Fig. 5.9 Out-of-sample cross-sectional ZCAPM mispricing errors comparing average one-month-ahead realized excess returns in percent (Y-axis) to average one-month-ahead predicted (fitted) excess returns in percent (X-axis) for 133 anomaly portfolios. The restricted analysis period is July 1973 to December 2016

for U.S. anomaly portfolios to replicate our previous analyses. The authors winsorized these anomaly returns at the NYSE 80th percentile to avoid skewness by a few mega stocks.

Using the same full sample period July 1972 to December 2021 as before, Table 5.4 contains the cross-sectional regression results. For the full analysis period July 1973 to December 2021 in Panel A, the results are comparable to our earlier tests in Panel A of Table 5.2 for the most part. The CAPM and multifactor models have difficulty pricing these test assets with only significant market and investment factor loadings (i.e., $\hat{\lambda}_m$ and $\hat{\lambda}_{CMA}$, respectively). The market price of return dispersion ($\hat{\lambda}_{RD}$) in the ZCAPM has a much higher t-statistic at 5.52 than factor loadings in other models, and like the multifactor models the market price of market factor loadings is significant (at the 10% level). Also, the R^2 value for the ZCAPM at 62% well exceeds other models with a maximum of 29%.

Table 5.4 Out-of-sample Fama-MacBeth cross-sectional tests of 153 anomaly portfolios for asset pricing models in the full sample period July 1972 to December 2021. Using 153 anomalous portfolios from Jensen, Kelly, and Pedersen (2023), this table contains results for the full sample period July 1972 to December 2021. Based on standard two-step Fama-MacBeth cross-sectional tests, we report out-of-sample (one-month-ahead) estimated market prices of risk denoted $\hat{\lambda}_k$ for the kth factor for the analysis period July 1973 to December 2021. Associated t-statistics are shown below estimated prices of risk. The asset pricing models are: CAPM, Fama and French three-factor model (FF3), Carhart four-factor model (C4), Fama and French five-factor model (FF5), Fama and French six-factor model (FF6), and ZCAPM. Factors in these models are denoted as m (CRSP index excess return, see footnote 1), *RD* (market return dispersion), *SMB* (size), *HML* (value), *MOM* (momentum), *RMW* (profitability), and *CMA* (capital investment). Results are shown for the full analysis period (Panel A) in addition to analysis subperiods July 1973 to December 2000 (Panel B) and January 2001 to December 2021 (Panel C)

Panel A: Full analysis period July 1973 to December 2021

Model	$\hat{\alpha}$	$\hat{\lambda}_m$	$\hat{\lambda}_{RD}$	$\hat{\lambda}_{SMB}$	$\hat{\lambda}_{HML}$	$\hat{\lambda}_{MOM}$	$\hat{\lambda}_{RMW}$	$\hat{\lambda}_{CMA}$	R^2
CAPM	0.21	0.33							0.01
	10.89	1.19							
FF3	0.20	0.56		−0.09	0.09				0.12
	12.50	2.48		−0.61	0.59				
C4	0.18	0.49		−0.10	0.12	0.24			0.13
	12.77	2.20		−0.67	0.83	1.28			
FF5	0.17	0.67		−0.04	0.05		0.15	0.26	0.29
	12.67	2.77		−0.25	0.33		1.10	2.09	
FF6	0.16	0.45		−0.02	0.10	0.27	0.17	0.18	0.29
	13.64	1.90		−0.11	0.74	1.46	1.26	1.57	
ZCAPM	0.16	0.46	0.56						0.62
	8.43	1.75	5.52						

Panel B: Analysis subperiod July 1973 to December 2000

Model	$\hat{\alpha}$	$\hat{\lambda}_m$	$\hat{\lambda}_{RD}$	$\hat{\lambda}_{SMB}$	$\hat{\lambda}_{HML}$	$\hat{\lambda}_{MOM}$	$\hat{\lambda}_{RMW}$	$\hat{\lambda}_{CMA}$	R^2
CAPM	0.27	0.34							0.03
	10.73	0.96							
FF3	0.25	0.64		−0.09	0.24				0.23
	11.85	2.32		−0.45	1.24				
C4	0.23	0.57		−0.14	0.31	0.39			0.26
	12.40	2.07		−0.69	1.63	1.59			
FF5	0.22	0.60		−0.12	0.25		0.08	0.37	0.34
	12.90	2.16		−0.64	1.39		0.41	2.12	
FF6	0.20	0.34		−0.16	0.31	0.44	0.07	0.29	0.37
	14.11	1.28		−0.82	1.76	1.89	0.33	1.73	
ZCAPM	0.18	0.42	0.72						0.77
	6.62	1.36	5.12						

contd.

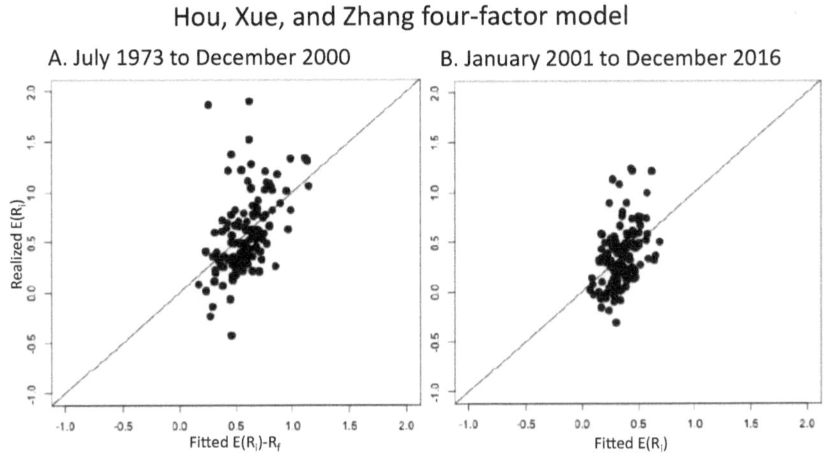

Fig. 5.10 Out-of-sample cross-sectional Hou, Xue, and Zhang four-factor model mispricing errors comparing average one-month-ahead realized excess returns in percent (Y-axis) to average one-month-ahead predicted (fitted) excess returns in percent (X-axis) for anomaly 133 portfolios. Two analysis subperiods are shown: Panel A. July 1973 to December 2000; and Panel B. January 2001 to December 2016

Table 5.4 continued

Panel C: Analysis subperiod January 2001 to December 2021

Model	$\hat{\alpha}$	$\hat{\lambda}_m$	$\hat{\lambda}_{RD}$	$\hat{\lambda}_{SMB}$	$\hat{\lambda}_{HML}$	$\hat{\lambda}_{MOM}$	$\hat{\lambda}_{RMW}$	$\hat{\lambda}_{CMA}$	R^2
CAPM	0.11	0.42							0.01
	4.23	0.90							
FF3	0.11	0.54		−0.12	−0.17				0.11
	5.56	1.43		−0.53	−0.86				
C4	0.09	0.47		−0.10	−0.21	0.09			0.12
	4.83	1.28		−0.43	−1.05	0.32			
FF5	0.08	0.95		0.06	−0.30		0.21	0.10	0.30
	4.59	2.24		0.26	−1.54		1.26	0.67	
FF6	0.08	0.67		0.08	−0.24	0.08	0.24	0.03	0.31
	4.96	1.59		0.39	−1.24	0.30	1.50	0.19	
ZCAPM	0.10	0.58	0.38						0.45
	4.45	1.27	2.71						

[1] In the ZCAPM, due to using average market excess returns rather than a proxy for market portfolio excess returns, the price of beta risk associated with CRSP index excess returns is denoted $\hat{\lambda}_a$ instead of $\hat{\lambda}_m$ in the other models

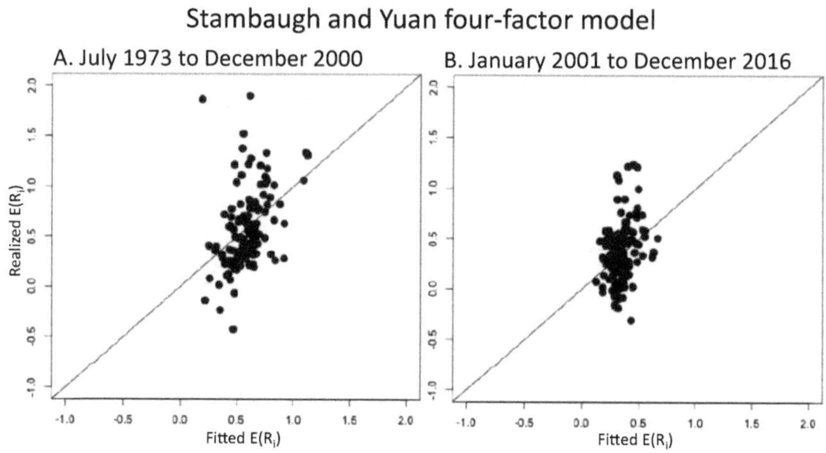

Fig. 5.11 Out-of-sample cross-sectional Stambaugh and Yuan four-factor model mispricing errors comparing average one-month-ahead realized excess returns in percent (Y-axis) to average one-month-ahead predicted (fitted) excess returns in percent (X-axis) for anomaly 133 portfolios. Two analysis subperiods are shown: Panel A. July 1973 to December 2000; and Panel B. January 2001 to December 2016

Subperiod analyses are shown in Panels B and C of Table 5.4. The results again are generally similar to Table 5.2. The ZCAPM continues to outperform other models in terms of both sizably higher statistical significance of market return dispersion loadings and higher goodness-of-fit. These differences are more evident in the earlier subperiod July 1973 to December 2000. As before, in the later subperiod January 2001 to December 2021, all models exhibit diminished pricing ability.

The graphs of mispricing errors in Figs. 5.13, 5.14 and 5.15 affirm the cross-sectional regression findings.[19] For the full analysis period in Fig. 5.13, we see that the ZCAPM does a good job with lower mispricing errors than the FF6 model. Comparing the two models in the earlier subperiod in Fig. 5.14, even stronger results in favor of the ZCAPM are

[19] As in Fig. 5.7 for the 133 portfolios, we construct graphs of 5-year moving averages of the mean returns and standard deviation of returns for the 153 anomaly portfolios over time. The graphs appear very similar to those in Fig. 5.7, with the exception of somewhat lower standard deviations of returns after 2005.

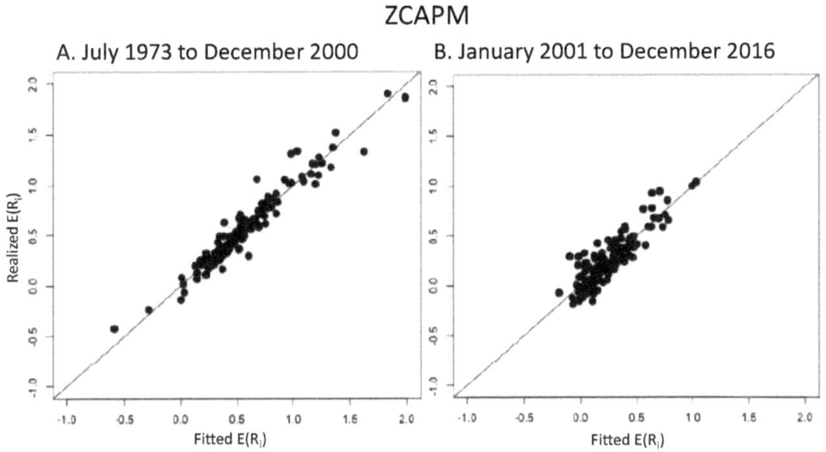

Fig. 5.12 Out-of-sample cross-sectional ZCAPM mispricing errors comparing average one-month-ahead realized excess returns in percent (Y-axis) to average one-month-ahead predicted (fitted) excess returns in percent (X-axis) for 133 anomaly portfolios. Two analysis subperiods are shown: Panel A. July 1973 to December 2000; and Panel B. January 2001 to December 2016

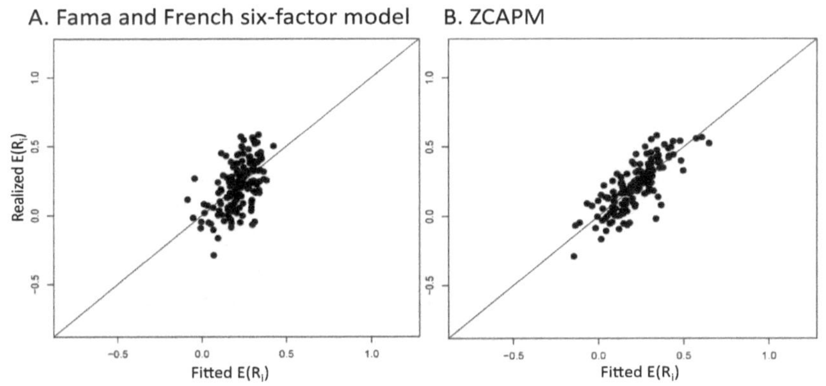

Fig. 5.13 Out-of-sample cross-sectional Fama and French six-factor model (Panel A) and ZCAPM (Panel B) mispricing errors comparing average one-month-ahead realized excess returns in percent (Y-axis) to average one-month-ahead predicted (fitted) excess returns in percent (X-axis) for 153 portfolios. The analysis subperiod is July 1973 to December 2021

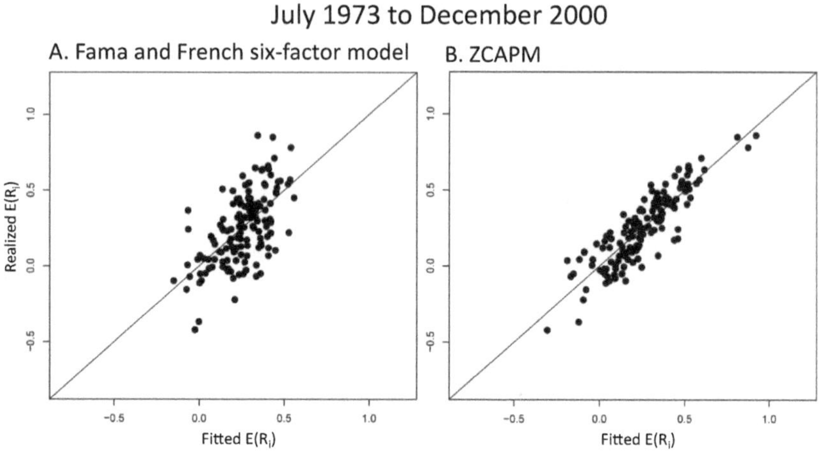

Fig. 5.14 Out-of-sample cross-sectional Fama and French six-factor model (Panel A) and ZCAPM (Panel B) mispricing errors comparing average one-month-ahead realized excess returns in percent (Y-axis) to average one-month-ahead predicted (fitted) excess returns in percent (X-axis) for 153 portfolios. The analysis subperiod is July 1973 to December 2000

produced. In the later subperiod in Fig. 5.15, the results are very different from the other graphs. The distribution of average realized and predicted anomaly returns is compressed into a smaller range of values with lower mean values. Compared to the earlier subperiod, due to the narrower range of dependent variable anomaly returns, it is not surprising that the FF6 model and ZCAPM have greater difficulty pricing anomalies in this subperiod. Subsequently, as before for the 133 portfolios in unreported analyses, we drop the financial crisis years 2008 and 2009 and repeat Fig. 5.15; however, the results again do not change much. As another test, we re-run Fig. 5.15 using only the post-financial crisis years from 2011 to 2021. As shown in Fig. 5.16, the plots of average mispricing errors for FF6 and the ZCAPM improve and look somewhat similar to the earlier subperiod results in Fig. 5.14 (i.e., the R^2 values for the FF6 and ZCAPM are 43% and 72%, respectively, which are consistent with earlier subperiod results in Panel B of Table 5.4). This noticeable improvement in the analysis period 2011 to 2021 was not evident upon repeating Fig. 5.16 for the 133 anomaly portfolios.

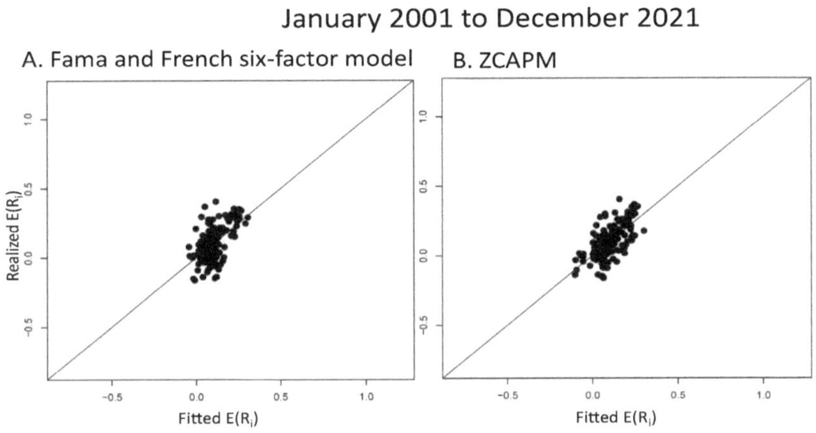

Fig. 5.15 Out-of-sample cross-sectional Fama and French six-factor model (Panel A) and ZCAPM (Panel B) mispricing errors comparing average one-month-ahead realized excess returns in percent (Y-axis) to average one-month-ahead predicted (fitted) excess returns in percent (X-axis) for 153 portfolios. The analysis subperiod is January 2001 to December 2021

Lastly, adding another sample period to our robustness tests, in unreported results available upon request from the authors, we ran the subperiod February 1952 to June 1973 for which daily returns are available for 116-out-of-153 anomaly portfolios.[20] Due to factor availability on Kenneth French's website, we test the CAPM, FF3, and C4 models. The ZCAPM factors are computed as before. Out-of-sample cross-sectional regression results yield: (1) significant momentum factor loadings (C4) and market dispersion factor loadings (ZCAPM) (i.e., $\hat{\lambda}_{MOM}$ and $\hat{\lambda}_{RD}$) with t-statistics of 3.39 and 4.38 respectively; and (2) R^2 values for C4 and ZCAPM equal to 36% and 82%, respectively. Average mispricing errors for C4 and ZCAPM tell the story in Fig. 5.17. The results indicate that the ZCAPM well explains mispricing errors but not the C4 model.

In sum, robustness checks using 153 anomaly portfolios from Jensen, Kelly, and Pedersen corroborate the results for the 133 portfolios from Chen and Zimmerman. Our findings confirm the superior pricing ability

[20] The number of anomalies drops considerably prior to this period.

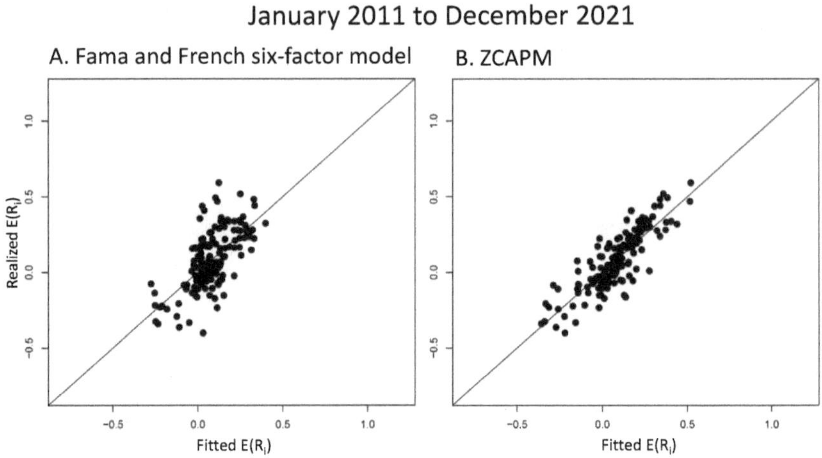

Fig. 5.16 Out-of-sample cross-sectional Fama and French six-factor model (Panel A) and ZCAPM (Panel B) mispricing errors comparing average one-month-ahead realized excess returns in percent (Y-axis) to average one-month-ahead predicted (fitted) excess returns in percent (X-axis) for 153 portfolios. The analysis subperiod is January 2011 to December 2021

of the ZCAPM in out-of-sample cross-sectional tests as well as graphs of average mispricing errors. In this sample of anomaly portfolios, average anomaly returns and their ranges change over time. Comparing Figs. 5.14 and 5.15 with subperiods before and after the year 2000, average anomaly returns become visibly lower and compressed over time. However, in the post-crisis period 2011–2021, average anomaly returns spread out once again with a wider dispersion that is comparable to the earlier subperiod in Fig. 5.14. In this regard, the increase in dispersion among anomaly returns in the years 2011–2021 appears to be due to more negative average returns in this subperiod than in the subperiod 2001–2021. These patterns of anomaly returns do not occur in the 133 portfolios; that is, average anomaly returns and their ranges are similar for the subperiods 2001 to 2021 and 2011 to 2021. We infer that anomaly returns are fluctuating over time and, in some cases, becoming negative.

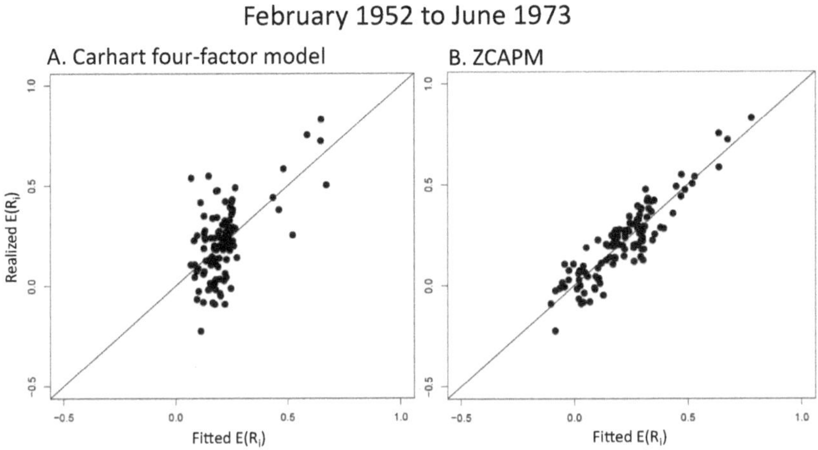

Fig. 5.17 Out-of-sample cross-sectional Carhart four-factor model (Panel A) and ZCAPM (Panel B) mispricing errors comparing average one-month-ahead realized excess returns in percent (Y-axis) to average one-month-ahead predicted (fitted) excess returns in percent (X-axis) for 153 portfolios. The analysis subperiod is February 1952 to June 1973

5.3 What Explains ZCAPM Outperformance?

In our cross-sectional regression tests as well as the graphical analyses of mispricing errors, we find that the ZCAPM well outperforms other prominent asset pricing models. A number of widely cited asset pricing models have difficulty pricing anomaly portfolios which implies that real mispricing exists among these portfolios. However, our ZCAPM results point to a different inference – namely, anomaly returns can be explained by risk factors, especially zeta risk associated with market return dispersion. Since our tests are completely out-of-sample (one-month-ahead), there is no possibility of manipulation or favoring one model over another in some way. What explains this outperformance?

Kolari, Liu, and Huang (2021) argued that total market return dispersion captures all of the long-short factors in different multifactor models. In effect, each long-short factor is itself a rough measure of return dispersion (e.g., small stock returns minus big stock returns is a return spread or dispersion). Relevant to this interpretation, by way of explaining the better performance of their three-factor model compared to the CAPM, Fama and French (1993) observed that "... the size and book-to-market factors can explain the differences in average returns across stocks, but the market factor is needed to explain why stock returns are on average above the 1-month T-bill rate" (Fama and French 1993, p. 38). Of course, as shown in Fig. 4.1 in Chapter 4, differences in average returns across stocks are directly related to the span of the parabola as measured by return dispersion. In this respect, the market return dispersion factor in the ZCAPM subsumes or encompasses all long-short portfolio returns that are component parts of total return dispersion. As the parabola changes over time, its level (as measured by average market returns) and width (corresponding to total market return dispersion) change. All assets' returns within the parabola are affected by these two market forces. Importantly, the empirical ZCAPM employs the expectation-maximization (EM) algorithm to take into account positive and negative sensitivity of asset returns to changes in the market dispersion factor.

Kolari, Liu, and Huang mathematically proved that the width or span of the mean-variance investment parabola of Markowitz (1952, 1959) is largely determined by cross-sectional return dispersion among asset returns in the market.[21] As mentioned earlier, given this new insight, they inferred that the average market return lies in the vicinity of the axis of symmetry in the middle of the parabola, rather than near the efficient frontier as supposed by many authors in the past. This picture of the stock market and investment parabola (see Fig. 4.1 in Chapter 4) is consistent with Fama and French's view that market returns give the overall level of stock returns (i.e., axis of symmetry) and their size and value factors capture differences in average returns across stocks (i.e, market return dispersion). More recently, Cooper, Gulen, and Ion (2024, p. 10) have argued that the asset growth factor in the Hou, Xue, and Zhang (2015) model and Fama and French (2015) five-factor model is significantly driven by macroeconomic shocks that, in turn, generate cross-sectional return dispersion in the market.[22]

[21] Mathematical proofs are provided using both random matrix theory and Markowitz equations.

[22] They investigated macroeconomic shocks to production, consumption, liquidity, uncertainty, financing costs, production networks, and sentiment. Relatedly, see our previous ZCAPM discussion in Sect. 4.1 of Chapter 4 on cross-sectional market volatility and macroeconomic shocks, including relevant literature citations

Thus, long-short factors represent different slices that lie within the total return dispersion in the market depicted by the vertical span of the parabola.

A number of multifactors are needed to proxy total market return dispersion, which explains why authors continue to add new multifactors in the effort to more fully capture total return dispersion. All of the multifactors are contained within the total return dispersion of the market. Ipso facto, as researchers find more long-short multifactors in the future, the resultant multifactor models should converge to the ZCAPM. However, because factors are not stable over time (e.g., the size factor can be positive in some years and negative in other years) and can diminish over time (e.g., long-short anomaly portfolio returns have decreased), their ability to consistently price stock returns is compromised. By contrast, regardless of anomaly returns, total market return dispersion is always large and dynamically changing and therefore continues to play an important role in asset pricing as the parabola evolves over time. For these reasons, Kolari, Liu, and Huang inferred that multifactor models are special cases of the ZCAPM that include selected return dispersion slices corresponding to long-short factor returns within the total return dispersion of the market.

The parabola is constantly fluctuating with changes in both the average market return and market return dispersion over time. These two market forces impact all assets within the parabola. Could these market forces vanish over time due to this publication? In our view, they are as likely to vanish as the mean-variance parabola itself. In previous tests of the CAPM using the market model, a general market index such as the CRSP index or S&P 500 index is commonly used to proxy the market portfolio on the efficient frontier of Markowitz's mean-variance parabola. If general market indexes lie approximately on the axis of symmetry of the parabola, as posited by ZCAPM theory, then the market model form of the CAPM excludes the cross-sectional standard deviation of returns in the market (or return dispersion), which is a very important second factor as we have seen in our cross-sectional tests of the ZCAPM. As shown earlier in Sect. 4.1.1 of Chapter 4, the ZCAPM is grounded in the zero-beta CAPM of Black (1972). He defined a second beta factor as " ... the minimum-variance, zero-beta portfolio of risky assets, where beta is defined using whatever market portfolio we use to represent the first factor" (Black, 1995, p. 170). Commenting on this second factor, Black reasoned:

> When Fama and French say that the line relating expected return and beta is flat, they are just saying that the expected excess return on the second factor

> is large.
> If we believe it's as large as they say, we won't fool around with their third and fourth factors,[23] for which they give no theory. We'll go for the gold in the second factor!

We believe that market return dispersion is tantamount to the second factor that Black was hypothesizing should exist. More precisely, as shown in Fig. 4.1 in Chapter 4, the difference or gap in returns between an efficient portfolio and inefficient, zero-beta portfolio (with equal return variance) is attributable to market return dispersion. Even if we cannot estimate these two portfolios and their associated returns in the real world, we know that their difference as expressed in Black's zero-beta CAPM can be approximated by the readily observable cross-sectional return dispersion of returns in the market. Because the theoretical ZCAPM is derived from the zero-beta CAPM of Black, it supports his model in addition to the foundational CAPM of Sharpe (1964), Lintner (1965), Mossin (1966), and Treynor (1961, 1962), mean-variance investment parabola of Markowitz, and related intertemporal, consumption, and production CAPMs of Merton (1973), Cochrane (1991), and Lucas (1978) and Breeden (1979), respectively. If indeed multifactor models are special cases of the more general empirical ZCAPM, then the ZCAPM represents a unifying theory that links general equilibrium models such as the CAPM and zero-beta CAPM to empirically designed multifactor models.[24]

In the context of the joint efficient market hypothesis, acceptance of the ZCAPM as a valid asset pricing model implies that prices efficiently reflect available information. As Fama (2013) recognized, stock market anomalies should not be interpreted as mispricing (see also Schwert (2003)). In this regard, he observed that anomalous returns could arise due to an invalid asset pricing model, market inefficiency, or both. Consistent with Fama's now famous efficient market hypothesis, our empirical ZCAPM evidence suggests that anomaly portfolio returns are manifestations of their inherent risks rather than mispricing. In one recent asset pricing study, the authors

[23] According to Black, these two factors correspond to the small-firm factor and price-to-book factor, respectively.

[24] According to Fama and French (1992, 1993, 1996), the linear factor structure in their multifactor models has some relation to the Arbitrage Pricing Model (APT) of Ross (1976) and Intertemporal CAPM (ICAPM) of Merton (1973); however, they noted that this economic interpretation is open to multiple alternative views and further inquiry.

opined that "... the credibility of the anomalies literature can improve via a close connection with economic theory" (Hou, Xue, and Zhang (2020, p. 2072)). We believe that the ZCAPM provides both theoretical and empirical grounds for better understanding anomalies in financial markets.

Finally, it is not surprising to us that cross-sectional market return dispersion can comprehensively explain large, diverse datasets of anomaly portfolio returns. After all, anomaly returns are measured by using long-short portfolio returns that are essentially return dispersions. Long position stocks tend to earn higher returns than short position stocks. In the context of the mean-variance parabola, higher yielding long stocks are likely to be located somewhere in the upper half of the parabola, whereas lower yielding short stocks would tend to be in the bottom half of the parabola. Ceteris paribus, as market return dispersion increases (decreases) and the parabola's span becomes wider (narrower), anomaly portfolio returns would increase (decrease). While a long-short asset pricing factor may well capture some anomaly portfolios' returns if they are similarly correlated, it is much less likely to be successful for a large, diverse set of anomaly portfolios. Of course, more long-short factors can be added to models to better explain a large dataset of long-short anomaly portfolio returns, but as discussed above, we know that factors are not stable and can diminish over time. Our empirical evidence shows that, in different analysis periods, the total return dispersion of all stocks in the market more comprehensively captures the return movements of large numbers of long-short anomaly portfolios than subsets of long-short (dispersion) factors. Thus, total return dispersion is an ever present and enduring market force that significantly affects the cross-section of average anomaly returns.

5.4 Summary and Implications

The empirical evidence in this chapter makes a number of important contributions to the understanding of anomaly portfolios and the field of asset pricing:

1. *Out-of-sample cross-sectional regression model tests of anomaly portfolios.* Using two large online datasets of anomaly portfolio returns, in out-of-sample cross-sectional regression tests, we showed that the ZCAPM well outperforms a variety of acclaimed multifactor models. Goodness-of-fit for the ZCAPM always exceeded multifactor models,

in many cases by large margins, and R^2 estimates were greater than 90% at times. Also, the statistical significance of market dispersion loadings in the ZCAPM (i.e., market price of risk) was exceptionally high with t-statistics often in the 3–7 range, which well exceeds those of extant multifactors' loadings.

2. *Out-of-sample average mispricing errors from cross-sectional regression models.* Average mispricing errors were visibly smaller for the ZCAPM estimated via EM regression than various multifactor models in repeated tests with different anomaly datasets and analysis periods. In general, anomaly portfolios cannot be explained by traditional OLS multifactor models—that is, they are anomalous to these models. However, the ZCAPM did a good job of reducing mispricing errors for large datasets consisting of diverse anomaly portfolios. Citing Lakonishok, Shleifer, and Vishney (1994), as Thaler (1999) has opined, the predictability of returns on the basis of different firm and market characteristics is controversial because "... no one has been able to specify an observable, as opposed to theoretical or metaphysical, risk measure that can explain the existing data pattern ..." (Thaler, 1999, p. 14). We believe that this controversy is resolved for the most part, as the average returns of a wide variety of anomalies are largely explained by the ZCAPM.
3. *Market efficiency.* Explaining anomaly portfolio returns represents a high bar for any asset pricing model. Behavioral finance posits that human behavior in psychology helps to explain anomalies for which asset pricing models fail.[25] As advanced by DeBondt and Thaler (1987), Lakonishok, Shleifer, and Vishny (1994), Thaler (1999), and others, mispricing due to cognitive biases in human behavior can help explain the anomalies. However, contrary to the behavioral explanation for the large number of anomalies, the success of the ZCAPM documented in this chapter supports the efficient market hypothesis of Fama (1970). In his 2013 Nobel Prize Lecture entitled "Two Pillars of Asset Pricing," Fama (2013) related efficient markets to asset pricing models. As he instructed, under the joint hypothesis, if empirical tests reject a model, the problem could be due to an inefficient market or a bad model of market equilibrium. Alternatively, if an asset pricing model of expected returns is useful in terms of

[25] The behavioral finance literature is large and growing. See Shiller (1981), DeBondt and Thaler (1987), Lakonishok, Shleifer, and Vishny (1994), Thaler (1999), and many others.

explaining actual returns, then prices must be efficient. As such, asset prices are determined by risk as ascertained by rational investors based on available market information. Our ZCAPM evidence suggests that the previously observed predictability of future returns for large samples of anomaly portfolios under study are explained by risk for the most part rather than mispricing.

4. *The ZCAPM and implications to asset pricing*. Since the ZCAPM is derived in a general equilibrium setting using the mean-variance investment parabola of Markowitz (1952, 1959) and zero-beta CAPM of Black (1972), the CAPM is not dead as proclaimed by Fama and French (1996) and others. Instead, the CAPM is alive and well in the form of the ZCAPM. Thus, the joint award of the 1990 Nobel Prize in Economic Sciences to Harry Markowitz and William Sharpe was not in vain.

What explains the outperformance of the empirical ZCAPM relative to prominent multifactor models in our cross-sectional tests? As Kolari, Liu, and Huang have argued, widely used long-short factors in multifactor models are themselves rough measures of market return dispersion. As such, long-short factors represent slices within the total cross-sectional dispersion of stock returns in the market. The ZCAPM captures all of the multifactors in its total market return dispersion factor that is associated with the span of mean-variance parabola (itself an approximation of the return spread between an efficient portfolio and its zero-beta inefficient counterpart in Black's zero-beta CAPM). In this sense, multifactor models can be viewed as special cases of the empirical ZCAPM that focus on selected slices within the cross-sectional distribution of market stock returns or span of the parabola. Thus, the ZCAPM represents a unifying model that links the general equilibrium CAPM and multifactor model branches of asset pricing literature.

Departing from other asset pricing models that rely upon ordinary least squares (OLS) regression, both positive and negative sensitivity to the market return dispersion factor (viz., zeta risk) are modeled in the empirical ZCAPM using the expectation-maximization (EM) algorithm. Ceteris paribus, as the span of the parabola increases (decreases), assets in the top half of the parabola experience higher (lower) returns, and those in the bottom half experience lower (higher) returns. The empirical ZCAPM takes into account these potential return patterns by means of a probability estimate of the direction of market return dispersion effects on an asset. This probability is incorporated in the ZCAPM's estimated zeta risk coefficient.

The evidence in this chapter has a number of implications for future research.

Replication. Given the strong performance of the empirical ZCAPM relative to leading asset pricing models, replication of our tests is warranted. In their book, Kolari, Liu, and Huang reported extensive empirical tests of the ZCAPM using test assets sorted on firm characteristics and industries. In other publications and academic conference presentations, they reported ZCAPM tests using historical data going back to the 1920s, empirical tests of stock returns in other countries, and additional results. In all of these tests, the ZCAPM consistently outperformed popular multifactor models. Yet publication of ZCAPM findings in top finance journals has eluded the authors over the past decade. Since many authors believe that published research findings on asset pricing factors are subject to serious question, replication studies should be conducted by other authors to confirm important results and avoid false discoveries. As mentioned in Chapter 4, our computer code for running the empirical ZCAPM is available online at GitHub in multiple programming languages.

Unpriced anomalies. Although the ZCAPM did a good job of pricing the broad datasets of anomalies under study, the possibility of anomalies not priced by the ZCAPM should be explored. Is the empirical ZCAPM a general market model able to price risk across the complete cross-section of stock returns? Or are there segments of the stock market that are anomalous to the ZCAPM? Of course, such anomalies would be interesting to study, especially from a behavioral standpoint.

Event studies. The empirical ZCAPM can be applied to event studies in which abnormal returns are estimated as the difference between out-of-sample realized and predicted returns. As Fama (2013) has observed, event studies are important to our understanding of asset pricing with respect to market efficiency and rational pricing due to risk versus behavioral finance and irrational pricing due to human behavior. According to Fama (1998b), to estimate abnormal returns, it is crucial to accurately measure risk when computing predicted returns for event stocks by means of an asset pricing model. Since the ZCAPM has lower mispricing error than other models, it should be able to more accurately measure abnormal returns, especially long-run abnormal returns for which risk adjustment over time is crucial.

Corporate finance. Work on the nexus between asset pricing and corporate finance is recommended. For example, the ZCAPM can be employed to estimate the cost of equity of firms as an input to the weighted average cost of capital. Tests of famous capital structure theories by Modigliani and Miller (1958, 1963), Hamada (1972), and others with respect to financial leverage could be revisited. Moreover, capital budgeting applications are possible.

Portfolio management. Future study should explore the practical implications of the ZCAPM to investment portfolio management. In their book, Kolari, Liu, and Huang apply the ZCAPM to the construction of portfolios based on their beta and zeta risks. Out-of-sample beta-zeta sorted portfolios are shown to form a latticework within the mean-variance investment parabola. This return/risk architecture suggests that investment managers can build portfolios that meet client risk preferences. Once upon a time, it was hoped that the CAPM would enable investment decisions based on beta-sorted portfolios. Low (high) beta portfolios would earn lower (higher) returns in the future. Investors could then choose beta portfolios that coincide with their risk preferences. But beta turned out to be unrelated to the cross-section of average stock returns. Perhaps this investment practice can be realized using the ZCAPM. A recent book by Kolari, Liu, and Pynnonen (2024) showed that the ZCAPM can be used to build high-performing investment portfolios. Certainly, research in this area is merited to potentially benefit professional and personal investment practices.

Determinants of market return dispersion. Considerable research has been devoted to understanding the intertemporal behavior of average stock market returns, which is the first moment in the distribution of stock returns. But what about the second moment? As noted earlier, previous studies have found that economic fundamentals are related to cross-sectional market return dispersion. In view of the importance of market return dispersion as an asset pricing factor in the ZCAPM, further study would be informative. In the context of the ZCAPM, what causes the span of the parabola to increase or decrease over time? In addition to macroeconomic variables, the impacts of interest rates, investor behavior, geopolitical conflicts, international events, etc. on market return dispersion should be explored. Moreover, are there different ways to compute market return dispersion (and related average market returns) that could lead to improved measurement of beta and zeta risks in the ZCAPM? Further research on market return dispersion is recommended.

Other asset classes. Our cross-sectional stock market tests of the ZCAPM can be extended to other asset classes, including bonds, commodities, and real estate. Given daily return information, the empirical ZCAPM can be estimated using average market returns and their return dispersion in each asset class market. Similarly, tests of mutual funds, exchange-traded funds, and other institutional portfolios are possible.

References

Back, K., N. Kapadia, and B. Ostdiek. 2013. Slopes as factors: Characteristic pure plays, Working paper, Rice University.

Back, K., N. Kapadia, and B. Ostdiek. 2015. Testing factor models on characteristic and covariance pure plays, Working paper, Rice University.

Bali, T., and G., R. F. Engle, and Y. Tang. 2017. Dynamic conditional beta is alive and well in the cross section of daily stock returns. *Management Science* 63: 3760–3779.

Barillas, F., and J. Shanken. 2018. Comparing asset pricing models. *Journal of Finance* 73: 715–754.

Black, F. 1972. Capital market equilibrium with restricted borrowing. *Journal of Business* 45: 444–454.

Black, F. 1995. Estimating expected return. *Financial Analysts Journal* 49: 36–38.

Bowles, B., A. V. Reed, M. C. Ringgenberg, and J. R. Thornock. 2023. Anomaly time, *Journal of Finance*, forthcoming.

Breeden, N. D. 1979. An intertemporal asset pricing model with stochastic consumption and investment opportunities. *Journal of Financial Economics* 7: 265–296.

Carhart, M. M. 1997. On persistence in mutual fund performance. *Journal of Finance* 52: 57–82.

Chen, A. Y., and M. Velikov. 2023. Zeroing in on the expected returns of anomalies. *Journal of Financial and Quantitative Analysis* 58: 968–1004.

Chen, A. Y., and T. Zimmermann. 2020. Publication bias and the cross-section of stock returns. *Review of Asset Pricing Studies* 10: 249–289.

Chordia, T., A. Goyal, and A. Saretto. 2020. Anomalies and false rejections. *Review of Financial Studies* 33: 2134–2179.

Cochrane, J. H. 1991. Production-based asset pricing and the link between stock returns and economic fluctuations. *Journal of Finance* 46: 209–237.

Cochrane, J. H. 1996. A cross-sectional test of an investment-based asset pricing model. *Journal of Political Economy* 104: 572–621.

Cochrane, J. H. 2005. *Asset Pricing. Revised.* Princeton, NJ: Princeton University Press.

Cooper, M., H. Gulen, and M. Ion. 2024. The use of asset growth in empirical asset pricing models. *Journal of Financial Economics* 151: 103746.

Daniel, K., and S. Titman. 2012. Testing factor-model explanations of market anomalies. *Critical Finance Review* 1: 103–139.

De Bondt, W., and R. Thaler. 1987. Further evidence on investor overreaction and stock market seasonality. *Journal of Finance* 42: 557–581.

Dempster, A. P., L. M. Laird, and D. B. Rubin. 1977. Maximum likelihood from incomplete data via the EM algorithm. *Journal of the Royal Statistical Society* 39: 1–38.

Fama, E. F. 2013. *Two Pillars of Asset Pricing*, Nobel Prize Lecture.

Fama, E. F., and K. R. French. 1992. The cross-section of expected stock returns. *Journal of Finance* 47: 427–465.

Fama, E. F., and K. R. French. 1993. Common risk factors in the returns on stocks and bonds. *Journal of Financial Economics* 33: 3–56.

Fama, E. F., and K. R. French. 1996. Multifactor explanations of asset pricing anomalies. *Journal of Finance* 51: 55–84.

Fama, E. F., and K. R. French. 2015. A five-factor asset pricing model. *Journal of Financial Economics* 116: 1–22.

Fama, E. F., and K. R. French. 2018. Choosing factors. *Journal of Financial Economics* 128: 234–252.

Fama, E. F., and K. R. French. 2020. Comparing cross-section and time-series factor models. *Review of Financial Studies* 33: 1892–1926.

Fama, E. F., and J. D. MacBeth. 1973. Risk, return, and equilibrium: Empirical tests. *Journal of Political Economy* 81: 607–636.

Ferson, W. E. 2019. *Empirical Asset Pricing: Models and Methods*. Cambridge, MA: The MIT Press.

Ferson, W. E., S. K. Nallareddy, and B. Xie. 2013. The "out-of-sample" performance of long-run risk models. *Journal of Financial Economics* 107: 537–556.

Ferson, W. E., S. Sarkissian, and T. Simin. 1999. The alpha force asset pricing model: A parable. *Journal of Financial Markets* 2: 49–68.

Giglio, S., and D. Xiu. 2021. Asset pricing with omitted factors. *Journal of Political Economy* 129: 1947–1990.

Green, J., J. R. Hand, and F. Zhang. 2017. The characteristics that provide independent information about average US monthly stock returns. *Review of Financial Studies* 30: 4389–4436.

Harvey, C. R., Y. Liu, and H. Zhu. 2016. and the cross-section of expected returns. *Review of Financial Studies* 29: 5–68.

Hou, K., C. Xue, and L. Zhang. 2015. Digesting anomalies: An investment approach. *Review of Financial Studies* 28: 650–705.

Hou, K., C. Xue, and L. Zhang. 2020. Replicating anomalies. *Review of Financial Studies* 33: 2019–2133.

Jagannathan, R., G. Skoulakis, and Z. Wang. 2010. *The analysis of the cross-section of security returns, in Handbook of Financial Econometrics*, vol. 2. Amsterdam, NL: Elsevier.

Jagannathan, R., and Z. Wang. 1996. The conditional CAPM and the cross-section of asset returns. *Journal of Finance* 51: 3–53.

Jensen, T. I., B. Kelly, and L. H. Pedersen. 2023. Is there a replication crisis in finance? *Journal of Finance* 78: 2465–2518.

Jones, P. N., and G. J. McLachlan. 1990. Algorithm AS 254: Maximum likelihood estimation from grouped and truncated data with finite normal mixture models. *Applied Statistics* 39: 273–282.

Kolari, J. W., J. Z. Huang, W. Liu, and H. Liao. 2024a. *A quantum leap in asset pricing: Explaining anomalous returns.* Palm Beach Gardens, FL: Presented at the annual conference meetings of the Southern Finance Association.

Kolari, J. W., J. Z. Huang, W. Liu, and H. Liao. 2024b. A quantum leap in asset pricing: Explaining anomalous returns, Presented at the annual conference meetings of the Southwestern Finance Association, San Antonio, TX. Awarded the Best Paper in Investments.

Kolari, J. W., W. Liu, and J. Z. Huang. 2021. *A New Model of Capital Asset Prices: Theory and Evidence.* Cham, Switzerland: Palgrave Macmillan.

Kolari, J. W., W. Liu, and S. Pynnonen. 2024. *Professional Investment Portfolio Management: Boosting Performance with Machine-Made Portfolios and Stock Market Evidence.* Cham, Switzerland: Palgrave Macmillan.

Lettau, M., and S. Ludvigson. 2001. Consumption, aggregate wealth, and expected stock returns. *Journal of Finance* 56: 815–849.

Lewellen, J., S. Nagel, and J. A. Shanken. 2010. A skeptical appraisal of asset pricing tests. *Journal of Financial Economics* 96: 175–194.

Lintner, J. 1965. The valuation of risk assets and the selection of risky investments in stock portfolios and capital budgets. *Review of Economics and Statistics* 47: 13–37.

Lo, A. W., and A. C. MacKinlay. 1990. Data snooping in tests of financial asset pricing models. *Review of Financial Studies* 3: 431–467.

Lucas, R. E. 1978. Asset prices in an exchange economy. *Econometrica* 46: 1429–1445.

MacKinlay, A. C., and M. P. Richardson. 1991. Using generalized method of moments to test mean-variance efficiency. *Journal of Finance* 46: 511–527.

Markowitz, H. M. 1952. Portfolio selection. *Journal of Finance* 7: 77–91.

Markowitz, H. M. 1959. *Portfolio Selection: Efficient Diversification of Investments.* New York, NY: Wiley.

Martin, I., and S. Nagel. 2021. Market efficiency in the age of big data. *Journal of Financial Economics* 45: 154–177.

McLachlan, G. J., and T. Krishnan. 2008. The EM Algorithm and Extensions (2nd ed.). Hoboken, NJ: Wiley.

McLachlan, G. J., and D. Peel. 2000. Finite Mixture Models. Hoboken, NJ: Wiley Interscience.

McLean, R. D., and J. Pontiff. 2016. Does academic publication destroy predictability? *Journal of Finance* 71: 5–32.

Merton, R. C. 1973. An intertemporal capital asset pricing model. *Econometrica* 41: 867–887.

Mossin, J. 1966. Equilibrium in a capital asset market. *Econometrica* 34: 768–783.

Ross, S. A. 1976. The arbitrage theory of capital asset pricing. *Journal of Economic Theory* 13: 341–360.

Schwert, G. W. 2003. Anomalies and market efficiency. In *Handbook of the Economics of Finance*, ed. G. M. Constantinides, M. Harris, and R. Stulz, 939–974. Amsterdam, NL: North-Holland.

Shanken, J. 1992. On the estimation of beta-pricing models. *Review of Financial Studies* 5: 1–33.

Shanken, J., and G. Zhou. 2007. Estimating and testing beta pricing models: Alternative methods and their performance in simulations. *Journal of Financial Economics* 84: 40–86.

Sharpe, W. F. 1964. Capital asset prices: A theory of market equilibrium under conditions of risk. *Journal of Finance* 19: 425–442.

Shiller, R. J. 1981. Do stock prices move too much to be justified by subsequent changes in dividends. *American Economic Review* 71: 421–436.

Simin, T. 2008. The poor performance of asset pricing models. *Journal of Financial and Quantitative Analysis* 43: 335–380.

Stambaugh, R. F., and Y. Yuan. 2017. Mispricing factors. *Review of Financial Studies* 30: 1270–1315.

Thaler, R. H. 1999. Mental accounting matters. *Journal of Behavioral Decision Making* 12: 183–206.

Treynor, J. L. 1961. Market value, time, and risk, Unpublished manuscript.

Treynor, J. L. 1962. Toward a theory of market value of risky assets. Unpublished manuscript.

CHAPTER 6

Further Tests of Asset Pricing Models and Anomaly Portfolio Returns

Abstract This chapter extends the cross-sectional tests of different asset pricing models in the previous chapter using different test asset portfolios. In Chapter 5, we conducted tests based on 133 U.S. anomaly portfolios constructed by Chen and Zimmerman (2020) and 153 anomaly portfolios by Jensen, Kelly, and Pedersen ((Jensen and Kelly, 2023)). Here, we report further evidence using other test asset portfolios. First, we employ commonly used portfolios in published asset pricing studies reviewed in Chapter 2. To do this, a variety of size, value, profitability, capital investment, and momentum stock portfolios are downloaded from Kenneth FrenchâŁ™s database website. With the exception of momentum portfolios, these test assets are not long/short portfolios as in the case of anomaly portfolios; instead, they are portfolios that are used in the construction of anomaly portfolios. For example, Fama and French (1992, 1993) sorted individual stocks by market capitalization into size deciles. The top/bottom three size deciles are used to construct the long/short size factor in their multifactor asset pricing models. Thus, we take a more granular look at the returns of long and short portfolios that are used in forming anomaly portfolios. Second, we utilize industry portfolios available on FrenchâŁ™s website. Industry portfoliosâŁ™ returns are notorious for being difficult to explain with any asset pricing model and therefore can be considered to be anomalous. Finally, we add to the previous chapter by testing a sample of 86 anomaly portfolio returns in Japan. These long/short portfolios are available online at the website provided by Jensen et al. As in Chapter 5, our goal is to show that the ZCAPM does a good job of explaining stock

J. W. Kolari et al., *Asset Pricing Models and Market Efficiency*,
https://doi.org/10.1007/978-3-031-92901-3_6

portfolios' returns. In turn, the efficient markets hypothesis holds in the sense that rational investors and systematic market risk explain stock returns. Behavioral explanations based on irrational investors subject to psychological biases are not needed to explain long/short portfolio stock returns for the most part.

6.1 Methodology

Data

We download daily returns for U.S. stock portfolios from Kenneth French's website.[1] The sample period is July 1972 to December 2021. This sample period is used to be consistent with the analyses of anomaly portfolio returns in Chapter 5. Portfolios are formed by sorting individual stocks on different firm and stock characteristics. We collect the following portfolio datasets: 25 size (market capitalization) and book-to-market equity portfolios, 25 size and profitability portfolios, 25 size and capital investment portfolios, 25 size and momentum portfolios, 25 book-to-market equity and profitability portfolios, 25 book-to-market equity and capital investment portfolios, and 25 profitability and capital investment portfolios. These portfolios are used to construct long/short size, value, profitability, momentum, and capital investment anomaly portfolios. For example, for the size anomaly, higher earning small stock portfolios are used to form the long portfolio, whereas lower earning large stocks are contained in the short portfolio. Thus, our analyses of these portfolios take a more granular look at anomalous returns based on long/short portfolios. We combine these portfolios into an aggregate portfolio of 175 test assets.

Also, we gathered a separate sample of 47 industry portfolios with daily returns available from July 1963 to December 2021. A number of researchers have recommended industry portfolios in asset pricing tests, including Lewellen, Nagel, and Shanken (2010), Daniel and Titman (2012), and others. These portfolios are exogenous to asset pricing factors in multifactor models, which invariably do not contain an industry factor. By contrast, our aggregate 175 portfolios are constructed based on characteristics that are used to build long/short asset pricing factors. Ferson, Sarkissian, and Simin (1999) have warned that an endogeneity problem can occur in

[1] See https://mba.tuck.dartmouth.edu/pages/faculty/ken.french/datalibrary.

asset pricing tests using test assets sorted on the same characteristics used to build factors in a multifactor model. Given the difficulty of explaining industry portfolio returns in extant asset pricing studies, we view them as anomalous portfolios.

As in Chapter 5, we download daily factors for the Fama and French and Carhart models from French's website. Daily factors for the Hou, Xue, and Zhang as well as Stambaugh and Yuan models are gathered from online databases made available by the authors (i.e., the sample period is restricted to July 1972 to December 2016).

Lastly, we consider the case of anomaly portfolios in Japan. Online daily return series for Japanese anomalies are downloaded from the website provided by Jensen, Kelley, and Pedersen (2023). Asset pricing factors in Japan are made available from a recent study by Kolari, Huang, Butt, and Liao (2022). A final sample of 86 anomalies is obtained for our analyses.

Cross-Sectional Regression Analyses

Here, we briefly review the standard two-step Fama and MacBeth (1973) procedure for cross-sectional regression analyses. Chapter 5 contains a more in-depth discussion. As before, we employ only out-of-sample tests as opposed to in-sample tests. In the first step, using 1-year of daily returns from July 1972 to June 1973, we begin by estimating a time-series regression for each asset pricing model using the test asset portfolios under consideration:

$$R_{it} - R_{ft} = \alpha_i + \sum_{k=1}^{K} b_{ik} F_{kt} + e_{it},\ t = 1, \ldots, T, \tag{6.1}$$

where $R_{it} - R_{ft}$ is the realized excess return on the ith test asset for day t, R_{ft} is the riskless rate proxied by the Treasury bill rate, α_i is the intercept term or alpha, F_{kt} are asset pricing factors for $k = 1, \ldots, K$ factors, b_{ik} are corresponding K beta risk loadings for the ith portfolio, $i = 1, \ldots, N$ correspond to the number of portfolios, $t = 1, \ldots, T$ is the estimation period, and $e_{it} \sim$ iid $(0, \sigma_i^2)$.

In the second step, using an out-of-sample approach with one-month-ahead returns, we estimate the following ordinary least squares (OLS) cross-sectional regression for the test asset portfolios:

$$\begin{aligned} R_{iT+1} - R_{fT+1} &= \hat{\alpha} + \lambda_1 \hat{b}_{i1} + \lambda_2 \hat{b}_{i2} \\ &\quad + \ldots + \lambda_K \hat{b}_{iK} + u_{iT+1},\ i = 1, \ldots, N, \end{aligned} \tag{6.2}$$

where $R_{iT+1} - R_{fT+1}$ is the realized excess return on the ith portfolio in out-of-sample (one-month-ahead) month $T+1$, $\hat{\alpha}$ is the intercept, $\hat{b}_{ik}$, $k = 1, \ldots, K$ are K beta risk loadings estimated for N anomaly portfolios in the estimation period $t = 1, \ldots, T$, λ_k are corresponding estimated market prices of beta risk loadings, and u_{iT+1} are zero mean and independent of the explanatory variables. Giglio and Xiu (2021) show that the asymptotic efficiency of OLS estimates in the above cross-sectional regression is not improved by other estimation methods (e.g., weighted least squares (WLS), generalized least squares (GLS), general method of moments (GMM), and maximum likelihood (ML) estimation).

This two-step procedure is rolled forward 1 month at a time and repeated until December 2016. Within the full analysis period from July 1973 to December 2021, we average the cross-sectional λ_k parameters. Using average λ_ks over time, t-values are computed to estimate their statistical significance. Additionally, from July 1973 to December 2021, we produce a monthly time series of one-month-ahead realized and predicted returns for each portfolio. Using these monthly returns series, we compute average values for each of the test asset portfolios. As in Jagannathan and Wang (1996) and Lettau and Ludwigson (2001, footnote 17, p. 1254), we regress average realized returns on average predicted returns to obtain R^2 estimates. Plots of resultant average realized and predicted returns are produced to graphically illustrate out-of-sample average mispricing errors for test asset portfolios.

Asset Pricing Models

As in Chapter 5 using anomaly portfolios, we test the following asset pricing models:

- CAPM market model with CRSP value-weighted index minus the Treasury bill rate as the market factor, or R_m;
- Fama and French (1992, 1993) three-factor model (FF3) based on augmenting the market model with a size factor (small minus large firms' stock returns, or *SMB*) and value factor (high book-to-market equity minus low book-to-market equity firms' stock returns, or *HML*);
- Carhart (1997) four-factor model (C4) based on augmenting the three-factor model with a momentum factor (firms with high past return stock returns minus low past stock returns, or *MOM*);

- Fama and French (2015) five-factor model (FF5) based on augmenting their three-factor model with a profitability factor (robust operating profitability minus weak operating profitability returns, *RMW*) and capital investment factor (conservative investment minus aggressive investment returns, or *CMA*);
- Fama and French (2018) six-factor model (FF6) based on augmenting their five-factor model with a momentum factor;
- Hou, Xue, and Zhang (2015) four-factor q model (HXZ4) based on augmenting the market model with a size factor (equity market capitalization, *ME*), profitability factor (return on equity, *ROE*), and capital investments factor (investment to assets ratio of the firm, *IA*);
- Stambaugh and Yuan (2017) four-factor model (SY4) based on augmenting the market model with a size factor (*SMB*), management factor (derived from rankings of stocks' returns with respect to six anomaly portfolios, *MGMT*), and a performance factor (derived from rankings of stocks' returns with respect to five anomaly portfolios, *PERF*); and
- Kolari, Huang, and Liu (2021) two-factor ZCAPM with CRSP value-weighted index minus the Treasury bill rate as the average market factor (a) plus the cross-sectional market volatility or dispersion of stocks (σ_a).

As reviewed in Chapter 4, for readers unfamiliar with the ZCAPM, the empirical form of the ZCAPM is as follows:

$$R_{it} - R_{ft} = \beta_{ia}(R_{at} - R_{ft}) + Z^{*}_{ia}\sigma_{at} + u_{it}, \quad t = 1, \ldots, T, \tag{6.3}$$

where $(R_{it} - R_{ft})$ is the excess stock returns for the ith stock or portfolio, $R_{at} - R_{ft}$ is average excess market returns, (σ_{at}) is cross-sectional market return dispersion, β_{ia} is the beta risk coefficient, Z^{*}_{ia} is the zeta risk coefficient, and other notation is as before. Unlike other asset pricing models that are estimated using standard ordinary least squares (OLS) regression, expectation-maximization (EM) regression is used to estimate the empirical ZCAPM.[2] Due to the estimation of a hidden or latent variable in the EM algorithm, the ZCAPM takes advantage of machine learning (ML). More-

[2] Chapter 4 contains an Appendix with details on the estimation of EM regression. See also Dempster, Laird, and Rubin (1977), Jones and McLachlan (1990), McLachlan and Peel (2000), McLachlan and Krishnan (2008), and others. Wikipedia provides an excellent discussion EM regression and citations to literature.

over, unlike other models, the second step OLS cross-sectional regression in the Fama-MacBeth procedure is estimated as follows:

$$R_{i,T+1} - R_{fT+1} = \lambda_0 + \lambda_a \hat{\beta}_{ia} + \lambda_{RD} \hat{Z}^*_{ia} N_{T+1} + u_{it}, \tag{6.4}$$

where N_{T+1} is the number of trading days in month $T + 1$ (i.e., 21 days), $Z^*_{ia} N_{T+1}$ is the monthly estimated zeta risk, and λ_{RD} is the monthly risk premium for zeta risk associated with market return dispersion. The OLS regression models do not require this rescaling of beta risk coefficients. In the empirical ZCAPM, zeta risk coefficient Z^*_{ia} is measured on a daily basis. Due to using monthly returns on the left-hand-side of Eq. (6.4), Z^*_{ia} is rescaled to measure monthly zeta risk premiums. Notably, the per unit zeta risk return premium $\hat{\lambda}_{RD}$ is unchanged.

Due to data limitations, the HXZ4 and SY4 models have a restricted sample period from July 1972 to December 2016. For this reason, we run all models during this sample period also.

6.2 Empirical Evidence

Table 5.1 in Chapter 5 summarizes the descriptive statistics for asset pricing factors in different models. Here, we begin by examining the ability of these models to explain the daily returns for two datasets of test asset portfolios: (1) 175 size and stock characteristics sorted portfolios, and (2) 47 industry portfolios. Our analyses consist of out-of-sample, Fama-MacBeth cross-sectional regression tests and graphs of portfolios' average mispricing errors (i.e., average realized monthly returns minus average predicted or fitted monthly returns). Finally, we contribute further empirical tests of anomaly portfolios by considering the case of Japan.

Cross-Sectional Regression Results: Full Analysis Period

Using 175 sorted portfolios sorted on firm and stock characteristics in the full analysis period, Table 6.1 gives the out-of-sample cross-sectional regression results for alternative asset models. In all models, the market price of market beta risk (denoted $\hat{\lambda}_m$) is not significant. With the exception of the ZCAPM, contrary to CAPM theory, estimated beta risk premiums are negative. Among the OLS multifactor models, only the market prices of size, profitability, and capital investment beta risks (or $\hat{\lambda}_{SMB}$, $\hat{\lambda}_{RMW}$, and

$\hat{\lambda}_{CMA}$, respectively) are statistically significant. The latter two beta risk premiums are significant at 1% and 5% levels, respectively. For the ZCAPM, the market price of market return dispersion loadings ($\hat{\lambda}_{RD}$) is more significant than the models with a t-statistic of 4.70. This statistic exceeds the 3 t-value threshold recommended by Harvey, Liu, and Zhu (2016) and Chordia, Goyal, and Saretto (2020) for the significance of factor loadings in multifactor models. Only the ZCAPM passes their hurdle rate for factors to avoid false discoveries.

In terms of goodness-of-fit as measured by R^2 values, the ZCAPM outperforms the other multifactor models. With an estimated R^2 value of 86%, the ZCAPM well outperforms the Fama and French six-factor model (FF6) at 65%. Other models have lower goodness-of-fit. Compared to the results for anomaly portfolios, the OLS multifactor models perform better in terms of noticeably higher goodness-of-fit. It is interesting to compare the results in Table 6.1 to those in Table 5.2 in previous Chapter 5 for 133 anomaly portfolios. The highest R^2 among the OLS multifactor models in Table 5.2 was 19%, which is much worse than the 65% achieved by the FF6 model in Table 6.1 We infer that, using OLS multifactor models, firm and stock sorted portfolios are much easier to explain than anomaly portfolios. In other words, the long/short anomaly portfolios in Table 5.1 in Chapter 5 are anomalous to the OLS multifactor models, but constituent portfolios

Table 6.1 Out-of-sample Fama-MacBeth cross-sectional tests of 175 portfolios sorted on firm and stock characteristics for asset pricing models in the full sample period July 1972 to December 2021

Model	$\hat{\alpha}$	$\hat{\lambda}_m$	$\hat{\lambda}_{RD}$	$\hat{\lambda}_{SMB}$	$\hat{\lambda}_{HML}$	$\hat{\lambda}_{MOM}$	$\hat{\lambda}_{RMW}$	$\hat{\lambda}_{CMA}$	R^2
CAPM	0.93	-0.16							0.22
	4.03	-0.66							
FF3	0.81	-0.13		0.20	0.16				0.32
	4.46	-0.58		1.65	1.36				
C4	0.94	-0.26		0.20	0.17	0.25			0.44
	5.48	-1.27		1.65	1.49	1.47			
FF5	0.73	-0.04		0.23	0.15		0.24	0.18	0.54
	4.01	-0.20		1.88	1.25		2.70	2.37	
FF6	0.98	-0.29		0.23	0.16	0.23	0.23	0.17	0.65
	5.88	-1.52		1.83	1.36	1.33	2.68	2.20	
ZCAPM	0.58	0.16	0.43						0.86
	2.72	0.71	4.70						

[1] In the ZCAPM, due to using average market excess returns rather than a proxy for market portfolio excess returns, the price of beta risk associated with CRSP index excess returns is denoted $\hat{\lambda}_a$ instead of $\hat{\lambda}_m$ in the other models

used to construct long and short positions in anomaly portfolios in Table 6.1 are much less anomalous.

Importantly, the goodness-of-fit of the ZCAPM is little changed in these two different sets of test asset portfolios—namely, 84% for anomaly portfolios in Table 5.1 versus 86% for firm and stock characteristic sorted portfolios in Table 6.1. It is clear that OLS multifactor models underperform the ZCAPM (i.e., EM multifactor model) in both sets of test portfolios but especially so for anomaly portfolios. Also, both anomaly portfolios in Table 5.2 and constituent portfolios used in their long/short portfolio construction in Table 6.1 are not anomalous to the ZCAPM. In effect, anomalies disappear after their returns are risk-adjusted using ZCAPM systematic market factors.

A downside of the factors in OLS multifactor models is that they are constructed from the same firm and stock characteristics used to form the test asset portfolios in Table 6.1. These models build factors directly related to the anomaly portfolios returns that they are seeking to explain. Thus, their performance is fairly good for these selected anomaly portfolios but not the general population of anomalies studied in Chapter 5. By contrast, EM regression estimation of the ZCAPM provides good results regardless of the chosen test asset portfolios. Thus, unlike other models, the ZCAPM is applicable to a more diverse set of anomalies as well as their constituent (or component) portfolios.

In Table 6.2, we report the cross-sectional regression results using 47 industry portfolios as test assets. Now the market price of risk of size beta risk ($\hat{\lambda}_{SMB}$) becomes insignificant, the market price of value beta risk ($\hat{\lambda}_{HML}$) continues to be insignificant, the market price of momentum ($\hat{\lambda}_{MOM}$) is now significant, and profitability and capital investment ($\hat{\lambda}_{RMW}$ and $\hat{\lambda}_{CMA}$, respectively) remain significant, albeit at lower levels than for the 175 test asset portfolios. Again the t-statistic for the market price of market return dispersion ($\hat{\lambda}_{RD}$) is more highly significant at 3.46 than the other factor loadings.

Using industry portfolios, the goodness-of-fit for all models diminishes relative to Table 6.1 with 175 size and firm characteristic sorted portfolios. Nonetheless, the ZCAPM outperforms the other models with an R^2 value of 57%. By comparison, the FF6 model has an R^2 estimate of 34%. The goodness-of-fit of other models drops markedly below this level. This out-of-sample (one-month-ahead) evidence confirms that the ZCAPM outperforms other multifactor models in terms of both the statistical significance of market prices of risk and explanatory power.

Table 6.2 Out-of-sample Fama-MacBeth cross-sectional tests of 47 industry portfolios sorted on firm and stock characteristics for asset pricing models in the full sample period July 1972 to December 2021

Model	$\hat{\alpha}$	$\hat{\lambda}_m$	$\hat{\lambda}_{RD}$	$\hat{\lambda}_{SMB}$	$\hat{\lambda}_{HML}$	$\hat{\lambda}_{MOM}$	$\hat{\lambda}_{RMW}$	$\hat{\lambda}_{CMA}$	R^2
CAPM	0.46	0.28							0.06
	2.19	1.15							
FF3	0.43	0.26		0.07	0.05				0.15
	1.95	0.98		0.43	0.36				
C4	0.44	0.25		0.06	–0.01	0.39			0.30
	2.01	1.00		0.44	–0.08	1.70			
FF5	0.34	0.35		0.07	0.05		0.23	0.17	0.16
	1.52	1.35		0.48	0.39		2.11	1.68	
FF6	0.52	0.17		0.06	0.02	0.37	0.22	0.14	0.34
	2.29	0.66		0.39	0.19	1.67	2.05	1.33	
ZCAPM	0.34	0.41	0.30						0.57
	1.66	1.71	3.46						

[1] In the ZCAPM, due to using average market excess returns rather than a proxy for market portfolio excess returns, the price of beta risk associated with CRSP index excess returns is denoted $\hat{\lambda}_a$ instead of $\hat{\lambda}_m$ in the other models

Cross-Sectional Regression Results: Restricted Analysis Period

We repeat the above cross-sectional tests with data series from July 1972 to December 2016. During this restricted sample period, we are able to download factors for both the Hou, Xue, and Zhang (HXZ4) and Stambaugh and Yuan (SY4) asset pricing models. We replicate the empirical tests in Tables 6.1 and 6.2 for all models and compare the results to HXZ4 and SY4 in Tables 6.3 and 6.4.

Using 175 test asset portfolios, Table 6.3 reports results that are similar to those in Table 6.1. As shown there, the HXZ4 and SY4 models perform similar to the C4 model of Carhart. The most significant factor loadings for the latter two models are achieved by the HXZ4 market price of capital investments beta risk ($\hat{\lambda}_{IA}$) with a t-statistic of 3.21 and the market price of management beta risk ($\hat{\lambda}_{MGMT}$) with a t-statistic of 3.18. Size and profitability beta risks ($\hat{\lambda}_{ME}$ and $\hat{\lambda}_{ROE}$, respectively) are both significant at the 5% level in the HXZ4 model, and size and performance beta risks ($\hat{\lambda}_{ME}$ and $\hat{\lambda}_{ROE}$, respectively) are significant at the 10% level in the SY4 model. The R^2 estimates for these two models are similar to C4.

The best performing OLS multifactor model is FF6 with an R^2 value of 72%. For this model, the market prices of size, value, profitability, and

Table 6.3 Out-of-sample Fama-MacBeth cross-sectional tests of 175 portfolios sorted on firm and stock characteristics for asset pricing models in the restricted sample period July 1972 to December 2016

Model	$\hat{\alpha}$	$\hat{\lambda}_m$	$\hat{\lambda}_{RD}$	$\hat{\lambda}_{SMB}$	$\hat{\lambda}_{HML}$	$\hat{\lambda}_{MOM}$	$\hat{\lambda}_{RMW}$	$\hat{\lambda}_{CMA}$	R^2
CAPM	1.42	−0.30							0.32
	5.97	−1.26							
FF3	1.24	−0.24		0.23	0.26				0.42
	6.50	−1.04		1.76	2.17				
C4	1.39	−0.39		0.23	0.29	0.27			0.54
	7.71	−1.85		1.78	2.38	1.53			
FF5	1.14	−0.13		0.26	0.25		0.23	0.25	0.63
	5.99	−0.61		2.03	2.06		2.43	3.08	
FF6	1.41	−0.40		0.26	0.28	0.26	0.23	0.23	0.72
	8.24	−2.08		1.99	2.24	1.40	2.60	2.89	
ZCAPM	1.02	−0.05	0.43						0.91
	4.60	−0.23	4.48						

Model	$\hat{\alpha}$	$\hat{\lambda}_m$	$\hat{\lambda}_{RD}$	$\hat{\lambda}_{SMB}$	$\hat{\lambda}_{ME}$	$\hat{\lambda}_{IA}$	$\hat{\lambda}_{ROE}$	$\hat{\lambda}_{MGMT}$	$\hat{\lambda}_{PERF}$	R^2
HXZ4	1.43	−0.41			0.28	0.33	0.35			0.54
	8.16	−2.10			2.06	3.21	2.47			
SY4	1.14	−0.13		0.24				0.00	0.00	0.46
	5.95	−0.61		1.85				3.18	1.82	

[1] In the ZCAPM, due to using average market excess returns rather than a proxy for market portfolio excess returns, the price of beta risk associated with CRSP index excess returns is denoted $\hat{\lambda}_a$ instead of $\hat{\lambda}_m$ in the other models

capital investments betas ($\hat{\lambda}_{SMB}$, $\hat{\lambda}_{HML}$, $\hat{\lambda}_{RMW}$, and $\hat{\lambda}_{ROE}$, respectively) are significant at 5% and 1% levels. The ZCAPM outperforms FF6 in terms of a relatively high market price of market return dispersion risk ($\hat{\lambda}_{RD}$) with a t-statistic of 4.48 and higher R^2 value of 91%. Thus, these test asset portfolios, which are exogenous to the ZCAPM but endogenous to the other multifactor models, are almost completely explained by the ZCAPM.

Lastly, we review the results for the 47 industry portfolios in the restricted sample period. The results for models in Table 6.4 are little changed from those in Table 6.2 Note that the HXZ4 and SY4 models have difficulty pricing these portfolios. They only achieve R^2 values of 14% and 10%, respectively, which is well below the C4 model at 34%. The statistical significance of the market prices of beta risks is noticeably lower than for the 175 portfolios in Table 6.3. Only the market prices of capital investments beta risk ($\hat{\lambda}_{IA}$) and management beta risk ($\hat{\lambda}_{MGMT}$) for the HXZ4 and SY4 models, respectively, are significant at the 5% level or lower.

Table 6.4 Out-of-sample Fama-MacBeth cross-sectional tests of 47 industry portfolios for asset pricing models in the restricted sample period July 1972 to December 2016

Model	$\hat{\alpha}$	$\hat{\lambda}_m$	$\hat{\lambda}_{RD}$	$\hat{\lambda}_{SMB}$	$\hat{\lambda}_{HML}$	$\hat{\lambda}_{MOM}$	$\hat{\lambda}_{RMW}$	$\hat{\lambda}_{CMA}$		R^2
CAPM	0.93	0.15								0.00
	4.19	0.59								
FF3	0.91	0.11		0.01	0.15					0.08
	3.86	0.39		0.05	1.12					
C4	0.91	0.11		0.00	0.09	0.36				0.32
	3.96	0.40		0.02	0.73	1.52				
FF5	0.76	0.24		0.02	0.14		0.29	0.25		0.10
	3.24	0.89		0.12	1.06		2.57	2.25		
FF6	0.96	0.03		-0.01	0.12	0.36	0.29	0.20		0.37
	4.11	0.13		-0.05	0.94	1.55	2.57	1.82		
ZCAPM	0.76	0.23	0.30							0.58
	3.53	0.94	3.24							
Model	$\hat{\alpha}$	$\hat{\lambda}_m$	$\hat{\lambda}_{RD}$	$\hat{\lambda}_{SMB}$	$\hat{\lambda}_{ME}$	$\hat{\lambda}_{IA}$	$\hat{\lambda}_{ROE}$	$\hat{\lambda}_{MGMT}$	$\hat{\lambda}_{PERF}$	R^2
HXZ4	1.00	0.03			0.08	0.30	0.27			0.14
	4.37	0.11			0.48	2.42	1.81			
SY4	0.72	0.31		0.03				0.00	0.00	0.10
	3.03	1.11		0.16				2.20	1.78	

[1] In the ZCAPM, due to using average market excess returns rather than a proxy for market portfolio excess returns, the price of beta risk associated with CRSP index excess returns is denoted $\hat{\lambda}_a$ instead of $\hat{\lambda}_m$ in the other models

Again the ZCAPM produces cross-sectional regression results that exceed other models in terms of a relatively high market price of market return dispersion risk ($\hat{\lambda}_{ME}$) with a t-statistic of 3.24 and higher R^2 value of 58%. While industry portfolios are better explained by the ZCAPM than by the other models, these portfolios are more difficult to explain than the 175 firm and stock characteristic sorted portfolios in addition to large samples of 133 and 153 anomaly portfolios in previous Chapter 5.

In sum, based on standard Fama-MacBeth out-of-sample cross-sectional regression tests, the ZCAPM outperforms OLS multifactor models popular in the literature. Industry portfolios are more difficult to explain than other test asset portfolios. Nonetheless, the ZCAPM performs reasonably well even for these portfolios.

Graphical Cross-Sectional Results: Full Analysis Period

As in Chapter 5 for anomaly portfolio returns, we estimate mispricing errors for the 175 firm and stock characteristic sorted portfolios from Kenneth French's database website in addition to 47 industry portfolios. Following Cochrane (1996) and Lettau and Ludvigson (2001)), mispricing errors are measured by the average predicted returns minus average realized (actual) returns of test asset portfolios. Predicted returns are estimated using the estimated one-month-ahead cross-sectional regression models discussed in the previous section. They are the fitted returns of the models in each one-month-ahead estimated regression. As the cross-sectional regression model is rolled forward one month at time through the sample period from July 1973 to December 2021, a monthly series of fitted (or predicted) returns are generated for each portfolio. The average of these monthly predicted (or fitted) returns is compared to the average monthly realized return over time. A graph of these out-of-sample return series is plotted with average realized returns on the Y-axis and average fitted returns on the X-axis. The 45 degree line in this graph indicates no pricing error. Portfolios that are close (distant) to this line have less (more) mispricing error. As mispricing errors decrease, the ability of a model increases in terms of explaining their out-of-sample returns.

In Fig. 6.1, we plot the average mispricing errors of 175 portfolios. Panel A gives the results for the Fama and French three-factor model (FF3), and Panel B shows the results for the Carhart four-factor model (C4). While these two models produce similar results, they exhibit sizable mispricing errors, especially for portfolios with relatively low or high returns among the test asset portfolios.

Figure 6.2 repeats these analyses for the Fama and French six-factor model (FF6) in Panel A and ZCAPM in Panel B. The FF6 model reduces the mispricing error in the previous figures with FF3 and C4 models' results. However, the ZCAPM has demonstrably lower mispricing errors than the FF6 model. The improvement in terms of lowering mispricing error is apparent throughout the distribution of average realized returns from low to high returns. We infer that the ZCAPM substantially reduces mispricing errors relative to the FF6 model.

Figures 6.3 and 6.4 display the mispricing results for 47 industry portfolios. In Panels A and B of Figs. 6.3 with results for the FF3 and C4 models, respectively, average mispricing errors are much higher for industry portfolios compared to the 175 firm and stock characteristic portfolios. Both

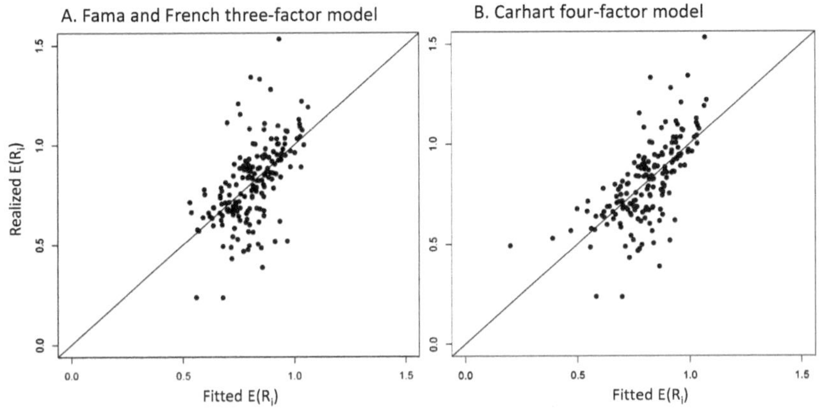

Fig. 6.1 Out-of-sample cross-sectional French three-factor model (Panel B) Carhart four-factor model (Panel A) and mispricing errors comparing average one-month-ahead realized excess returns in percent (Y-axis) to average one-month-ahead predicted (fitted) excess returns in percent (X-axis) for 175 size and firm characteristic portfolios. The full analysis period is July 1973 to December 2021

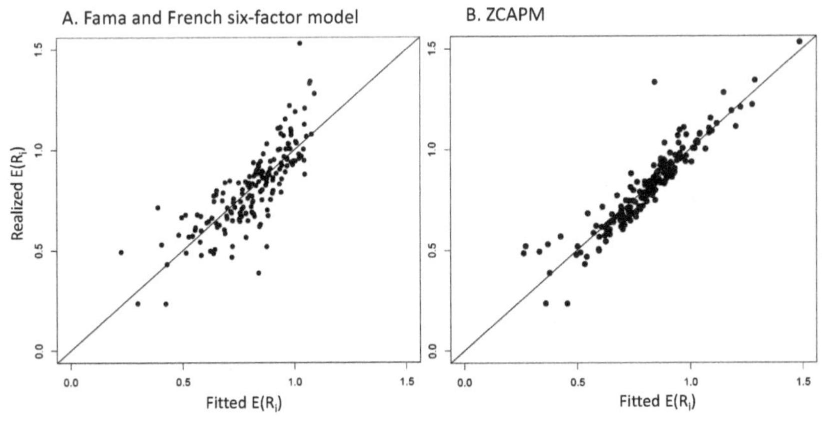

Fig. 6.2 Out-of-sample cross-sectional Fama and French six-factor model (Panel A) and ZCAPM (Panel B) mispricing errors comparing average one-month-ahead realized excess returns in percent (Y-axis) to average one-month-ahead predicted (fitted) excess returns in percent (X-axis) 175 size and firm characteristic portfolios. The full analysis period is July 1973 to December 2021

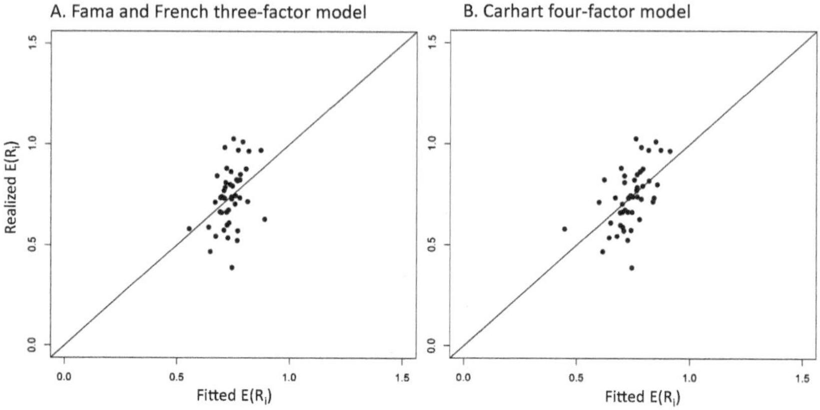

Fig. 6.3 Out-of-sample cross-sectional Fama and French three-factor model (Panel A) and Carhart four-factor model (Panel B) mispricing errors comparing average one-month-ahead realized excess returns in percent (Y-axis) to average one-month-ahead predicted (fitted) excess returns in percent (X-axis) for 47 industry portfolios. The full analysis subperiod is July 1973 to December 2021

models do a poor job of explaining these portfolios' average returns. The results for the FF6 and ZCAPM are shown in Panels A and B, respectively, of Fig. 6.4. Again the ZCAPM outperforms the FF6 model. As shown there, some low return portfolios are difficult to price for the ZCAPM. In unreported results, we find that these portfolios tend to have relatively low numbers of stocks that increase their idiosyncratic risk and related difficulty in pricing.

Graphical Cross-Sectional Results: Restricted Analysis Period

The above analyses are repeated for the restricted analysis period July 1972 to December 2016 that was used in Hou, Xue, and Zhang (HXZ4) and Stambaugh and Yuan (SY4) analyses. The models are estimated for the first 1-year period from July 1972 to June 1973. The first one-month-ahead cross-sectional model is estimated in July 1973. The analyses are rolled forward one month at time to December 2016.

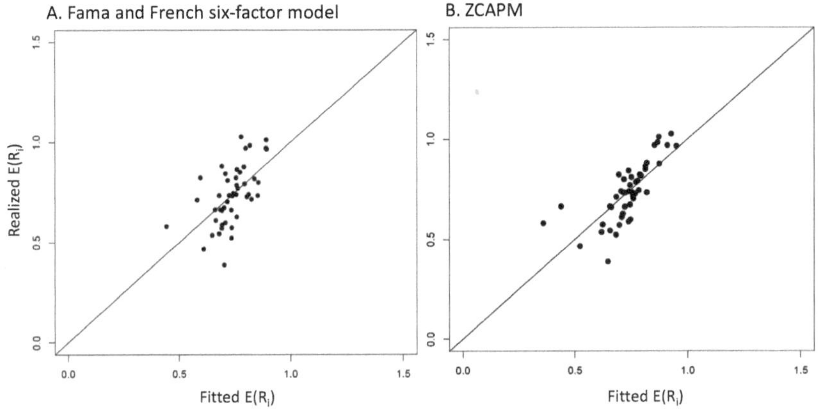

Fig. 6.4 Out-of-sample cross-sectional Fama and French six-factor model (Panel A) and ZCAPM (Panel B) mispricing errors comparing average one-month-ahead realized excess returns in percent (Y-axis) to average one-month-ahead predicted (fitted) excess returns in percent (X-axis) for 47 industry portfolios. The full analysis subperiod is July 1973 to December 2021

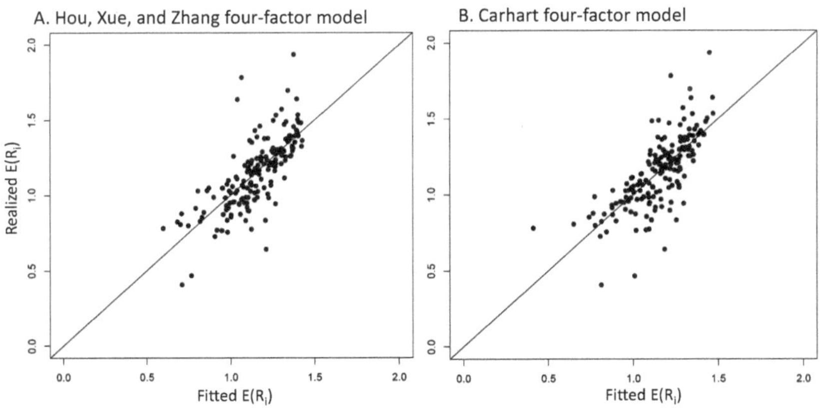

Fig. 6.5 Out-of-sample cross-sectional Hou, Xue, and Zhang four-factor model (Panel A) and Carhart four-factor model (Panel B) mispricing errors comparing average one-month-ahead realized excess returns in percent (Y-axis) to average one-month-ahead predicted (fitted) excess returns in percent (X-axis) for 175 size and firm characteristic portfolios. The restricted analysis period is July 1973 to December 2016

Figure 6.5 displays the results for the HXZ4 model in Panel A and C4 model in Panel B. These models again perform similarly. Figure 6.6 shows that the SY4 model performs similar to the C4 model also.

As before, the FF6 model in Panel A of Fig. 6.7 improves the average mispricing errors over the other models but underperform the ZCAPM in Panel B. Average mispricing errors for the ZCAPM appear to be even smaller than in the full analysis period shown in Fig. 6.2. Only one portfolio lies well off the line out of 175 portfolios, which is most likely a portfolio containing small cap stocks with considerably idiosyncratic risk. Overall, the ZCAPM does a convincing job of explaining these portfolios' returns.

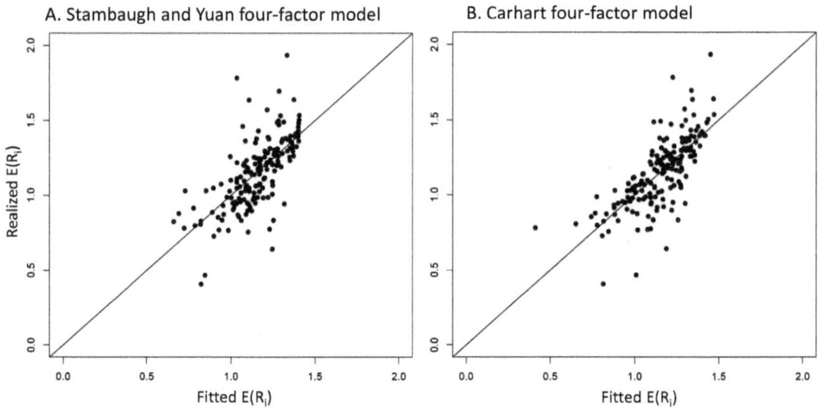

Fig. 6.6 Out-of-sample cross-sectional Stambaugh and Yuan (Panel A) and Carhart four-factor model (Panel B) mispricing errors comparing average one-month-ahead realized excess returns in percent (Y-axis) to average one-month-ahead predicted (fitted) excess returns in percent (X-axis) for 175 size and firm characteristic portfolios. The restricted analysis period is July 1973 to December 2016

Figures 6.8, 6.9, and 6.10 provide the graphical results for average mispricing errors using 47 industry portfolios. All models have greater difficulty in pricing these portfolios compared to the 175 firm and stock characteristic portfolios. Even so, the ZCAPM performs better than the other multifactor models with lower average mispricing errors.

In sum, the results for the restricted period corroborate those for the restricted period. The ZCAPM consistently has lower mispricing errors than

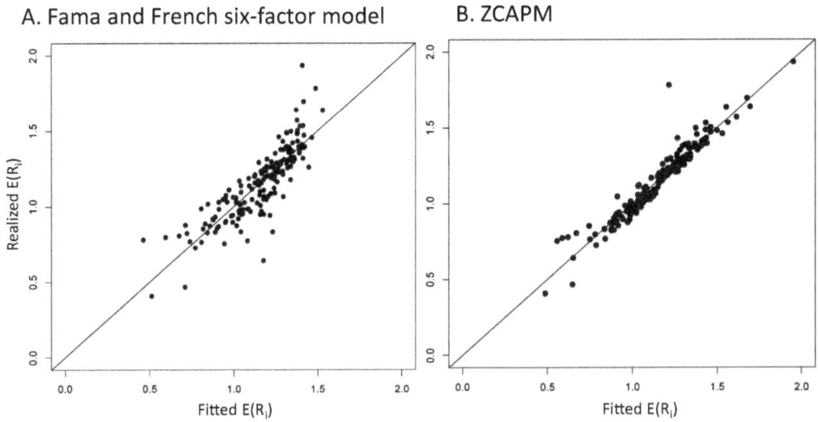

Fig. 6.7 Out-of-sample cross-sectional Fama and French six-factor model (Panel A) and ZCAPM (Panel B) mispricing errors comparing average one-month-ahead realized excess returns in percent (Y-axis) to average one-month-ahead predicted (fitted) excess returns in percent (X-axis) for 175 size and firm characteristic portfolios. The restricted analysis period is July 1973 to December 2016

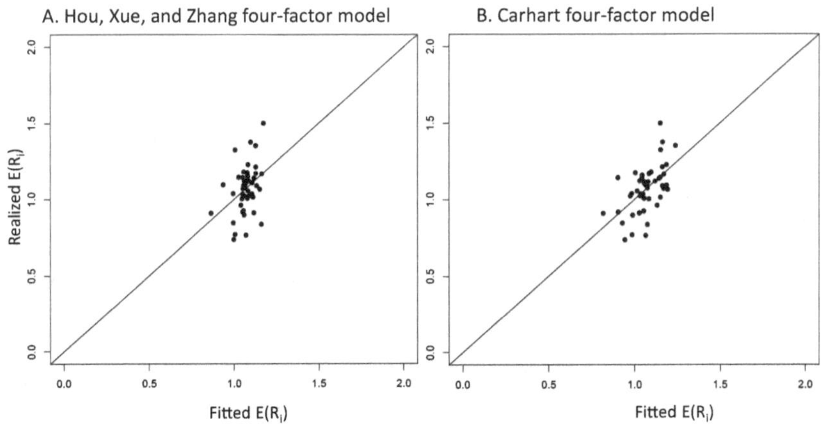

Fig. 6.8 Out-of-sample cross-sectional Hou, Xue, and Zhang four-factor model (Panel A) and Carhart four-factor model (Panel B) mispricing errors comparing average one-month-ahead realized excess returns in percent (Y-axis) to average one-month-ahead predicted (fitted) excess returns in percent (X-axis) for 47 industry portfolios. The restricted analysis period is July 1973 to December 2016

the other models. We infer that these out-of-sample tests of the different models confirm the superior ability of the ZCAPM to explain test asset portfolios returns.

Further Evidence on Anomaly Portfolios: The Case of Japan

We next investigate anomaly portfolio returns in Japan. We download 153 anomaly portfolio returns from Jensen, Kelly, and Pedersen (2023) that are available online at Error! Hyperlink reference not valid. et al. make available data series for 193 countries. Asset pricing factors for Japan are generously provided by Kolari, Huang, Butt, and Liao (2022), who apply different models including the ZCAPM to other countries. They use Thomson Reuters Datastream to download individual stock prices, total returns, market capitalizations of stocks, and book values of firms. Fairly good sample sizes from approximately 550 to 1,900 individual stocks per year are included in their analyses. The CAPM is estimated for the market factor using value-weighted returns of individual sample stocks in excess of the USA. Treasury bill rate. Fama and French as well as Carhart factors are as follows: size factor (*SMB*), value factor (*HML*), and momentum factor (*MOM*).[3] For the ZCAPM, the daily cross-sectional standard deviation of all individual stock returns is computed using value-weighted returns. Taking the intersection of these daily return data series for anomaly portfolios and factors yields a sample period from February 3, 1986 to September 2020. In this sample period, some anomalies are dropped due to insufficient return data, which trims the final sample to 86 anomaly portfolios.

Based on these data series, we run out-of-sample Fama-MacBeth cross-sectional regressions to estimate the market prices of factor loadings for each model. Table 6.5 reports the results for Japanese stock market anomalies. Only the market price of market return dispersion loadings ($\hat{\lambda}_{RD}$) for the ZCAPM is statistically significant (at the 5% level) with a t-statistic of 4.70. The market, size, value, and momentum factors, which are employed in the CAPM, Fama and French three-factor model, and Carhart four-factor model, are not significant. These results are similar to the Japanese stock

[3] These long/short size, value, and momentum factors are computed similar to Fama and French and Carhart. Individual stocks are sorted into decile portfolios based on these firm and stock characteristics. Following Kenneth French's website for the construction of factors, long/short portfolios are formed from selected deciles to build the factors. All factors use value-weighted returns.

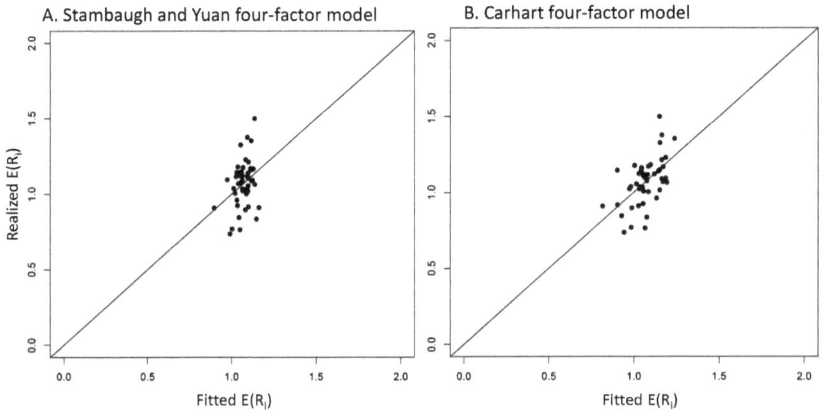

Fig. 6.9 Out-of-sample cross-sectional Stambaugh and Yuan (Panel A) and Carhart four-factor model (Panel B) mispricing errors comparing average one-month-ahead realized excess returns in percent (Y-axis) to average one-month-ahead predicted (fitted) excess returns in percent (X-axis) for 175 size and firm characteristic portfolios. The restricted analysis period is July 1973 to December 2016

market tests for industry portfolios in Kolari et al. (with the exception that the value factor was significant at the 10% level in the Carhart four-factor model). Notice that the ZCAPM has a relatively high R^2 value of 90% . The other models achieve at most an R^2 value of 28% . Thus, the ZCAPM has much better goodness-of-fit on an out-of-sample basis than other multifactor models. Indeed, anomaly portfolio returns in Japan are almost completely explained by the ZCAPM.

Turning to the graphical analyses of average mispricing errors, Figs. 6.11 and 6.12 confirm the explanatory power of the ZCAPM over the CAPM and multifactor models. The latter well-known models have almost no ability to explain anomaly portfolio returns in Japan. However, the ZCAPM does a good job in this respect. Corroborating our U.S. stock market anomaly results, we conclude that anomaly portfolio returns in Japan are well explained by the ZCAPM but not other models.

Table 6.5 Out-of-sample Fama-MacBeth cross-sectional tests of 86 anomaly portfolios in Japan for asset pricing models in the period February 3, 1986 to September 24, 2020

Model	$\hat{\alpha}$	$\hat{\lambda}_m$	$\hat{\lambda}_{RD}$	$\hat{\lambda}_{SMB}$	$\hat{\lambda}_{HML}$	$\hat{\lambda}_{MOM}$	R^2
CAPM	0.10	−1.58					0.02
	3.43	−1.57					
FF3	0.11	−0.14		−0.23	0.07		0.26
	4.24	−0.16		−0.52	0.14		
C4	0.11	−0.15		−0.15	−0.14	0.78	0.28
	4.01	−0.17		−0.31	−0.27	0.97	
ZCAPM	0.06	−1.32	0.29				0.90
	1.93	−1.32	2.37				

[1] In the ZCAPM, due to using average market excess returns rather than a proxy for market portfolio excess returns, the price of beta risk associated with CRSP index excess returns is denoted $\hat{\lambda}_a$ instead of $\hat{\lambda}_m$ in the other models

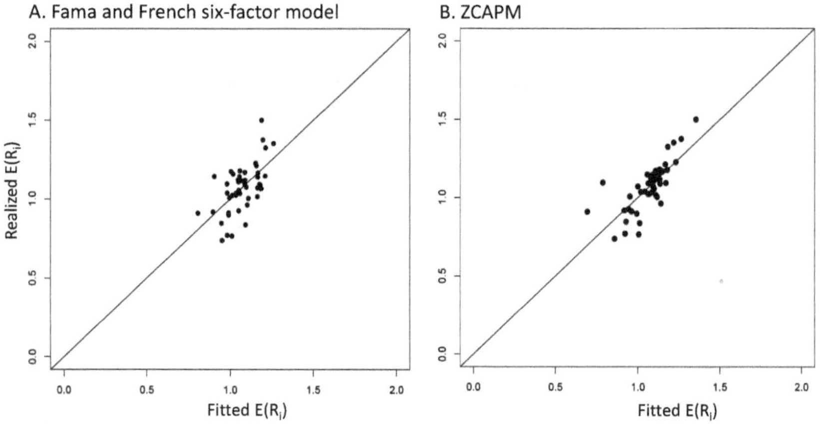

Fig. 6.10 Out-of-sample cross-sectional Fama and French six-factor model (Panel A) and ZCAPM (Panel B) mispricing errors comparing average one-month-ahead realized excess returns in percent (Y-axis) to average one-month-ahead predicted (fitted) excess returns in percent (X-axis) for 47 industry portfolios. The restricted analysis period is July 1973 to December 2016

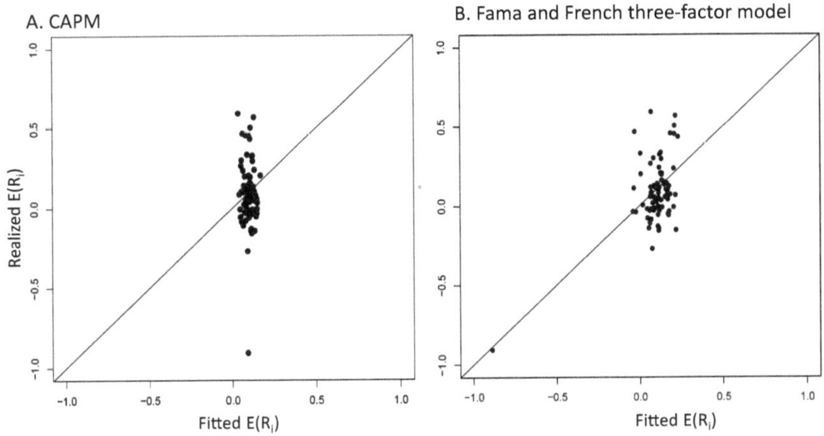

Fig. 6.11 Out-of-sample cross-sectional CAPM (Panel A) and Fama and French three-factor model (Panel B) mispricing errors comparing average one-month-ahead realized excess returns in percent (Y-axis) to average one-month-ahead predicted (fitted) excess returns in percent (X-axis) for 86 anomaly portfolios in Japan. The analysis period is February 1987 to September 2020

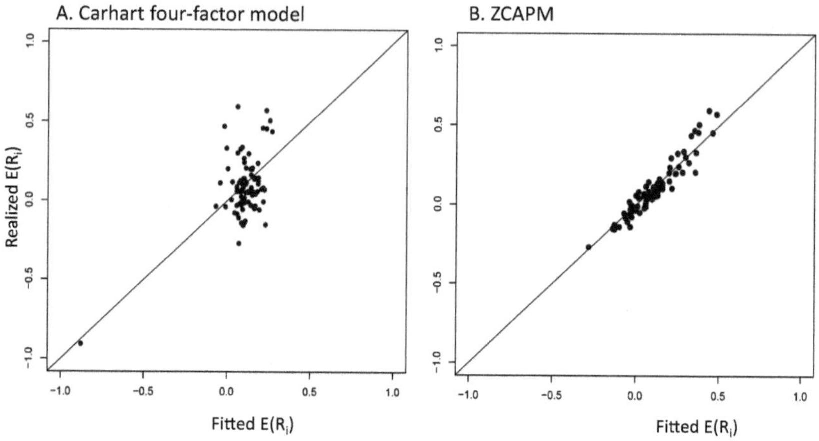

Fig. 6.12 Out-of-sample cross-sectional Carhart four-factor model (Panel A) and ZCAPM (Panel B) mispricing errors comparing average one-month-ahead realized excess returns in percent (Y-axis) to average one-month-ahead predicted (fitted) excess returns in percent (X-axis) for 86 anomaly portfolios in Japan. The analysis period is February 1987 to September 2020

6.3 Summary

This chapter extended tests of long/short anomaly portfolio returns in Chapter 5 to the returns of portfolios in either the long or short positions of anomaly portfolios. These more granular tests of anomaly portfolios are useful in better understanding the pricing ability of different asset pricing models. Also, we included long/short momentum portfolios' returns that are notorious for being difficult to explain by models. Because asset pricing models typically have difficulty pricing industry portfolios, we added these portfolios to our tests. Finally, we gathered a dataset of anomaly portfolios in Japan made available online by Jensen, Kelly, and Pedersen (2023), which extends our analyses to other countries beyond the USA. All time-series regressions of different asset pricing models are estimated using daily stock returns in one year and rolled forward over time by one month at a time. Subsequently, standard Fama-MacBeth out-of-sample cross-sectional regressions and graphical analyses of average mispricing errors are used to evaluate different asset pricing models.

For U.S. stock returns, with the exception of the industry portfolios, our empirical results are similar to those based on anomaly portfolios returns. In all tests, the ZCAPM consistently outperformed the CAPM and prominent OLS-based multifactor models, including the Fama and French (1992, 1993, 2015, and 2018) three-, five-, and six factor models in addition to four-factor models by Carhart (1997), Hou, Xue, and Zhang (2015), and Stambaugh and Yuan (2017). Like the anomaly portfolios in Chapter 5, the ZCAPM did a good job of explaining the stock returns of firm and stock characteristic sorted portfolios. Other models were less successful with only the Fama and French six-factor model exhibiting a fair level of explanatory power. In the restricted analysis period, the ZCAPM's R^2 value was over 90% for these portfolios, which is nearing a perfect goodness-of-fit. Thus, we infer that the ZCAPM not only can explain long/short anomaly portfolio returns but their constituent long and short positions also.

The results for industry portfolios were weaker for all models. Only the ZCAPM achieved an estimated R^2 value in excess of 50%. Also, only the market price of zeta risk in the ZCAPM was significant with a t-statistic in excess of 3 as recommended to identify valid factors (e.g., see Harvey, Liu, and Zhu (2016) and Chordia, Goyal, and Saretto (2020)). One potential problem with the industry portfolios is that the number of stocks in some portfolios was fairly small in some portfolios over time. This sample size issue increased the idiosyncratic risk of these portfolios, thereby decreasing the ability of asset pricing models to price them using systematic market risks. Despite this drawback, the ZCAPM appeared to provide some degree of pricing performance. The only other model to provide some pricing ability for industry portfolios (albeit less than the ZCAM) was the Fama and French six-factor model. Other models performed badly.

Our firm and stock characteristic sorted portfolio results support the efficient markets hypothesis of Fama (1965, 1970, 2013). Given these stock portfolios' risk profiles using the ZCAPM, the cross- section of their average returns was well explained. On a consistent basis, other well-known multifactor models did not perform as well as the ZCAPM. Indeed, in many cases commonly used multifactor models supported the behavioral school of finance, wherein psychological biases are needed to explain anomalous stock returns (e.g., Daniel, Hirshleifer, and Subrahmanyam (1997) and Barberis, Shleifer, and Vishny (1998)). Taking into account the ZCAPM, stock returns appear to be efficiently priced by rational investors' assessments of their systematic risks, such that behavioral explanations are not needed.

The result for anomaly portfolios is Japan corroborate our U.S. results. The ZCAPM outperformed the CAPM, Fama and French three-factor model and Carhart four-factor model. It was the only model with significant factor loadings (viz., the zeta risk coefficient related to the market return dispersion factor). Also, the ZCAPM's explanatory power in these out-of-sample cross-sectional regression tests was 90%, which well exceeded other models with 28% at most. Graphs of average mispricing errors confirmed this exceptional explanatory power with relatively small magnitudes of mispricing errors across the anomaly portfolios.

The consistent empirical evidence in favor of the ZCAPM over other asset pricing models that have gained worldwide attention in finance literature and practice suggests that the ZCAPM warrants further study. The ZCAPM not only does a good job of explaining long/short anomaly portfolio returns as documented in Chapter 5 but can explain the returns of portfolios sorted into firm and stock characteristics that are utilized in the construction of long/short anomaly portfolios. The repeated outperformance of the ZCAPM in tests of these portfolios raises an important question: Is the ZCAPM a more valid asset pricing model? In our opinion, the answer based on these findings as well as those in Kolari, Liu, and Huang (2021), Kolari, Liu, and Pynnonen (2024), and related studies, is a resounding yes. Other multifactor models do not take into account total market return dispersion; instead, they focus on slices of total return dispersion that are incomplete and confusing. Rather than use selected segments of total return dispersion as captured by long/short factors in multifactor models, a more parsimonious and powerful approach is to simply use the total market return dispersion as in the ZCAPM. The ZCAPM is a next generation asset pricing model that capitalizes on machine learning (ML) to enhance predictive artificial intelligence (AI).

Our results for industry portfolios suggest that future research is needed to better understand why their returns are more difficult to explain for asset pricing models. While a small number of stocks in some industry portfolios is one possible explanation for their weaker results, other issues could be problematic, such as industry or sector rotations in the market that regularly occur over time. These rotations are commonly discussed by market professionals. For example, collapsing oil prices due to changing industry conditions can cause oil producing companies to experience large losses in their stock prices (which happened in 2015), and vice versa with sudden increases in oil prices. These industry-specific events are not taken into account in asset pricing models, as no industry factor has been developed by researchers to the authors' knowledge. To potentially fill this gap in the literature, the authors have ongoing research on the construction of a significant long/short industry factor. Some preliminary results are promising.

References

Barberis, N., A. Shleifer, and R. Vishny. 1998. A model of investor sentiment. *Journal of Financial Economics* 49: 307–343.

Carhart, M. M. 1997. On persistence in mutual fund performance. *Journal of Finance* 52: 57–82.

Chen, A. Y., and T. Zimmermann. 2020. Publication bias and the cross-section of stock returns. *Review of Asset Pricing Studies* 10: 249–289.

Chen, A. Y., and T. Zimmermann. 2022. Open source cross-sectional asset pricing. *Critical Finance Review* 11: 207–264.

Chordia, T., A. Goyal, and A. Saretto. 2020. Anomalies and false rejections. *Review of Financial Studies* 33: 2134–2179.

Cochrane, J. H. 1996. A cross-sectional test of an investment-based asset pricing model. *Journal of Political Economy* 104: 572–621.

Daniel, K., D. Hirshleifer, and A. Subrahmanyam. 1997. A theory of overconfidence, self-attribution, and security market under- and over-reactions. Unpublished working paper. University of Michigan.

Daniel, K., and S. Titman. 2012. Testing factor-model explanations of market anomalies. *Critical Finance Review* 1: 103–139.
Dempster, A. P., N. M. Laird, and D. B. Rubin. 1977. Maximum likelihood from incomplete data via the EM algorithm. *Journal of the Royal Statistical Society* 39: 1–38.
Fama, E. F. 1965. The behavior of stock-market prices. *The Journal of Business* 38: 34–105.
Fama, E. F. 1970. Efficient capital markets: A review of theory and evidence. *Journal of Finance* 35: 383–417.
Fama, E. F. 2013. *Two Pillars of Asset Pricing*, Nobel Prize Lecture.
Fama, E. F., and K. R. French. 1992. The cross-section of expected stock returns. *Journal of Finance* 47: 427–465.
Fama, E. F., and K. R. French. 1993. Common risk factors in the returns on stocks and bonds. *Journal of Financial Economics* 33: 3–56.
Fama, E. F., and K. R. French. 2015. A five-factor asset pricing model. *Journal of Financial Economics* 116: 1–22.
Fama, E. F., and K. R. French. 2018. Choosing factors. *Journal of Financial Economics* 128: 234–252.
Fama, E. F., and J. D. MacBeth. 1973. Risk, return, and equilibrium: Empirical tests. *Journal of Political Economy* 81: 607–636.
Ferson, W. E., S. Sarkissian, and T. Simin. 1999. The alpha force asset pricing model: A parable. *Journal of Financial Markets* 2: 49–68.
Giglio, S., and D. Xiu. 2021. Asset pricing with omitted factors. *Journal of Political Economy* 129: 1947–1990.
Harvey, C. R., Y. Liu, and H. Zhu. 2016. and the cross-section of expected returns. *Review of Financial Studies* 29: 5–68.
Hou, K., C. Xue, and L. Zhang. 2015. Digesting anomalies: An investment approach. *Review of Financial Studies* 28: 650–705.
Jagannathan, R., and Z. Wang. 1996. The conditional CAPM and the cross-section of asset returns. *Journal of Finance* 51: 3–53.
Jensen, T. I., B. Kelly, and L. H. Pedersen. 2023. Is there a replication crisis in finance? *Journal of Finance* 78: 2465–2518.
Jones, P. N., and G. J. McLachlan. 1990. Algorithm AS 254: Maximum likelihood estimation from grouped and truncated data with finite normal mixture models. *Applied Statistics* 39: 273–282.
Kolari, J. W., J. Z. Huang, H. A. Butt, and H. Liao. 2022. International tests of the ZCAPM asset pricing mode. *Journal of International Financial Markets, Institutions, and Money* 79: 101607.
Kolari, J. W., J. Z. Huang, W. Liu, and H. Liao. 2022. Further tests of the ZCAPM asset pricing model. Journal of Risk and Financial Management 15: 1–23. Reprinted in Kolari, J. W., and S. Pynnonen. 2022. Eds., Frontiers of Asset Pricing (MDPI, Basel, Switzerland).

Kolari, J. W., J. Z. Huang, W. Liu, and H. Liao. 2025. A quantum leap in asset pricing: Explaining anomalous returns. *Journal of Risk and Financial Management* 18: 362. https://doi.org/103390/jrfm18070362.

Kolari, J. W., W. Liu, and J. Z. Huang. 2021. *A New Model of Capital Asset Prices: Theory and Evidence*. Cham, Switzerland: Palgrave Macmillan.

Kolari, J. W., W. Liu, and S. Pynnonen. 2024. *Professional Investment Portfolio Management: Boosting Performance with Machine-Made Portfolios and Stock Market Evidence*. Cham, Switzerland: Palgrave Macmillan.

Lettau, M., and S. Ludvigson. 2001. Consumption, aggregate wealth, and expected stock returns. *Journal of Finance* 56: 815–849.

Lewellen, J., S. Nagel, and J. A. Shanken. 2010. A skeptical appraisal of asset pricing tests. *Journal of Financial Economics* 96: 175–194.

McLachlan, G. J., and T. Krishnan. 2008. *The EM Algorithm and Extensions*, 2nd ed. New York, NY: Wiley.

McLachlan, G., and D. Peel. 2000. *Finite Mixture Models*. New York, NY: Wiley Interscience.

Modigliani, F., and M. H. Miller. 1958. The cost of capital, corporation finance and the theory of investment. *American Economic Review* 48: 261–297.

Modigliani, F., and M. H. Miller. 1963. Corporation income taxes and the cost of capital: A correction. *American Economic Review* 53: 433–443.

Stambaugh, R. F., and Y. Yuan. 2017. Mispricing factors. *Review of Financial Studies* 30: 1270–1315.

PART IV

Asset Pricing Model Validity

CHAPTER 7

Empirical Tests on the Validity of Asset Pricing Models

Abstract Previous chapters have shown that well-known asset pricing models published in top tier finance journals do a poor job of explaining anomaly portfolio returns. In stark contrast, a recent but lesser known model dubbed the ZCAPM by Kolari, Liu, and Huang (2021) almost completely explains anomaly stock returns. These findings call into question the validity of prominent asset pricing models. That is, commonly used multifactor models appear to be missing factors that are needed to explain anomaly returns. To test this possibility, in this chapter we employ a new out-of-sample cross-sectional regression coefficient test of alpha mispricing error terms. According to Jensen (1968), the alpha parameter in the estimation of a time-series regression for an asset pricing model measures mispricing error which arises primarily due to missing factors in the model. Many authors test for the presence of mispricing errors using the Gibbons, Ross, and Shanken (GRS) (1989) test for the joint zero equality of alphas across a sample of test assets (e.g., stock portfolios). Notably, this test is restricted to linear model tests on an in-sample basis. Extending the GRS test of alphas, a recent study by Kolari, Huang, Liu, and Liao (2014) proposed a novel out-of-sample alpha test. More specifically, alpha parameters for tests assets estimated by a time-series regression model are used as a factor loading in a standard out-of-sample (one-month-ahead) Fama and MacBeth (1973) cross-sectional regression. If the alpha loading is significant, it means that missing factors exist in the time-series regression asset pricing model. Kolari et al. found that, even if in-sample GRS tests indicate that alphas are jointly zero with no apparent mispricing error and

J. W. Kolari et al., *Asset Pricing Models and Market Efficiency*,
https://doi.org/10.1007/978-3-031-92901-4_7

missing factors, out-of-sample alpha tests can suggest missing factors exist. In this chapter, we compare out-of-sample alpha test results for the CAPM, prominent multifactor models, and the recent ZCAPM. Our analyses use a variety of different test assets. Across these test asset samples, we find that mispricing errors are consistently lower in the ZCAPM compared to other models. For most test assets, the ZCAPM shows evidence of no missing factors. Thus, we conclude that the ZCAPM is not plagued by a missing factor problem as in the case of the CAPM and popular multifactor models. By inference, while our evidence supports the ZCAPM as a valid asset pricing model, well-known multifactor models are not supported. Also, due to the ability of the ZCAPM to well explain the cross-section of average stock returns, our empirical evidence suggests that the stock market is efficient.

7.1 Out-of-Sample Testing of Jensen's Alpha for Model Validity

To evaluate asset pricing models, many researchers utilize the Gibbons, Ross, and Shanken (GRS) test for the joint equality of alpha (denoted α) for a sample of test assets. Alpha is the intercept parameter in the time-series regression run to estimate an asset pricing model. Jensen (1968) observed that, if alpha is positive and significant, missing factors must exist that cause mispricing error in the model (i.e., positive or negative alphas imply asset under-pricing or over-pricing, respectively). Hence, so-called *Jensen's alpha* provides a way to test the validity of the CAPM and multifactor models.

If an asset pricing model reduces alpha to be closer to zero compared to other competing models, it is considered to be a better model. For example, the Fama and French (1992; 1993) three-factor model augmenting the CAPM market factor with size and value factors had a much smaller alpha than the CAPM. Indeed, using stock portfolios sorted on size and value firm characteristics, based on GRS tests, Fama and French found that the alpha was significantly no different from zero. For other test assets, however, alpha is reduced compared to the CAPM but nonzero. In their quest to reduce alpha, researchers have added more factors to alternative multifactor models, including the Carhart (1997) four-factor model, Fama and French (2015; 2018) five- and six-factor models as well as four-factor models by Hou, Xue, and Zhang (2015), Stambaugh and Yuan (2017), and others. Commenting on this literature, Cochrane (2011) has referred to the growing number of multifactors in asset pricing models as a *factor zoo*.

Unfortunately, the GRS test has a number of recognized drawbacks.. Citing numerous studies in the literature, Hollstein and Prokopzuk (2022) highlighted the following potential pitfalls of the GRS test: (1) look-ahead bias due to using information that investors do not have, (2) inappropriate constant-beta assumptions, (3) rejection of models due to disparities between historical average factor returns and unobservable risk premia, and (4) nonoptimal statistical properties. In light of these problems, they recommended that researchers utilize Fama and MacBeth (1973) cross-sectional regression tests to better assess the validity of different asset pricing models.[1]

Another drawback pointed out by Kolari et al. (2024) is that the GRS test is performed on an in-sample basis. This limitation is particularly egregious. Consider an investor that develops a trading rule (e.g., based on momentum in stocks) to construct high earning stock portfolios. Even though the trading rule may do well on an in-sample basis, it is not proven on an out-of-sample basis. As a practical matter, the investor needs to apply the trading rule to stocks on an out-of-sample basis and then check the performance in the future (e.g., next month). In-sample trading is not an investable stock trading strategy. Out-of-sample tests are needed to verify investment results and validate real world trading strategies. Numerous researchers, including Simin (2008), Ferson, Nallareddy, and Xie (2013), Barillas and Shanken (2018), Fama and French 2018), and others, have argued that, to virtually eliminate data snooping issues, cross-sectional regression analyses of asset pricing models should be conducted on an out-of-sample basis using future returns after factor loadings are estimated.

In line with the aforementioned recommendations for testing alphas, Kolari, Huang, Liu, and Liao (2024) proposed a new alpha test based on out-of-sample cross-sectional regression analyses. Using the standard two-step Fama-MacBeth approach, a time-series regression asset pricing model is initially estimated to obtain estimates of alpha:

$$R_{it} - R_{ft} = \alpha_i + \sum_{k=1}^{K} b_{ik} F_{kt} + e_{it}, \tag{7.1}$$

[1] In this regard, as discussed in Chapter 5, Giglio and Xiu (2021) found that the asymptotic efficiency of OLS estimates in cross-sectional regression analyses is not improved by using other estimation methods, such as weighted least squares (WLS), generalized least squares (GLS), general method of moments (GMM), and maximum likelihood (ML) estimation.

where $R_{it} - R_{ft}$ is the realized excess return on the ith test asset for day t, R_{ft} is the riskless rate proxied by the Treasury bill rate, α_i is the intercept term or Jensen's alpha, F_{kt} are asset pricing factors for $k = 1, \ldots, K$ factors, b_{ik} are corresponding K beta risk loadings for the ith portfolio, $i = 1, \ldots, N$ correspond to the number of portfolios, $t = 1, \ldots, T$ is the estimation period, and $e_{it} \sim$ iid $(0, \sigma_i^2)$. Rolling forward the time-series regression one month at a time yields a series of α_i intercepts and b_{ik} beta loadings. Subsequently, these parameters are incorporated in a cross-sectional regression as independent variables. More specifically, they proposed the following out-of-sample OLS cross-sectional regression:

$$R_{iT+1} - R_{fT+1} = \alpha + \eta_\alpha \hat{\alpha}_i + \lambda_1 \hat{b}_{i1} + \lambda_2 \hat{b}_{i2} + \ldots + \lambda_K \hat{b}_{iK} + u_{iT+1}, i = 1, \ldots, N, \quad (7.2)$$

where $R_{iT+1} - R_{fT+1}$ is the realized excess return on the ith portfolio in out-of-sample (one-month-ahead) month $T + 1$, α is the intercept (i.e., a level return that equals the common return to all test assets not captured by the explanatory variables), λ_k are corresponding estimated market prices of beta risk loadings, $u_{iT+1} \sim$ iid $(0,\sigma_i^2)$, and other notation is as before. Their innovative inclusion of the $\hat{\alpha}_i$ parameter in the cross-sectional regression enables the estimation of the η_α coefficient. The latter coefficient measures the sensitivity of one-month-ahead returns of stock portfolios to mispricing error due principally to missing factors contained in Jensen's alpha.

The Kolari et al. alpha test has a number of advantages. First, it is easy to implement using standard two-step Fama-MacBeth regression methods. Second, unlike the GRS test that applies only to linear models, it can be applied to both linear and nonlinear models. Third, it extends the in-sample GRS test to an out-of-sample test of alphas. Fourth, as discussed earlier, it has good statistical properties inherent in OLS cross-sectional regression analyses. Fourth, it provides new information about the validity of a model not provided by the GRS test. Fifth, and last, its interpretation is straightforward.

To interpret the η_α coefficient in cross-sectional regression relation (2), it is important to recognize that the independent variables α_i and b_{ik} have different units of measurement. Alpha is measured in terms of percent returns, whereas betas are dimensionless with no units of measurement. For this reason, their corresponding coefficients have different units of measurement also. The λ_k coefficients are factor mimicking portfolio returns in percent terms. By contrast, the η_α coefficient is a dimensionless sensitivity coefficient with respect to alpha. As the authors mathematically prove, η_α reflects the change in excess stock returns per unit change in α_i returns. In this regard, readers may incorrectly suppose that η_α is a factor mimicking portfolio return as in the case of λ_k. Instead, η_α represents the proportionate contribution of alpha mispricing errors to the out-of-sample excess returns of sample test assets. Also, the combined term $\eta_\alpha \hat{\alpha}_i$ measures the out-of-sample risk premium in return terms due to missing factors' returns (and other potential non-factor related returns).

In forthcoming cross-sectional regression tests, we employ six different asset pricing models:

- CAPM market model with CRSP value-weighted index minus the Treasury bill rate as the market factor (*M*);
- Fama and French (1992; 1993) three-factor model (FF3) that augments the market model with a size factor (i.e., small minus large firms' stock returns, or *SMB*) and value factor (i.e., high book-to-market equity minus low book-to-market equity firms' stock returns, or *HML*);
- Carhart (1997) four-factor model (C4) that augments the three-factor model with a momentum factor (i.e., firms with high past return stock returns minus low past stock returns, or *MOM*);
- Fama and French (2015) five-factor model (FF5) that augments their three-factor model with a profitability factor (i.e., robust operating profitability minus weak operating profitability returns, *RMW*) and capital investment factor (i.e., conservative investment minus aggressive investment returns, or *CMA*)[2];
- Fama and French (2018) six-factor model (FF6) that augments their five-factor model with a momentum factor; and
- Kolari, Liu, and Huang (2021) two-factor ZCAPM based on the market factor and the total market return dispersion factor (i.e., the cross-sectional standard deviation of stocks in the market, or *RD*).

Based on the above test procedures, we initially estimate time-series regression (7.1) for these models using one year of daily returns. Subsequently, we estimate one-month-ahead cross-sectional regression (7.2) both without and with the inclusion of α_i and its corresponding η coefficient, re-

[2] This model is similar to the *q*-factor model of Hou, Xue, and Zhang (2015).

spectively. We denote models augmented with α_i coefficients by adding the letter A (e.g., CAPM is CAPM-A, . . ., ZCAPM is ZCAPM-A).

Except for the ZCAPM, all of the asset pricing models contain an alpha intercept in their regression specification. As discussed in Chapter 4, the empirical ZCAPM does not have an alpha intercept. To estimate an alpha for the ZCAPM, we use the average of the residual error terms in its expectation-maximization (EM) regression. Precedent for this approach for estimating alpha can be found in Fama and French (2020), who used average residual error terms for a mathematical asset pricing model with no intercept to provide an estimate of alpha. In typical OLS regression asset pricing models, average residual errors are approximately zero; however, for both EM regression estimation of the ZCAPM and the Fama and French mathematical asset pricing model, average residual errors are nonzero.

Data

For our analyses, we utilize a variety of different test assets. First, from Chapter 5, we employ daily returns for 133 anomaly portfolios made available by Chen and Zimmerman (2022) from July 1972 to December 2021. Second, as in Chapter 6, we use 47 industry portfolios that have proven to be anomalous to most asset pricing models. Third, 1,000 individual stocks with the largest market capitalization at year end from July 1964 to December 2021 are gathered. According to Ang, Liu, and Schwarz (2020), more efficient tests of whether factors are priced are possible with individual stocks compared to portfolios, especially for two-step cross-sectional regression coefficients. Because asset pricing models generally have difficulty in pricing individual stocks, we consider them to be anomalous assets. Fourth, and last, we repeat the empirical tests of 175 firm and stock sorted portfolios in Kolari, Huang, Liu, and Liao (2024). The authors tested these portfolios for the CAPM and multifactor models but did include the ZCAPM in their tests. Here we report new results that include the ZCAPM. Fifth, and last, we conduct tests using the 86 anomaly portfolios in Japan from Chapter 6.

7.2 Empirical Results

Similar to Kolari et al. (2024), we find that the estimated market prices of risk, or λ_k, for different factor loadings are unchanged for the most part by adding α_i coefficients and associated sensitivity coefficient $\hat{\eta}_\alpha$ to the different asset pricing models. It is apparent that alpha contains missing factors that are unrelated (or uncorrelated) to existing factors in each model. Tables 7.1, 7.2, 7.3 and 7.4 give the empirical results of out-of-sample tests of Jensen's alpha for different test assets.

Table 7.1 Alpha mispricing error tests of different asset pricing models due to missing factors: Out-of-sample Fama-MacBeth cross-sectional tests for 133 anomaly portfolios in the sample period July 1972 to December 2021 This table reports cross-sectional regression alpha mispricing error tests for different asset pricing models using 133 anomaly portfolios in Chen and Zimmerman (2022) for the sample period July 1972 to December 2021. In Chapter 5, we reported the results for these models without alpha mispricing error tests. Based on standard two-step Fama-MacBeth cross-sectional tests, we report out-of-sample (one-month-ahead) estimated market prices of risk denoted $\hat{\lambda}_k$ for the kth factor for the analysis period July 1973 to December 2021. Associated t-statistics are shown below estimated prices of risk. The asset pricing models are: CAPM, Fama and French three-factor model (FF3), Carhart four-factor model (C4), Fama and French five-factor model (FF5), Fama and French six-factor model (FF6), and ZCAPM. Factors in these models are denoted as m (CRSP index excess return, RD (market return dispersion), SMB (size), HML (value), MOM (momentum), RMW (profitability), and CMA (capital investment). Corresponding market prices of risk, or λ_k, for $1, \ldots, K$ factor loadings (and associated t-statistics) are shown in the table. Each cross-sectional regression relation is run after augmentation with Jensen's $\hat{\eta}_\alpha$ coefficients that are estimated for each respective time-series asset pricing model regression. The letter A is added to each model to denote the additional estimation of sensitivity coefficient $\hat{\eta}_\alpha$ related to $\hat{\alpha}_i$ coefficients

Model	$\hat{\alpha}$	$\hat{\eta}_\alpha$	$\hat{\lambda}_m$	$\hat{\lambda}_{RD}$	$\hat{\lambda}_{SMB}$	$\hat{\lambda}_{HML}$	$\hat{\lambda}_{MOM}$	$\hat{\lambda}_{RMW}$	$\hat{\lambda}_{CMA}$	R^2
CAPM-A	0.27	0.44	0.29							0.96
	9.53	7.89	1.37							
FF3-A	0.25	0.42	0.35		–0.06	0.27				0.88
	11.21	10.59	2.01		–0.31	1.81				
C4-A	0.23	0.42	0.24		–0.11	0.25	0.29			0.94
	11.03	11.98	1.40		–0.58	1.78	1.25			
FF5-A	0.24	0.43	0.37		0.06	0.15		0.26	0.26	0.86
	11.32	12.29	2.17		0.33	0.93		1.95	2.39	
FF6-A	0.22	0.43	0.23		0.06	0.19	0.38	0.27	0.24	0.94
	11.04	13.67	1.36		0.35	1.33	1.58	2.26	2.20	
ZCAPM-A	0.26	0.35	0.01	0.81						0.95
	9.70	2.60	1.31	7.65						

Table 7.2 Alpha mispricing error tests of different asset pricing models due to missing factors: Out-of-sample Fama-MacBeth cross-sectional tests for 47 industry portfolios in the sample period July 1972 to December 2021
This table reports cross-sectional regression alpha mispricing error tests for different asset pricing models using 47 industry downloaded from Kenneth French's online database for the sample period July 1972 to December 2021. Based on standard two-step Fama-MacBeth cross-sectional tests, we report out-of-sample (one-month-ahead) estimated market prices of risk denoted $\hat{\lambda}_k$ for the kth factor for the analysis period July 1973 to December 2021. Associated t-statistics are shown below estimated prices of risk. The asset pricing models are: CAPM, Fama and French three-factor model (FF3), Carhart four-factor model (C4), Fama and French five-factor model (FF5), Fama and French six-factor model (FF6), and ZCAPM. Factors in these models are denoted as m (CRSP index excess return), RD (market return dispersion), SMB (size), HML (value), MOM (momentum), RMW (profitability), and CMA (capital investment). Corresponding market prices of risk, or λ_k, for $1, \ldots, K$ factor loadings (and associated t-statistics) are shown in the table. Each cross-sectional regression relation is run after augmentation with Jensen's $\hat{\eta}_\alpha$ coefficients that are estimated for each respective time-series asset pricing model regression. The letter A is added to each model to denote the additional estimation of sensitivity coefficient $\hat{\eta}_\alpha$ related to $\hat{\alpha}_i$ coefficients

Model	$\hat{\alpha}$	$\hat{\eta}_\alpha$	$\hat{\lambda}_m$	$\hat{\lambda}_{RD}$	$\hat{\lambda}_{SMB}$	$\hat{\lambda}_{HML}$	$\hat{\lambda}_{MOM}$	$\hat{\lambda}_{RMW}$	$\hat{\lambda}_{CMA}$	R^2
CAPM-A	0.57	0.21	0.45							0.87
	2.73	4.33	1.90							
FF3-A	0.63	0.20	0.33		0.13	0.13				0.74
	2.96	4.46	1.30		0.87	1.02				
C4-A	0.67	0.18	0.29		0.12	0.05	0.19			0.73
	3.20	4.23	1.19		0.81	0.41	0.91			
FF5-A	0.61	0.19	0.35		0.12	0.14		0.21	0.16	0.76
	2.74	4.38	1.40		0.81	1.09		1.94	1.55	
FF6-A	0.76	0.19	0.19		0.11	0.09	0.17	0.22	0.13	0.73
	3.44	4.46	0.79		0.75	0.71	0.79	1.98	1.29	
ZCAPM-A	0.64	-0.03	0.02	0.31						0.83
	3.09	-0.23	1.65	3.35						

Table 7.3 Alpha mispricing error tests of different asset pricing models due to missing factors: Out-of-sample Fama-MacBeth cross-sectional tests for 1,000 individual largest market capitalization stocks in the sample period July 1964 to December 2021. This table reports cross-sectional regression tests for 1,000 individual largest market capitalization stocks for the sample period July 1964 to December 2021. Based on standard two-step Fama-MacBeth cross-sectional tests, we report out-of-sample (one-month-ahead) estimated market prices of risk denoted $\hat{\lambda}_k$ for the kth factor for the analysis period July 1964 to December 2021. Associated t-statistics are shown below estimated prices of risk. The asset pricing models are: CAPM, Fama and French three-factor model (FF3), Carhart four-factor model (C4), Fama and French five-factor model (FF5), Fama and French six-factor model (FF6), and ZCAPM. Factors in these models are denoted as m (CRSP index excess return, *RD* (market return dispersion), *SMB* (size), *HML* (value), *MOM* (momentum), *RMW* (profitability), and *CMA* (capital investment). Corresponding market prices of risk, or λ_k, for $1, \ldots, K$ factor loadings (and associated t-statistics) are shown in the table. Each cross-sectional regression model relation is re-run after augmentation with Jensen's $\hat{\eta}_\alpha$ coefficients from its respective time-series asset pricing model regression. The letter A is added to each model to denote the additional estimation of sensitivity coefficient $\hat{\eta}_\alpha$ related to $\hat{\alpha}_i$ coefficients

Model	$\hat{\alpha}$	$\hat{\eta}_\alpha$	$\hat{\lambda}_m$	$\hat{\lambda}_{RD}$	$\hat{\lambda}_{SMB}$	$\hat{\lambda}_{HML}$	$\hat{\lambda}_{MOM}$	$\hat{\lambda}_{RMW}$	$\hat{\lambda}_{CMA}$
CAPM-A	0.53	0.10	0.09						
	(4.15)	(4.56)	(0.52)						
CAPM	0.57		0.10						
	(4.20)		(0.60)						
FF3-A	0.45	0.10	0.15		–0.00	0.14			
	(3.92)	(4.67)	(1.02)		(–0.02)	(1.52)			
FF3	0.47		0.15		0.05	0.09			
	(4.05)		(1.01)		(0.55)	(0.94)			
C4-A	0.45	0.09	0.14		0.01	0.10	0.01		
	(4.07)	(4.84)	(0.95)		(0.11)	(1.21)	(0.04)		
C4	0.50		0.12		0.06	0.05	0.09		
	(4.34)		(0.87)		(0.75)	(0.65)	(0.66)		
F5-A	0.43	0.09	0.20		0.02	0.09		0.20	0.06
	(3.85)	(4.64)	(1.39)		(0.26)	(1.00)		(2.84)	(0.85)
FF5	0.45		0.20		0.07	0.04		0.18	0.06
	(4.04)		(1.40)		(0.84)	(0.42)		(2.64)	(0.94)
FF6-A	0.44	0.09	0.17		0.02	0.06	0.03	0.20	0.04
	(4.05)	(4.82)	(1.28)		(0.28)	(0.75)	(0.25)	(2.83)	(0.66)
FF6	0.48		0.16	0.07		0.02	0.11	0.17	0.04
	(4.36)		(1.18)	(0.86)		(0.22)	(0.84)	(2.62)	(0.66)
ZCAPM-A	0.53	0.07	0.09	0.16					
	(4.22)	(1.72)	(0.55)	(3.43)					
ZCAPM	0.53		0.11	0.15					
	(4.18)		(0.66)	(3.45)					

Table 7.4 Alpha mispricing error tests of different asset pricing models due to missing factors: Out-of-sample Fama-MacBeth cross-sectional tests for 175 firm and stock sorted test asset portfolios in the sample period July 1964 to December 2021
This table reports cross-sectional regression alpha mispricing error tests for the the ZCAPM using 175 firm and stock sorted portfolios downloaded from Kenneth French's online database for the sample period July 1964 to December 2021. Kolari, Liu, Huang, and Liu (2024) used these test asset portfolios to conduct tests of the CAPM and OLS multifactor models. Here extend their analyses by providing results for the ZCAPM, which was not tested in their study. First, using one year of daily returns from July 1963 to June 1964, we estimate empirical ZCAPM (see Chapters 4–6) by means of expectation-maximization (EM) regression analyses. Second, using out-of-sample (one-month-ahead) excess returns in July 1964, we run a Fama and MacBeth (1973) cross-sectional regression using the estimated risk loadings (coefficients) from the time-series regression for the ZCAPM. This two-step process is rolled forward one month at a time to December 2021. Averages of estimated market prices of risk for average market beta loadings and market return dispersion loadings, or λ_m and λ_{RD}, and associated t-statistics are shown in the table. The ZCAPM is re-run after augmentation with Jensen's α_i estimates (denoted ZCAPM-A), which are computed as the average of the residual error terms. The sensitivity coefficient with respect to α_i coefficients is denoted η_α. Daily riskless U.S. Treasury bill rates and CRSP value-weighted returns are downloaded from French's website. Daily measures of cross-sectional return dispersion for the ZCAPM are computed as the cross-sectional value-weighted standard deviation of returns for all common stocks on CRSP. Estimated R^2 values are computed using a single equation cross-sectional regression for the entire analysis period. The model is rerun with the additional estimation of sensitivity coefficient $\hat{\eta}_\alpha$ related to $\hat{\alpha}_i$ coefficients. We denote this model as ZCAPM-A

Model	Intercept	η_α	λ_a	λ_{RD}	R^2
ZCAPM-A	0.51	0.14	0.14	0.44	0.94
	(2.72)	(1.48)	(0.72)	(5.43)	
ZCAPM	0.56		0.10	0.44	0.89
	(2.95)		(0.49)	(5.47)	

133 Anomaly Portfolios

For the 133 anomaly portfolios in Table 7.1, focusing on column three with $\hat{\eta}_\alpha$ coefficients and associated t-values, we see that this alpha sensitivity coefficient is highly statistically significant in all models. For the CAPM augmented with $\hat{\alpha}_i$ coefficients, or CAPM-A, the t-statistic for $\hat{\eta}_\alpha = 0.44$ is 7.89, which strongly supports the inference that missing factors are contained in the time-series regression $\hat{\alpha}_i$ estimates. Likewise, the augmented Fama and French three-factor model (FF3-A), Carhart four-factor model (C4-A), and Fama and French five-, and six-factor models (FF5-A and FF6-A) have t-statistics for $\hat{\eta}_\alpha$ in the range of 8.81 to 13.61. These very large t-values imply that missing factors exist for these models. The augmented ZCAPM-A has the lowest t-value associated with $\hat{\eta}_\alpha$ at 2.60 that is significant at the 5 percent level; nonetheless, it, is much less significant than in the other models.

It is interesting that the R^2 values in Table 7.1 for models augmented with $\hat{\alpha}_i$ coefficients are very high at over 90 percent in most cases. The CAPM-A and ZCAPM-A have near perfect goodness-of-fit with R^2 estimates of96 percent and 95 percent, respectively. Recall from cross-sectional regression tests of these models using 133 anomaly portfolios in Table 5.2 in Chapter 5 that the CAPM had an R^2 value of only 1 percent. After augmenting the CAPM with $\hat{\alpha}_i$ coefficients, the R^2 value jumps dramatically. In Chapter 5, the FF6 model (without alpha augmentation) had an R^2 value of only 19 percent, whereas the ZCAPM is much higher at 84 percent.

The magnitudes of estimated $\hat{\eta}_\alpha$s in Table 7.1 range from a low of 0.35 for the ZCAPM-A to a high of 0.44 for the CAPM-A. The augmented FF6-A model has an $\hat{\eta}_\alpha$ estimate of 0.43. These $\hat{\eta}_\alpha$ estimates indicate that mispricing error contained in α_i intercepts accounts for 35 percent to 44 percent of out-of-sample test asset portfolio excess returns. Thus, it is apparent that mispricing errors in alphas are important in explaining out-of-sample anomaly portfolio excess returns.

In sum, our results suggest that all models have missing factors. However, the missing factor problem is statistically much more significant in the case of the CAPM and well-known OLS multifactor models than for the ZCAPM.

47 Industry Portfolios

Table 7.2 reports the missing factor test results for the 47 industry portfolios. There we see that all augmented models have highly significant estimated $\hat{\eta}_\alpha$ coefficients with t-values in the range of 4.23 to 4.46, with the exception of the ZCAPM. Unlike the anomaly portfolios, the $\hat{\eta}_\alpha$ coefficient for the ZCAPM is negative and insignificant. These results indicate that, in contrast to the other models, no missing factors exist in the ZCAPM. Again R^2 values are noticeably boosted for all models relative to their values without $\hat{\alpha}_i$ coefficient augmentation reported in Table 6.2 of Chapter 6.

1,000 Individual Stocks with Largest Market Capitalization

Table 7.3 contains the results for 1,000 individual stocks with the largest market capitalization among the population of CRSP database stocks on the last trading day of each sample year. Again focusing on the $\hat{\eta}_\alpha$ coefficient results in column three, with the exception of ZCAPM-A, all $\hat{\alpha}_i$ augmented models have significant $\hat{\eta}_\alpha$ sensitivity coefficients at the 5 percent level. Like the industry portfolios, the only significant market price of risk for the OLS multifactor models is λ_{RMW} associated with profitabililty loadings (i.e., t-statistics in the range of 2.62 to 2.84), and the market price of risk λ_{RD} associated with market return dispersion loadings. The latter market price of risk λ_{RD} achieves the highest t-statistic of 3.43 and 3.45 in the ZCAPM and ZCAPM-A models, respectively. These t-statistics exceed the 3.0 threshold recommended by Harvey, Liu, and Zhu (2016) and Chordia, Goyal, and Saretto (2020) for avoiding false discoveries.

As in Kolari et al. (2024), the estimated λ_k estimates for different factor loadings are unchanged by the addition of $\hat{\alpha}_i$ estimates and sensitivity coefficients $\hat{\eta}_\alpha$ for the most part. Hence, potential missing factors contained in $\hat{\alpha}_i$ coefficients have little or no correlation with other factors in the models. Notice that we do not report R^2 values due the unavailability of daily returns of many individual stocks throughout the entire sample. Overall, contrary to other models, our findings support the ZCAPM as a complete model with no missing factors.

To investigate further, we compute zeta risk premiums equal to $Z^*_{ia}\sigma_{at}$ for each individual stock in the one year estimation periods.[3] A total of 690 one month rolling estimates of zeta risk premiums is obtained for each of

[3] See the time-series regression form of the empirical ZCAPM in Eq. (4.11) of Chapter 4.

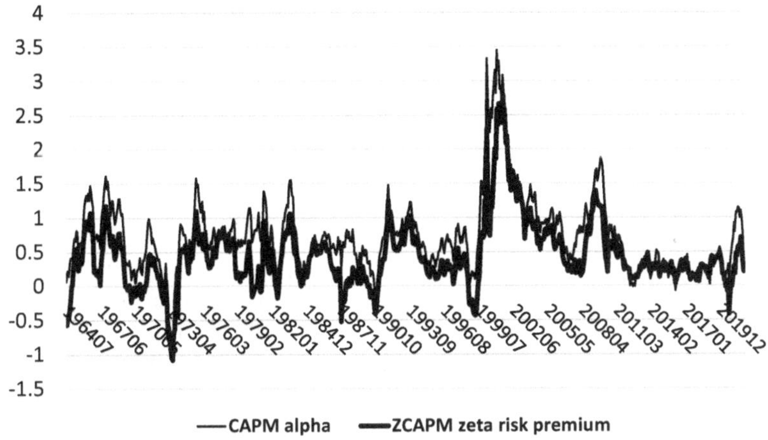

Fig. 7.1 This graph in the one-month rolling mean CAPM alpha ($\bar{\alpha}$) values and mean zeta risk premiums ($Z^*_{iM}\sigma_{Mt}$) over time estimated from time-series regressions of the CAPM and the empirical ZCAPM using one year of daily excess returns for 1,000 individual stocks with largest market capitalization at year-end of this estimation window. Values are scaled to monthly percent returns. The time-series regression for each model is initially estimated using daily returns from July 1963 to June 1964, and subsequent regressions are estimated by rolling forward one month at a time until November 2021 to obtain series of 690 values

the 1,000 stocks (i.e., a matrix containing 690 rows over time and 1,000 columns of stock portfolios).[4] In each year for the 1,000 stocks, the mean zeta risk premium is computed to generate 690 mean estimates over time.

Averaging these results for the 1,000 stocks, Fig. 7.1 illustrates mean CAPM alphas and mean zeta risk premiums over time. Exceptionally, the magnitudes of these two series are almost the same over time with an estimated correlation coefficient of $\rho = 0.98$. In other words, zeta risk premiums and CAPM alphas are almost identical to one another! These results are similar to those for 222 test asset portfolios studied by Kolari et al. (2024), who found that CAPM alphas were almost the same as zeta risk

[4] To compute the zeta risk premium equal to $Z^*_{i,a}\sigma_{at}$, we begin by calculating market return dispersion, or σ_{at}, in percent terms. We estimate $Z^*_{i,a}$ in each one year estimation period for a given portfolio and multiply it by the average daily σ_{at} during the year. To convert from daily to monthly zeta risk premiums, this quantity is multiplied by 21.

premiums in the ZCAPM over time. Based on these findings, we infer that zeta risk premiums almost completely explain CAPM alphas that contain mispricing factors' risk premiums.

175 Firm and Stock Sorted Portfolios

We next repeat the mispricing error tests in Kolari et al. (2024) for 175 firm and stock sorted portfolios downloaded from Kenneth French's online database. In their tests, very significant $\hat{\eta}_\alpha$ sensitivity coefficients were obtained for OLS multifactor models in our previous tables. Adding to their tests, we provide results for the ZCAPM, which was excluded in their analyses. As shown in Table 7.4, the $\hat{\eta}_\alpha$ estimate is not significant. Thus, our results indicate that, unlike prominent multifactor models, the ZCAPM has no missing factors.

86 Anomaly Portfolios in Japan

In Chapter 6, we reported out-of-sample, Fama-MacBeth cross-sectional regression tests of different asset pricing models for 86 anomaly portfolios in Japan. Here we repeat those tests but augment the cross-sectional regressions with $\hat{\alpha}_i$ coefficients from the models. Table 7.5 shows the results. The $\hat{\eta}_\alpha$ estimates for the CAPM-A, FF3-A, and C4-A models are significant with t-statistics of 2.45, 2.25, and 2.26, respectively. Only the ZCAPM-A model has an insignificant $\hat{\eta}_\alpha$ estimate. All R^2 estimates are very high at 98 percent. Unlike the results for U.S. anomaly portfolios in Table 7.1, these results indicate that the ZCAPM has no missing factors.

Implications to Model Validity

The clear implication of our out-of-sample cross-sectional regression tests for the significance of missing factors is that, compared to other well-known asset pricing models under study, the ZCAPM is the most complete asset pricing model with little or no evidence of a missing factor. When testing the 133 anomaly portfolios, we did find some evidence of a missing factor in the ZCAPM but not in other test assets, including industry portfolios, individual stocks, firm and stock sorted portfolios, and Japanese anomaly portfolios. Of course, anomaly portfolios are test assets that are difficult price for an asset pricing model and earn abnormally high returns over time on a persistent basis. Even so, given the much lower t-value for sensi-

Table 7.5 Alpha mispricing error tests of different asset pricing models due to missing factors: Out-of-sample Fama-MacBeth cross-sectional tests for 86 Japan anomaly portfolios in the sample period July 1972 to December 2021
This table reports cross-sectional regression alpha mispricing error tests for different asset pricing models using 86 Japan anomaly portfolios in Jensen, Kelly, and Pedersen (2023) for the sample period July 1972 to December 2021. In Chapter 6, we reported the results for these models without alpha mispricing error tests. Based on standard two-step Fama-MacBeth cross-sectional tests, we report out-of-sample (one-month-ahead) estimated market prices of risk denoted $\hat{\lambda}_k$ for the kth factor for the analysis period July 1973 to December 2021. Associated t-statistics are shown below estimated prices of risk. The asset pricing models are: CAPM, Fama and French three-factor model (FF3), Carhart four-factor model (C4), Fama and French five-factor model (FF5), Fama and French six-factor model (FF6), and ZCAPM. Factors in these models are denoted as m (CRSP index excess return, RD (market return dispersion), SMB (size), HML (value), and MOM (momentum). Corresponding market prices of risk, or λ_k, for $1, \ldots, K$ factor loadings (and associated t-statistics) are shown in the table. Each cross-sectional regression relation is run after augmentation with Jensen's $\hat{\eta}_\alpha$ coefficients that are estimated for each respective time-series asset pricing model regression. The letter A is added to each model to denote the additional estimation of sensitivity coefficient $\hat{\eta}_\alpha$ related to $\hat{\alpha}_i$ coefficients

Model	$\hat{\alpha}$	$\hat{\eta}_\alpha$	$\hat{\lambda}_m$	$\hat{\lambda}_{RD}$	$\hat{\lambda}_{SMB}$	$\hat{\lambda}_{HML}$	$\hat{\lambda}_{MOM}$	R^2
CAPM-A	0.07	0.16	−1.22					0.98
	2.20	2.45	−1.20					
FF3-A	0.09	0.14	0.14		−0.40	0.39		0.98
	3.02	2.25	0.16		−0.97	0.92		
C4-A	0.08	0.14	0.18		−0.31	0.31	0.20	0.98
	3.00	2.26	0.21		−0.71	0.71	0.34	
ZCAPM-A	0.07	0.24	−1.07	0.24				0.98
	2.48	1.24	−1.16	2.15				

tivity coefficient $\hat{\eta}_\alpha$ in the case of the ZCAPM compared to other models, mispricing factors are considerably less significant for the ZCAPM than the other multifactor models.

Based on these findings, we recommend future research on the exploration of possible improvements in the empirical specification of the ZCAPM to eliminate mispricing factors in anomaly portfolios. For example, as suggested in Kolari, Liu, and Pynnonen (2024, Chapters 7–10), the ZCAPM can be enhanced by replacing the CRSP market index as the proxy for the average market return by a portfolio closer to the global minimum variance portfolio in the Markowitz (1959) mean-variance investment portfolio. Further research is warranted on the market factors in the empirical specification of the ZCAPM. Moreover, because the ZCAPM employs the EM algorithm to estimate the probability of a hidden or latent variable related to the sensitivity of security returns to market return dispersion and related zeta risk, it falls within the field of machine learning (ML) and artificial intelligence. It may be possible to improve the EM algorithm procedures in the ML estimation of the empirical ZCAPM.

Lastly, the traditional in-sample GRS joint alpha test can be supplemented with the Kolari et al. (2024) out-of-sample, cross-sectional regression alpha test. In their paper, Fama and French (1993) found that joint alphas for 25 size and value sorted portfolios were approximately zero for the three-factor model in their sample period. Kolari et al. (2024) repeated the GRS test using a longer sample period but found joint alphas were not zero. In both of these in-sample GRS sample periods, they reported that out-of-sample η_α coefficients were significant. Hence, even if joint alphas are zero based on the in-sample GRS test, it is useful to conduct out-of-sample cross-sectional regression tests of alpha coefficients.

7.3 Summary and Implications

In this chapter, we tested the validity of different asset pricing models using a new cross-sectional regression test of alpha mispricing error by Kolari, Liu, Huang, and Liao (2024). Unlike the in-sample GRS test of jointly equal alphas applied by many researchers, the cross-sectional alpha test is out-of-sample and can be used for not only linear models but nonlinear models. Easy to implement with standard two-step Fama-MacBeth regression methods, alpha coefficients estimated for an asset pricing model in a time-series regression are incorporated as an independent variable in a cross-sectional regression. The coincident estimated sensitivity coefficient (denoted $\hat{\eta}_\alpha$) indicates the significance of alpha mispricing error (due to missing factors not contained in an asset pricing model) on out-of-sample returns (e.g., returns in the next month after alphas are estimated in the time-series regression for a model). More precisely, it measures the proportionate contribution of missing factors in a model to the future returns of sample test assets.

We conducted out-of-sample tests of alphas for the following models: CAPM, Fama and French three-, five-, and six-factor models, Carhart four-factor model, and ZCAPM. Different test assets were used: 133 anomaly portfolios, 47 industry portfolios, 1,000 individual stocks with the highest market capitalizations, 175 firm and stock sorted portfolios, and 86 anomaly portfolios in Japan. With the exception of the ZCAPM, all of the models exhibited highly significant $\hat{\eta}_\alpha$ sensitivity coefficients with respect to alpha mispricing terms. Thus, we inferred that missing factors exist in most models. By contrast, for different test assets, the $\hat{\eta}_\alpha$ sensitivity coefficients were normally insignificant for the ZCAPM. Only for the 133 anomaly portfolios was $\hat{\eta}_\alpha$ significant (but less significantly than other models). These results strongly support the ZCAPM as a valid asset pricing model. Other models consistently failed out-of-sample alpha mispricing tests.

Some important implications of our findings are as follows.

- Both cross-sectional tests of factor loading significance and goodness-of-fit as well as maximum Sharpe ratio tests based on time-series regression models can be supplemented with our cross-sectional regression test for missing factors.
- Even if in-sample GRS tests of alpha are jointly zero, out-of-sample cross-sectional alpha tests can imply that missing factors exist in an asset pricing model.
- Consistent with recent cross-sectional test results by Hollstein and Prokopczuk (2022), prominent equity pricing models did not well explain the cross-section of stock returns due to existence of missing factors.
- Empirical tests using a recent asset pricing model dubbed the ZCAPM imply that little or no mispricing error was apparent in cross-sectional regression tests of alpha sensitivity coefficients $\hat{\eta}_\alpha$. Also, graphical analyses showed that zeta risk premiums in the ZCAPM are almost identical to CAPM alphas over time. These findings suggest that, with the exception of anomaly stock portfolios, no missing factors exist in the ZCAPM. By implication, significant alpha tests for the CAPM and prominent multifactor models are not due to a trivial mechanical relation between alphas and out-of-sample cross-sectional returns. In view of its superior asset pricing performance in cross-sectional tests, further research on the ZCAPM is recommended.
- Our results imply that alpha mispricing errors in the CAPM are almost completely explained by zeta risk premiums in the ZCAPM. A common criticism is that Jensen's alpha is large and positive thereby

invalidating the CAPM. By adding zeta risk to the CAPM, this problem is resolved for the most part.

- How do other proposed multifactor models perform in out-of-sample cross-sectional alpha tests? Further research is needed to answer this question.
- If the ZCAPM almost completely captures missing stock pricing factors, the ongoing intensive search by researchers for missing long/short factors in asset pricing models can be discontinued. Also, there is little apparent need to search for behavioral explanations of abnormal stock returns not explained by multifactor models. Our ZCAPM results suggest that the rational investors price stocks based on systematic risk factors related to average market returns and the market dispersion of stock returns. Because fairly accurate prices with minimal error are obtained from available market information employed by the ZCAPM, our empirical results suggest that the stock market is efficient.

References

Ang, A., J. Liu, and K. Schwarz. 2020. Using stocks or portfolios in tests of factor models. *Journal of Financial and Quantitative Analysis* 55: 709–750.

Barillas, F., and J. Shanken. 2018. Comparing asset pricing models. *Journal of Finance*, 715 –754.

Carhart, M. M. 1997. On persistence in mutual fund performance. *Journal of Finance* 52: 57–82.

Chen, A. Y., and T. Zimmerman. 2022. Open source cross-sectional asset pricing. *Critical Finance Review* 11: 207–264.

Chordia, T., A. Goyal, and A. Saretto. 2020. Anomalies and false rejections. *Review of Financial Studies* 33: 2134–2179.

Cochrane, J. H. 2011. Presidential address: Discount rates. *Journal of Finance* 56: 1047–1108.

Fama, E. F., and K. R. French. 1992. The cross-section of expected stock returns. *Journal of Finance* 47: 427–465.

Fama, E. F., and K. R. French. 1993. Common risk factors in the returns on stocks and bonds. *Journal of Financial Economics* 33: 3–56.

Fama, E. F., and K. R. French. 2015. A five-factor asset pricing model. *Journal of Financial Economics* 116: 1–22.

Fama, E. F., and K. R. French. 2018. Choosing factors. *Journal of Financial Economics* 128: 234–252.

Fama, E. F., and K. R. French. 2020. Comparing cross-section and time-series factor models. *Review of Financial Studies* 33: 1892–1926.

Fama, E. F., and J. D. MacBeth. 1973. Risk, return, and equilibrium: Empirical tests. *Journal of Political Economy* 81: 607–636.

Ferson, W. E., S. K. Nallareddy, and B. Xie. 2013. The "out-of-sample" performance of long-run risk models. *Journal of Financial Economics* 107: 537–556.

Gibbons, M. R., S. A. Ross, and J. Shanken. 1989. A test of the efficiency of a given portfolio. *Econometrica* 57: 1121–1152.

Giglio, S., and D. Xiu. 2021. Asset pricing with omitted factors. *Journal of Political Economy* 129: 1947–1990.

Harvey, C. R., Y. Liu, and H. Zhu. 2016. and the cross-section of expected returns. *Review of Financial Studies* 29: 5–68.

Hollstein, F., and M. Prokopczuk. 2022. Testing factor models in the cross section. *Journal of Banking and Finance* 145: 106626.

Hou, K., C. Xue, and L. Zhang. 2015. Digesting anomalies: An investment approach. *Review of Financial Studies* 28: 650–705.

Jensen, M. C. 1968. The performance of mutual funds in the period 1945–1964. *Journal of Finance* 23: 389–416.

Kolari, J. W., W. Liu, and J. Z. Huang. 2021. *A New Model of Capital Asset Prices: Theory and Evidence.* Cham, Switzerland: Palgrave Macmillan.

Kolari, J. W., J. Z. Huang, W. Liu, and H. Liao. 2024. A cross-sectional asset pricing test of model validity. *Applied Economics* 56, forthcoming.

Kolari, J. W., W. Liu, and S. Pynnonen. 2024. *Professional Investment Portfolio Management: Boosting Performance with Machine-Made Portfolios and Stock Market Evidence.* Cham, Switzerland: Palgrave Macmillan.

Markowitz, H. M. 1959. *Portfolio Selection: Efficient Diversification of Investments.* New York, NY: Wiley.

Simin, T. 2008. The poor performance of asset pricing models. *Journal of Financial and Quantitative Analysis* 43: 335–380.

Stambaugh, R. F., and Y. Yuan. 2017. Mispricing factors. *Review of Financial Studies* 30: 1270–1315.

PART V

Conclusion

CHAPTER 8

Machine Learning in Asset Pricing: The Dominance of the ZCAPM

Abstract The empirical results in this book have shown that machine learning is a powerful new approach to asset pricing that can boost predictive performance of asset pricing models. The ZCAPM of Kolari, Liu, and Huang (2021) takes advantage of machine learning in estimating the empirical ZCAPM via the expectation-maximization (EM) algorithm in regression analyses. The ZCAPM contains a hidden or latent variable that determines the positive versus negative sensitivity of asset returns to changes in the cross-sectional return dispersion of assets in the market. It is unknown if a stock will be positively or negatively affected the market return dispersion at any given time. In estimating the empirical ZCAPM regression, the EM algorithm incorporates information about asset returns over the past year. From this information, it estimates a probability (or p value) that an asset or portfolio of assets will have a positive sensitivity to market return dispersion. As it turns out, from an artificial intelligence perspective, this hidden probability is crucial to the predictive success of the ZCAPM in explaining stock market anomalies in our out-of-sample cross-sectional regression tests. Without it, the model would not work in predicting anomaly portfolio returns. Here we review the material in previous chapters. Hundreds of long/short portfolios of stock market anomalies have been constructed by researchers. Because asset pricing models cannot explain their abnormally high average stock returns, these portfolios are considered to be anomalies. Importantly, the inability of prominent asset pricing models to explain economically interesting anomalies strikes a major blow to the famous efficient market hypothesis (EMH) of Nobel Prize winner Professor Eugene Fama.

J. W. Kolari et al., *Asset Pricing Models and Market Efficiency*,
https://doi.org/10.1007/978-3-031-92901-3_8

Asset prices should be related to their market risks. If systematic market risks in asset pricing models cannot explain their prices, the EMH is rejected. In its place, behavioral theories have proposed irrational investor behavior grounded in inherent biases in human behavior to potentially explain stock market anomalies' returns. Given the rising tide of anomalies, which are outpacing the ability of multifactor models in asset pricing to keep up with them, behavioralists have gained a solid footing in the anomalies literature. The stock market evidence documented in this book sheds new light on the longstanding yet increasing debate between efficient markets and behavioral theories of asset pricing. We compared the most prominent asset pricing models in the finance literature in terms of their ability to predict in out-of-sample tests the stock market returns of hundreds of anomaly portfolios. Also, we included in our tests the ZCAPM a lesser known asset pricing model that employs expectation-maximization (EM) algorithm optimization methods to estimate a hidden signal variable. Strikingly, the ZCAPM is the only model that does a good job of predicting the returns of large numbers of stock market anomaly portfolios (i.e., long/short portfolios based on accounting and market characteristics of firms). Virtually all of the anomalies tested are explained by the ZCAPM on an out-of-sample basis. Our ZCAPM evidence reverses the above mentioned trends in asset pricing and market efficiency. Given that the ZCAPM can explain anomalies' abnormally high returns over time, our results strongly support the EMH. In turn, behavioral explanations of anomalies are not needed. Also, since prominent multifactor models cannot predict anomaly returns over time, the ZCAPM dominates these models in terms of asset pricing ability. In further tests of model validity, we confirm that the ZCAPM has lower out-of-sample mispricing errors among anomaly portfolios than commonly-used, popular multifactor models. Important implications of our findings are discussed with respect to asset pricing and market efficiency in particular and the field of finance in general. Lastly, we provide closing remarks on the findings of this book.

8.1 The Rise of Anomalies

Professor Eugene Fama (1965, 1970) proposed the efficient market hypothesis (EMH). He argued that asset prices should reflect all available information. Rational investors evaluate information that is incorporated into prices in the market. As computers, the internet, smart phones, big data, etc. have become ubiquitous in society, prices should become more efficient compared to the past. In his 2013 Nobel Prize lecture, he proposed two pillars of asset pricing consisting of market efficiency and asset pricing models. If asset pricing models could explains asset returns, we can conclude that markets are efficient. However, the failure of asset pricing models implies either the models are bad or the market is inefficient. In this book, we will show that the failure of widely-used multifactor models is due a bad model problem and, therefore, not due to market inefficiency.

Responding to the failure of asset pricing models to explain the growing number of stock market anomalies, behavioral theories have gained traction. Kahneman and Tversky (1979) posited that investors are more sensitive to losses than gains (i.e., prospect theory). DeBondt and Thaler (DeBondt and Thaler 1985, DeBondt and Thaler 1987) proposed that investors tend to overweight recent information and underweight past information, which helps to explain stock price reversals over time. Shiller (1981) was awarded the Nobel Prize in Economics with Fama in 2013 due to his work on speculative bubbles in markets, market crashes, and potential psychological factors that contribute to such episodes. Other research by Daniel, Hirshleifer, and Subrahmanyam (1998) and Barberis, Shleifer, and Vishney (1998) developed behavioral models of asset pricing based on biases in human psychology. Investor overconfidence, over- and underreaction, over- and underweighting data, sentiment, and other biases are employed to better understand patterns in asset prices over time. Practitioners have implemented trading strategies that seek to exploit market anomalies due to behavioral biases.

Trading strategies seek to form long/short stock portfolios that earn abnormally high average returns. For example, momentum portfolios are comprised of long positions in past winner stocks and short positions in past loser stocks. Fama and French (1993) created long/short portfolios that are long small stocks and short big stocks as well as long value stocks and short growth stocks. They used these portfolios as asset pricing factors in their three-factor model to help explain size and value anomalies. The success of their model prompted other researchers to add more long/short factors to models to explain other anomalies. Unfortunately, as factors are added as predictors in ordinary least squares (OLS) regression models, various multifactors become increasingly correlated with one another. In this case, the parameter (or systematic risk measures) become unstable and can switch signs from positive to negative and vice versa. The R^2 estimates of goodness-of-fit can begin to decline after taking into account the declining degrees of freedom in the regression model. Overfitting can lead to an unstable covariance matrix that decreases out-of-sample model performance. Thus, multifactor models are naturally limited in the extent to which they can be augmented with hundreds of factors to explain hundreds of anomalies.

There are two possible solutions to the problem of overfitted multifactor models. One solution is to build a parsimonious multifactor model that contains relatively powerful factors with the ability to explain hundreds of anomalies. The ZCAPM in this book falls into this category. Only two factors – namely, an average market return and the cross-sectional return dispersion of the market (viz., the first and second moments of daily stock returns in the market) – are needed in the ZCAPM to do an excellent job of explaining hundreds of long/short stock portfolio anomalies.

A second solution is to build complex models using machine learning that are not bound by statistical restrictions. Focusing on the out-of-sample predictability of returns, such models could capture nonlinearities, interrelationships, and other complexities among many factors in asset pricing. Along these lines, a recent paper by Kelly, Malamud, and Zhou (2024) makes the case that complex models based on machine learning with many predictor variables outperform simpler models in terms of predicting future returns. The authors documented some evidence to support this proposition by predicting the CRSP value-weighted index using 15 predictors in the sample period 1926 to 2020. However, large predictor sets with greater complexity were not tested. Also, pertinent to the present book, no prediction analyses of long/short trading strategies for anomaly portfolios are provided. Even so, they emphasized the need for machine learning methods that go beyond the typical linear OLS regression setup of traditional multifactor models. We agree. The ZCAPM's use of the EM algorithm to estimate a hidden signal variable may well be unfamiliar to PhD level finance academics and Quants in professional finance circles, but it is well known in the hard sciences and is consistent with the current trend toward machine learning in asset pricing that seeks to predict out-of-sample returns.

Concerning the artificial intelligence (AI) difficulty of prediction in scientific studies, Breiman (2001) has noted:

> Prediction is rarely perfect. There are usually many unmeasured variables whose effect is referred to as *noise*. But the extent to which the model box emulates nature's box is a measure of how well our model can reproduce the natural phenomenon producing the data. (Breiman, 2001, p. 204)

8.2 Anomaly Stock Portfolios

An increasing number of anomalies were reported by academic researchers over the past 20 years. While concerning to the asset pricing community, McLean and Pontiff (2016) observed that many anomalies tended to diminish and even vanish over time. On an out-of-sample basis, academic publications of anomalies reduced their mispricing. Apparently, practitioners used the anomalies to implement trading strategies that tended to arbitrage away their abnormal profits. Moreover, Chen and Velikov (2023) conducted tests of anomalies after taking into account trading costs and found that their returns decayed after publication.

Even though Jacobs and Müller (2020) confirmed the declining trend of anomalies in the U.S. stock market, extensive tests in 39 international markets indicated that anomalies persisted over time. Additionally, after adjusting for publication bias, Chen and Zimmerman (2020) documented that post-publication returns had only declined about 12.3% on average among U.S. stock market anomalies. Consistent with this study, Bowles, Reed, Ringgenberg, and Thornock (2024) reported that U.S. market anomalies persist immediately after corporate events. They reconciled their findings with diminishing anomalies by pointing out that previous studies have used stale information on a quarterly or annual basis that accounts for declining returns.

Contradicting the anomalies literature, Hou, Zu, and Zhang (2020) contended that, because many anomalies cannot be replicated, these anomalies were false discoveries. They found that, especially for anomalies based on small microcap stocks and trading frictions (e.g., liquidity), replication failed. Also, the authors argued that academic journals do not publish papers with insignificant long/short stock portfolios. A smaller set of papers with significant anomalies achieved publication. In this regard, researchers may have engaged in p-hacking (i.e., data mining) to find significant anomalies in the data.

Further deepening the anomalies debate, Jensen, Kelly, and Pedersen (2023) computed alphas for anomaly portfolio returns using the CAPM market model. After doing so, the risk-adjusted returns of anomalies did not diminish over time. Their analyses showed that the anomaly factors could be replicated and hold in out-of-sample tests. Challenging the international findings of Jacobs and Müller, their results were consistent across 93 countries. Interestingly, they were able to group 153 anomalies into 13 clusters. Rather than hundreds of anomalies, there are only 13 anomaly types or classes. Another study by Favero, Melone, and Tamoni (2023) tested risk-adjusted anomaly returns and produced evidence that supports Jensen et al. Finally, evidence in other studies by Lu, Stambaugh, and Yuan (2017) and Anginer, Ray, Seyhun, and Xiu (2024) confirmed that risk-adjusted anomaly returns persist over time.

8.3 Prominent Multifactor Models and Anomaly Portfolios

Fama and French (1992, 1993) proposed the now famous three-factor model with market, size, and value factors to help explain the size and value anomalies. Small (value) stocks tend to earn higher returns over time than big (growth) stocks. The size and value factors are long/short portfolios known as *multifactors*. For test asset portfolios sorted on size and value firm characteristics, the three-factor model substantially reduced alpha mispricing error (i.e., the intercept parameter). While a major advance in empirical asset pricing, the model had little or no theoretical foundation other than some association with Ross' (1976) arbitrage pricing theory (APT) and Merton's (1973) intertemporal CAPM (ICAPM).

Carhart (1997) expanded the three-factor by adding a momentum factor. Momentum was shown to be a useful long/short portfolio in explaining mutual fund stock returns. Some years later, Fama and French (2015) added profitability and capital investment factors. These two factors were very similar to those in the Hou, Xue, and Zhang's (2015) four-factor q model (augmented with market and size factors).

Similar to the present book, Hou, Xue, and Zhang raised the bar on multifactor model tests by using a large number (viz., 80) long/short anomaly portfolios as test assets. Their q-factor model lowered alpha mispricing error relative to the three-factor model as well as four-factor model containing the momentum factor. Also, the model better explained the momentum anomaly, which they considered to be the most anomalous (unexplained) portfolio in the market.

Stambaugh and Yuan (2017) employed 11 well-known anomalies to form two clusters that were used to construct two new management and performance factors. They tested the resultant four-factor using the same 80 anomaly portfolios in Hou et al. Results tended to favor their model over the Fama and French five-factor as well as Hou et al. four-factor models. Not to be outdone, Fama and French (2018) advanced their six-factor model by adding a momentum factor to their five-factor model.

A major pitfall in traditional multifactor models is the construction of factors from the anomaly portfolios themselves. A resultant model augmented with new anomaly-derived factors performs well in terms of explaining the anomaly portfolios under study; however, it is not proven to work in explaining the returns of other anomalies. Behavioralists continue to discover new anomalies all the time. The current "whack-a-mole" approach to building multifactor models is doomed to failure over time as the factor zoo population grows. Also, anomaly factors tend to shine brightly for a while and then fade in the market, an on-off switching process that can repeat over time for any particular anomaly. Relevant to this discussion, the ZCAPM does not have this issue. Its two factors—specifically, the mean market return and cross-sectional standard deviation of returns—can be used to price all test assets, not only selected anomalies du jour. These systematic risk factors are always "on" so to speak and well explain all long/short stock portfolio anomalies.

A new trend in asset pricing is to use machine learning to conquer the factor hoards. For example, Fama and French (2020) derived cross section factors from cross-sectional regressions. This machine learning approach employs cross-sectional regressions of anomaly portfolios to let the data estimate the so-called *cross section factors*. Encouragingly, cross section factor models outperformed traditional multifactor models in terms of reducing alpha mispricing error. Another study by Lettau and Pelger (2020) employed Principal Components Analysis (PCA) to identify hidden or latent factors in a machine learning context. PCA utilizes statistical dimension reduction methods to find the major factors that explain stock returns. They found smaller mispricing errors for a five-factor PCA model compared to traditional models.

A troubling issue in machine learning (ML) models is that no theory is provided to justify the cross section and PCA factors. In this respect, our ZCAPM relies on ML to estimate the hidden or latent probability (p) of the directional effect of zeta risk on security returns; however, the ZCAPM has strong theoretical foundations in Markowitz (1959) portfolio theory, Sharpe's (1964) CAPM equilibrium pricing theory, and Black's zero-beta CAPM extension of the ZCAPM to risky borrowing rates and short selling. The estimated probability of positive (or negative) sensitivity to market return dispersion is linked to the upper (lower) half of the mean-variance investment parabola. In the ZCAPM, theory guides the specification of factors in the model, not strictly big data and statistical computation.

Another issue in ML models is in-sample rather than out-of-sample tests. Scientifically speaking, out-of-sample tests are more consistent with artificial intelligence (AI) which is predictive in nature. Most asset pricing researchers rely mainly on in-sample Gibbons, Ross, and Shanken (GRS) (1989) tests of the joint equality of alphas for a model. Relatively few studies provide out-of-sample test results that are predictive. Of course, passing out-of-sample tests is much more difficult than in-sample tests. We need to raise the scientific bar on asset pricing model tests by putting more emphasis on AI and prediction ability.

As a final comment, the development of asset pricing models outlined above suggests that competition is fairly intense among researchers to specify the best model. Unfortunately, in all likelihood due to this competition, our ZCAPM has been rejected at all the top finance journals over the past decade. These rejections are unusual in light of the fact that empirical evidence consistently and repeatedly shows that the ZCAPM outperforms all multifactor models in different test assets and sample periods, many times by large margins.

Years ago, Kolari, Liu, and Huang (2012) had early success with the ZCAPM by winning a Best Paper in Investments award at the Financial Management Association Conference (Atlanta, GA), the largest academic and professional finance conference in the world. More recently, Kolari, Huang, Liu, and Liao (2024a, 2024b) have presented anomalies evidence in this book at regional conferences by the Southern Finance Association (Palm Beach Gardens, FL) and Southwestern Finance Association (San Antonio, TX). Over a decade after our earlier award, it was gratifying to win the Best Paper in Investments award at the latter conference. Even so, finance conferences sponsored by top tier finance journals as well as the journals themselves have repeatedly rejected our ZCAPM papers for presentation and publication. As a large body of empirical results accumulated in our published books and papers[1], it has become clear that the ZCAPM empirically dominates popular multifactor models published in the top finance journals. We can only surmise that the ZCAPM is perceived to be a threat to authors of these models, which continue to share widespread acceptance in finance by academics and practitioners.

[1] See Kolari, Liu, and Huang (2021), Kolari, Liu, and Pynnonen (2024, 2023) and references cited therein.

8.4 The ZCAPM and Previous Tests of Anomaly Portfolios

We reviewed the derivation of the theoretical ZCAPM and specification of the empirical ZCAPM in the book by Kolari, Liu, and Huang (2021). As already mentioned, the ZCAPM utilizes the mean market return and cross-sectional standard deviation of returns in the market as systematic risk factors. The coincident systematic risks measure beta and zeta risks, respectively. The cross-sectional return dispersion factor defines the width or span of the Markowitz mean-variance investment parabola. Ceteris paribus, as the parabola increases in width, the returns of asset located in the top (bottom) half of the parabola experience increases (decreases), and vice versa as the parabola decreases in width. Naturally, the mean market return is located somewhere in the middle of the parabola along the axis of symmetry that divides the parabola into two symmetric halves.

The empirical ZCAPM introduces a dummy variable to capture the opposite effects of zeta risk on assets in the top versus bottom halves of the parabola. To estimate the probability (p) that the dummy variable is positive (as opposed to negative), we applied the expectation-maximization algorithm in the regression estimation of beta and zeta risk coefficients. It is important to recognize that p is a hidden or latent variable estimated in the EM algorithm via machine learning (ML) based on prior daily data series for security returns in addition to the mean market and cross-sectional return dispersion factors. With an estimate of p in hand for the ith test asset portfolio, the zeta risk coefficient (Z^*) can be estimated. Thus, the two-factor, nonlinear ZCAPM using the EM algorithm differs markedly from traditional linear multifactor models estimated by means of OLS regression. Like cross section factor and PCA models, the ZCAPM depends on ML for its estimation.

Previous empirical evidence published by Kolari et al. in their book showed that the empirical ZCAPM dominated popular multifactor models in out-of-sample cross-sectional regression tests. Decidedly lower mispricing errors in these out-of-sample tests were apparent in graphs of realized returns compared to predicted (or fitted) returns. The zeta risk coefficient in the ZCAPM was much more significant in the cross-sectional regression analyses than any of the various factors in traditional multifactor models. Finally, the goodness-of-fit (or R^2 values) for the ZCAPM well exceeded those for other multifactor models. In some test asset portfolios, the out-of-sample R^2 values approached near perfect goodness-of-fit. The findings documented in their book support the inference that the ZCAPM is the best performing asset pricing model in extant finance literature.

8.5 The ZCAPM and Large Online Datasets of Anomaly Portfolios

Chen and Zimmerman (2022) and Jensen, Kelly, and Pedersen (2023) have posted online open source datasets for over 250 anomaly portfolios on the internet. Researchers have sifted through the population of stocks trading in the market to ferret out these portfolios in terms of the inability of asset pricing models to explain them. Can the ZCAPM explain these difficult-to-price anomalous portfolios?

Our analyses reported the results of out-of-sample cross-sectional regression tests for 133 anomaly portfolios from Chen and Zimmerman. Using these test asset portfolios, the ZCAPM well outperformed other prominent multifactor models. Both goodness-of-fit estimates of R^2 values and estimates of market prices of risk (i.e., λ) for zeta risk were exceptional relative to other models. R^2 estimates at times exceeded 90 percent which nears perfect explanatory power, a remarkable achievement on an out-of-sample basis! The λ coefficients associated with zeta risk loadings (or Z^*) often had t-statistics in the range of 3 to 7, which is very high compared to other models' significance of market prices of risk. Generally speaking, this high level of significance is unmatched in the asset pricing literature. Further results for 153 anomaly portfolios from Jensen et al. corroborated these findings.

Next, we generated graphs of the out-of-sample predicted (or fitted) excess returns of anomaly portfolios using the ZCAPM compared to their actual or realized excess returns. In these graphs, a 45 degree line depicts perfect out-of-sample prediction of actual returns. To the extent that anomaly portfolios lie off the line, the magnitudes of mispricing errors can be assessed for an asset pricing model. In brief, compared to established multifactor models, the ZCAPM consistently had much small mispricing errors than other models. Due to their ease of interpretation, these mispricing graphs provided particularly compelling evidence in favor of the ZCAPM.

It is extraordinary that the ZCAPM explained virtually all of the anomalies in the cross section of average stock returns. These stunning findings support the efficient market hypothesis (EMH) of Fama (1970). Conversely, traditional multifactor models do a poor job of explaining anomaly portfolio returns for the most part. We infer that the anomalies are indeed anomalous to these models. However, they are not anomalous to the ZCAPM. By implication, rational investors price stocks based on their systematic market risks as reflected by beta and zeta risks in the ZCAPM rather than mispricing. Ergo, behavioral theories of asset pricing are not needed to explain the long/short portfolio returns of stocks in the large datasets under study.

Interpreting the outperformance of the ZCAPM, we argued that the cross-sectional market return dispersion factor in the ZCAPM encapsulates the growing list of factors utilized in multifactor models. Size, value, momentum, and other factors are long/short portfolios that can be considered to be rough measures of return dispersion. Each of these factors represents a slice of the total market dispersion. As these factors are added to multifactor models, the sum of their dispersions will gradually approach the total market dispersion as measured by the cross-sectional standard deviation of all stock returns in the market on any given day. In effect, multifactor models are special cases of the ZCAPM. Also, because the ZCAPM is a special case of the zero-beta CAPM and its derivative CAPM, multifactor models are related to the CAPM. Ironically, multifactor models were widely advocated after Fama and French (1996) declared the CAPM dead; unexpectedly, multifactor models turn out to be related to the CAPM by their link to the ZCAPM and its market return dispersion factor.

8.6 The ZCAPM and Further Tests of Anomaly Portfolios

In further tests, we increased the list of test assets to include long or short portfolio constituents of long/short factors, individual stocks, industry portfolios, and anomaly portfolios in Japan. In general, the results were similar to those for the online anomaly datasets discussed above. The ZCAPM continued to outperform traditional multifactor models in all of these tests. Interestingly, the ZCAPM performed very well with 86 anomaly portfolios in Japan (downloaded from the online data website by Jensen, Kelly, and Pedersen). According to our findings, the ZCAPM was able to price stocks in different countries. Among the different tests assets, industry portfolios were most difficult to price. Further research is needed to develop and test a potential new systematic risk factor related to industry or sector risk.

8.7 Validity Tests of Asset Pricing Models

In a recent paper, Kolari, Huang, Liu, and Liao (2024) developed a validity test for asset pricing models. Using Fama and MacBeth (1973) two-step equations, the authors inserted the alpha mispricing parameter from the first step time-series regression of a model into the second step cross-sectional regression. The coefficient $\hat{\eta}$ (associated with alpha) estimated in this second regression tests whether missing factors exist in the time-series regression model. If η is statistically significant, a missing factor exists. Using a wide variety of test assets, the ZCAPM was the only model to have insignificant $\hat{\eta}$ coefficients in most cases. Traditional multifactor models showed statistically significant evidence of missing factors. Of course, if their factors do not completely span the total cross-sectional distribution of stock returns in the market (i.e., total market dispersion) in the ZCAPM, some missing part of return dispersion would remain. These comparative tests strongly support the ZCAPM as the most valid asset pricing model.

8.8 Implications to Asset Pricing and Market Efficiency

Our results have important implications to future asset pricing research and market efficiency.

(a) Research is recommended on the ZCAPM itself. We used the value-weighted average return on the CRSP index as the mean market return factor. Another possibility is a proxy for the global minimum variance portfolio (denoted G), which lies at the vertex of the parabola on the axis of symmetry. In a recent book, Kolari, Liu, and Pynnonen (2023, Chapter 7) constructed a proxy for G using U.S. stock returns. Using the weighting scheme for portfolio G, a cross-sectional market dispersion factor was computed also. The Sharpe ratio of G was substantially higher than that of the CRSP index. In empirical tests, they found that the ZCAPM was improved by these changes. Is is possible that proxies for G could be improved to further enhance the ZCAPM? Furthermore, since the ZCAPM utilizes machine learning (ML) in its EM algorithm augmented regression estimation, it may be possible to make advances in its estimation procedures.

(b) Our tests revealed that industry portfolios are difficult to price. It is possible that an industry factor would improve matters. Despite the fact that practitioners routinely assess the industry risk of individual firms in stock price evaluations, no industry factor exists at the present time to the authors' knowledge. Further research on this gap in the literature would be useful.

(c) The ZCAPM can be used to construct relatively efficient portfolios that earn high returns per unit total risk. Kolari, Liu, and Pynnonen reported considerable evidence on this potential investment opportunity. Their results confirmed that efficient portfolios based on beta and zeta risk can earn relatively high out-of-sample returns over time. While the authors worked with a large pension fund for a few years to build efficient portfolios, our joint work was interrupted by management changes at the fund. It would be beneficial to partner with a securities firm or pension fund to implement ZCAPM machine learning technology to build high earning portfolios for individuals, businesses, and government agencies. Given the problems in the pension industry with keeping up with pensioner liabilities, we believe that the ZCAPM could provide a viable solution to improving pension investment outcomes for many people.

(d) In view of the ZCAPM's ability to explain anomaly portfolio returns, a question remains about the possible existence of anomalies that are not explained by the ZCAPM (excluding industry portfolios). Such anomalies, if they exist, would be interesting to study, especially from the perspective of behavioral theories. Perhaps inefficiencies do exist in the stock market. They may be persistent or transitory in nature. Future study of possible ZCAPM anomalies is recommended.

8.9 Closing Remarks

Machine learning (ML) is increasingly being applied to the field of asset pricing. Studies on systematic risk measurement, estimation of hidden or latent variables, and other topics central to asset pricing are becoming part of mainstream finance these days. The frontiers of asset pricing are being pushed back by new econometric methods, big data, high speed computers, and human ingenuity to integrate these technologies. Also, artificial intelligence (AI) is rapidly developing to improve out-of-sample predictive power in asset pricing. We believe that AI will be the next step in the evolutionary process.

In this book, we have sought to explain stock market anomalies constructed as long/short stock portfolios. Consistent with the growing practice of AI, our focus has been on the *predictability out of sample* of anomaly portfolio returns, rather than in-sample analyses that are not predictive. Commenting on the rising tide of anomaly portfolios in the finance literature, Cochrane (2011) aptly called this phenomenon the *factor zoo* in which factors are defined as long/short portfolios. So many factor anomalies have been proposed over the past 40 years that multifactor models have been overwhelmed and unable to keep up with them. In the early 1990s, Fama and French's (1993) three-factor model was able to account for size and value stock market anomalies. As asset pricing researchers added more and more factors to multifactor models in attempts to address anomalies, behavioral finance researchers have identified a growing list of anomalies that numbers in the hundreds at the present time.

As the factor zoo has grown, some researchers have sought to develop parsimonious multifactor models that can explain large numbers of anomalies. Most of their analyses are in-sample tests, as opposed to more investable out-of-sample tests. In keeping with parsimonious modeling, the ZCAPM of Kolari, Liu, and Huang (2021) only has two factors—namely, the mean market return and the cross-sectional standard deviation of returns of all stocks in the market (or market return dispersion). These factors are simply the first and second moments of returns of stocks in the market on any given day. Unlike the increasing array of multifactor models, the ZCAPM is derived mathematically as a special case of Black's (1972) zero-beta CAPM. It therefore is based on theory as opposed to ad hoc empirical specification. Also, different from other asset pricing models that include volatility factors, the ZCAPM posits that some stocks will react positively to increases in market return dispersion or volatility, and that other stocks will react negatively. Unfortunately, the direction of stock return sensitivity for any individual stock or portfolio of stocks is hidden or unobservable.

To solve the above missing variable problem, Kolari, Liu, and Huang applied the expectation-maximization algorithm in a regression model dubbed the ZCAPM. The EM algorithm is well-known in hard sciences. In the case of the ZCAPM, EM is used to estimate the probability that the stock return sensitivity to market return dispersion is positive (or negative) for any given security. With this hidden or latent variable estimated via machine learning, the empirical ZCAPM can be specified. We are aware that many researchers are accustomed to a linear OLS model specification in line with traditional multifactor models. However, the ZCAPM breaks new ground in asset pricing by using a nonlinear EM regression specification based on machine learning. We believe that the ZCAPM is a next generation asset pricing technology.

Extensive empirical tests in this book confirmed that the ZCAPM constitutes a quantum leap in asset pricing. Using large online datasets of anomaly portfolios, we showed that, whereas traditional multifactor models do a poor job of explaining anomalies for the most part, the ZCAPM performs quite well and effectively explains all of the hundreds of anomalies in out-of-sample (one-month-ahead) cross-sectional tests. This high level of explanatory power is surprising as even random chance would argue for some anomaly portfolios to be left unexplained. Interestingly, our anomaly datasets contained a number of momentum portfolios that are widely recognized as the most difficult explain in the factor zoo. Even so, the ZCAPM was able to measure their systematic risks and successfully estimate fitted or predicted returns in the next month. Our tests suggest that even the long-standing momentum puzzle in finance is resolved by the ZCAPM.

In view of these findings, research is needed that tests the ZCAPM against other asset pricing models, further develops the ZCAPM by incorporating machine learning and artificial intelligence to enhance its capabilities, and seeks to find anomalies not explained by the ZCAPM. Just as the CAPM led to many derivative models, including the intertemporal, consumption, production, international, and conditional CAPM, we believe that the ZCAPM is a building block for other related machine learning models that move beyond the boundaries of traditional multifactor models.

Postscript—The greatest stock market anomaly nowadays is the fact that the ZCAPM is not well known even though it consistently dominates published models in top tier finance journals in terms of better explaining the cross section of average stock returns.

References

Anginer, D., S. Ray, H. N. Seyhun, and L. Xu. 2024. Expensive anomalies. *Journal of Empirical Finance* 75: 101440.

Barberis, M., A. Shleifer, and R. Vishny. 1998. A model of investor sentiment. *Journal of Financial Economics* 49: 307–343.

Black, F. 1972. Capital market equilibrium with restricted borrowing. *Journal of Business* 45: 444–454.

Bowles, B., A. V. Reed, M. C. Ringgenberg, and J. R. Thornock. 2024. Anomaly time. *Journal of Finance* 79: 3543–3579.

Breiman, L. 2001. Statistical modeling: The two cultures. *Statistical Science* 16: 199–231.

Carhart, M. M. 1997. On persistence in mutual fund performance. *Journal of Finance* 52: 57–82.

Chen, A. Y., and M. Velikov. 2023. Zeroing in on the expected returns of anomalies. *Journal of Financial and Quantitative Analysis* 58: 968–1004.

Chen, A. Y., and T. Zimmermann. 2020. Publication bias and the cross-section of stock returns. *Review of Asset Pricing Studies* 10: 249–289.

Chen, A. Y., and T. Zimmerman. 2022. *Open source cross-sectional asset pricing Critical Finance Review* 11: 207–264.

Cochrane, J. H. 2011. Presidential address: Discount rates. *Journal of Finance* 56: 1047–1108.

Daniel, K., D. Hirshleifer, and A. Subrahmanyam. 1997. A theory of overconfidence, self-attribution, and security market under- and over-reactions. Unpublished working paper. University of Michigan.

DeBondt, W., and R. Thaler. 1985. Does the stock market overreact? *Journal of Finance* 40: 793–805.

DeBondt, W. F. M., and R. Thaler. 1987. Further evidence of stock market overreaction and seasonality. *Journal of Finance* 42: 557–581.

Fama, E. F. 1965. The behavior of stock-market prices. *The Journal of Business* 38: 34–105.

Fama, E. F. 1970. Efficient capital markets: A review of theory and evidence. *Journal of Finance* 35: 383–417.

Fama, E. F., and K. R. French. 1992. The cross-section of expected stock returns. *Journal of Finance* 47: 427–465.

Fama, E. F., and K. R. French. 1993. The cross-section of expected returns. *Journal of Financial Economics* 33: 3–56.

Fama, E. F., and K. R. French. 1996. The CAPM is wanted, dead or alive. *Journal of Finance* 51: 1947–1958.

Fama, E. F., and K. R. French. 2015. A five-factor asset pricing model. *Journal of Financial Economics* 116: 1–22.

Fama, E. F., and K. R. French. 2018. Choosing factors. *Journal of Financial Economics* 128: 234–252.

Fama, E. F., and K. R. French. 2020. Comparing cross-section and time-series factor models. *Review of Financial Studies* 33: 1892–1926.

Fama, E. F., and J. D. MacBeth. 1973. Risk, return, and equilibrium: Empirical tests. *Journal of Political Economy* 81: 607–636.

Gibbons, M. R., S. A. Ross, and J. Shanken. 1989. A test of the efficiency of a given portfolio. *Econometrica* 57: 1121–1152.

Hou, K., C. Xue, and L. Zhang. 2015. Digesting anomalies: An investment approach. *Review of Financial Studies* 28: 650–705.

Hou, K., C. Xue, and L. Zhang. 2020. Replicating anomalies. *Review of Financial Studies* 33: 2019–2133.

Howe, J. S. 1986. Evidence on stock market overreaction. *Financial Analysts Journal* 42: 74–77.

Jacobs, H., and S. Müller. 2020. Anomalies cross the globe: Once public, no longer existent? *Journal of Financial Economics* 135: 213–230.

Jensen, M. C. 1968. The performance of mutual funds in the period 1945–1964. *Journal of Finance* 23: 389–416.

Jensen, T. I., B. Kelly, and L. H. Pedersen. 2023. Is there a replication crisis in finance? *Journal of Finance* 78: 2465–2518.

Kahneman, D., and A. Tversky. 1979. Prospect theory: An analysis of decision under risk. *Econometrica* 47: 263–291.

Kelly, B., S. Malamud, and K. Zhou. 2024. The virtue of complexity in return prediction. *Journal of Finance* 79: 459–503.

Keynes, J. M., 1936. The General Theory of Employment Interest and Money. London: MacMillan.

Kolari, J. W., J. Z. Huang, W. Liu, and H. Liao. 2024. *A quantum leap in asset pricing: Explaining anomalous returns.* Palm Beach Gardens, FL: Presented at the annual conference meetings of the Southern Finance Association.

Kolari, J. W., J. Z. Huang, W. Liu, and H. Liao. 2024b. A quantum leap in asset pricing: Explaining anomalous returns, Presented at the annual conference meetings of the Southwestern Finance Association, San Antonio, TX. Awarded the Best Paper in Investments.

Kolari, J. W., W. Liu, and J. Z. Huang. 2012. A new asset pricing model based on the zero-beta CAPM, Presented at the at the annual conference meetings of the Financial Management Association, Atlanta. Awarded the Best Paper in Investments.

Kolari, J. W., W. Liu, and J. Z. Huang. 2021. *A New Model of Capital Asset Prices: Theory and Evidence.* Cham, Switzerland: Palgrave Macmillan.

Kolari, J. W., W. Liu, and S. Pynnonen. 2024. *Professional Investment Portfolio Management: Boosting Performance with Machine-Made Portfolios and Stock Market Evidence.* Cham, Switzerland: Palgrave Macmillan.

Kolari, J. W., and S. Pynnonen. 2023. *Investment Valuation and Asset Pricing: Models and Methods.* Cham, Switzerland: Palgrave Macmillan.

Lettau, M., and M. Pelger. 2020. Factors that fit the time series and cross-section of stock returns. *Review of Financial Studies* 33: 2274–2325.

Lintner, J. 1965. The valuation of risk assets and the selection of risky investments in stock portfolios and capital budgets. *Review of Economics and Statistics* 47: 13–37.

Lu, X., R. F. Stambaugh, and Y. Yuan. 2017. Anomalies abroad: Beyond data mining, NBER working paper 23809, Cambridge, MA.
Markowitz, H. M. 1959. *Portfolio Selection: Efficient Diversification of Investments.* New York, NY: Wiley.
McLean, R. D., and J. Pontiff. 2016. Does academic publication destroy predictability? *Journal of Finance* 71: 5–32.
Merton, R. C. 1973. An intertemporal capital asset pricing model. *Econometrica* 41: 867–887.
Mossin, J. 1966. Equilibrium in a capital asset market. *Econometrica* 34: 768–783.
Ross, S. A. 1976. The arbitrage theory of capital asset pricing. *Journal of Economic Theory* 13: 341–360.
Sharpe, W. F. 1964. Capital asset prices: A theory of market equilibrium under conditions of risk. *Journal of Finance* 19: 425–442.
Stambaugh, R. F., and Y. Yuan. 2017. Mispricing factors. *Review of Financial Studies* 30: 1270–1315.
Treynor, J. L. 1961. Market value, time, and risk, Unpublished manuscript.
Treynor, J. L. 1962. Toward a theory of market value of risky assets, Unpublished manuscript.

Index

J. W. Kolari et al., *Asset Pricing Models and Market Efficiency*,
https://doi.org/10.1007/978-3-031-92901-4_

FSC
www.fsc.org
MIX
Papier | Fördert
gute Waldnutzung
FSC® C083411

Kolibri 360 GmbH
Ferdinand-Jühlke-Straße 7
99095 Erfurt, Deutschland
produktsicherheit@kolibri360.de